Thomas Hardy

THE SOCIOLOGICAL IMAGINATION

But I would like to state that the geographical limits of the stage here trodden were not absolutely forced upon the writer by circumstances; he forced them upon himself from judgement.

* * *

Thus, though the people in most of the novels (and in much of the shorter verse) are dwellers in a province bounded on the north by the Thames, on the south by the English Channel, on the east by a line running from Hayling Island to Windsor Forest, and on the west the Cornish coast, they were meant to be typically and essentially those of any and every place where 'Thought's the slave of life, and life time's fool'—beings in whose hearts and minds that which is apparently local should be really universal. THOMAS HARDY, General Preface to the Wessex Edition (1912).

Thomas Hardy
The Sociological Imagination

NOORUL HASAN

First published 1982

First published in the United Kingdom 1982

Published by
THE MACMILLAN PRESS LTD
London and Basingstoke

Associated companies in
Delhi   Dublin   Hong Kong   Johannesburg
Lagos   Melbourne   New York   Singapore
Toronto

ISBN 0 333 32628 8

Printed in India

For CANDY
SUNNY
BABY
CHOTA

Foreword

A recent British survey showed that Hardy is now extremely popular with young people. F. R. Leavis's refusal to include Hardy in his great tradition is not acceptable to most contemporary readers. During the last decade literary criticism has thrown fresh light on Hardy's genius, on the tensions and contradictions in his art. In spite of his pessimism he was a man of courage and vitality. His second wife, in a letter, wrote of him sitting late in life in his study composing a most dismal poem with great spirit.

In his Macmillan introduction to *Tess of the d'Urbervilles*, P. N. Furbank calls Hardy a late nineteenth century emotionalist. He stands towards the humanist, didactic, 'teaching' tradition of fiction—the school of Dickens and George Eliot—somewhat in the relation that Mahler or Strauss did to the Beethoven tradition in music.

Hardy was deeply and radically divided. He could not make sense of the world, and his novels, in their contraries, reflect his scepticism. Those who look for 'organic' unity in his novels will be disappointed, for his greatness lies in his refusal to show harmonies where none exist. Optimism about ordinary people and the self-renewing qualities of country traditions is balanced by pessimism about the break-down of the old agricultural order and the indifference of the universe to pain and death.

In his introduction to *Poems of Thomas Hardy*, T. R. M. Creighton says that the poetry presents a composite picture of Hardy's mind: a mind concerned not to explain but to declare itself, able to sustain logical discrepancies within an intuitive framework. Noorul Hasan's sensitive account of Hardy's treatment of rural society similarly emphasises and justifies this intuitive genius. Dr Hasan supports Hardy's belief that the novelist is better equipped to understand social reality than the historian. The novelist responds not only to facts but also to the deep and often contradictory motives and emotions which underlie human conduct. Dr Hasan's book is undoubtedly an important addition to our understanding of the drama of warring values in Hardy's fiction.

C. B. Cox

Preface

Thomas Hardy once referred to himself as an Ancient Mariner. Many a 'guest' has testified to his Mariner-like powers of inducing a willing suspension of disbelief. Virginia Woolf, who had chosen to read *The Mayor of Casterbridge* on her journey to Max Gate in the summer of 1926 to visit Hardy, found herself strangely affected by the felt condition of the novel. Asked by Hardy if it had held her interest, 'I stammered that I could not stop reading it, which was true, but sounded wrong.' It required Virginia Woolf's alertness of feeling to intuit and affirm that Hardy was an irresistibly great novelist despite his rather uncertain reputation at that time. T. S. Eliot, inhibited by the critical habits of his generation and unable to place Hardy in perspective, dismissed him rashly as an unrewarding and sentimental writer. He is said to have suffered qualms of conscience later about his strictures on Hardy. The Ancient Mariner had had his revenge. Today Hardy's status as a major novelist is assured. Over half a century after his death we have sure intimations of his immortality in the increasing critical concern about his imagined world. My own courage to write on Hardy comes from a persistent personal awareness of his genius. I have stressed his intuitive understanding of the complementariness of fact and fiction in human experience. Fiction for Hardy is a human necessity for making sense of the world. His perception of the inevitability of fictional modes in man's response to his world not only gives Hardy a subtler understanding of the shapes of human history but also a new confidence in the novel.

This book is based on my 1978 Manchester doctoral thesis. I am grateful to the Commonwealth Scholarship Commission in the United Kingdom for the generous award of a Commonwealth Academic Staff Scholarship which enabled me and my family to spend three most rewarding and delightful years in England. I owe a special debt of gratitude to my research supervisor, Professor C. B. Cox, for saving me from several errors of taste and judgment by his frank and unsparing criticism and for his always cheerful encouragement. I am further indebted to him for the honour he has done me by

writing the Foreword to this book. I am grateful to
Dr M. E. Rose of the History Department at Manchester
University for a long and helpful discussion I had with him
about the condition of rural England of Hardy's time. To my
friend Grevel Lindop of the English Department at Manchester I am grateful for many stimulating conversations about
the writer we both admire. I recall with gratitude that many
of my ideas about Hardy gained clarity and focus in the course
of a conversation with Professor Samuel Hynes of Princeton
University in Southampton in Spring 1978. A word of thanks
goes to Mr R. N. R. Peers, Curator of the Dorset County
Museum, from whom I received considerable assistance in
my search for relevant Hardy material in the museum. I am
especially indebted to my friend Brijraj Singh of Delhi University whose encouragement and initiative facilitated the publication of this book. I am grateful to my friend and colleague
Paul Pimomo for his valuable contribution to the making of
this book and for his vital friendship in stressful times. I am
grateful, too, to my friends K. O. N. Nambiar and S. M. Nayar
for their assistance and encouragement. My irrepayable debts
to my brave wife and our three children, who accompanied
us on sometimes perilous sojourns into the Hardy country,
are acknowledged in the dedication.

Grateful acknowledgements and thanks are due to the
Trustees of the Thomas Hardy Memorial Collection in the
Dorset County Museum, Dorchester, for permission to quote
from Thomas Hardy's *Commonplace Books*.

I further wish to thank the following for their kind permission to quote from works of which they own the copyright:
the Trustees of the Hardy Estate and Macmillan, London
and Basingstoke for permission to quote from *The Life of
Thomas Hardy* (1962) by F. E. Hardy; Faber & Faber Ltd.
for permission to quote from *The Dyer's Hand and Other Essays*
(1963) and *Secondary Worlds* (1968) both by W. H. Auden, and
from *The Great Web: The Form of Hardy's Major Fiction* (1974)
by Ian Gregor.

Shillong   NOORUL HASAN
May 1981

Contents

CONTENTS

CHAPTER 1

Thomas Hardy and Views of Rural History

The novels of Thomas Hardy are inescapably an evocative cultural statement about the quality of life in a rural community. They do relate to the condition of rural England in the latter half of the nineteenth century as acknowledged not only by some of Hardy's famous critics but by Hardy himself. But *history, truth, fiction* are problematical concepts and much of the wonder of Hardy's enduring fictions depends on the way in which they extend, complicate, and wrestle with the meaning of these concepts. The Wessex novels take the form not of historical fiction, but of fiction as research into the history of rural culture. It would not do, therefore, to place them in a given historical context. Critical accounts which proceed from such an historical context miss out on the obliquity of Hardy's historical imagination. Hardy's fiction involves, but is not conterminous with, the factual history of Dorsetshire in the closing decades of the nineteenth century. In making local history their primary focus Hardy's historical critics have misjudged the creative centre of his fiction. They have paid insufficient attention to Hardy's metaphor-making powers and his astute understanding of the inherence of metaphors in the workings of folk consciousness. I shall argue that Hardy's novels celebrate a wider rediscovery of the metaphor of rural community in life and art in the nineteenth century, that they are indeed the finest flowers of this pervasive sociological apprehension. For a supporting context, let us consider some peculiarities of rural sociology, the dominance of the metaphor of community in the nineteenth-century sociological imagination, and Hardy's own revealing asides on history, truth, and fiction.

One important sociological characteristic of rural England, as of most rural societies, is that it seems always to have been looking back to an ideal past. This has led some to doubt if rural England ever existed in its pristine, unspoilt form, which is a legitimate suspicion. There can be little doubt, however, that for better or worse the English countryside had entered a new phase of civilisation in the nineteenth century and, consequently, there came about during this century an increasingly nostalgic quest for a lost rural identity. The resurgent rural consciousness is touched with a new sense of crisis and self-awareness. It is so central a consciousness in much of the most remarkable literature and social thinking of the century that it assumes the pervasiveness and force of a vital tradition. Nineteenth-century rural literature, therefore, is not a pastoral survival but a correlate of contemporary structures of feeling. It is the product of perceived experience. It does not fall back upon stereotype images of an immobile rural existence but is adequately motivated by the felt particularity of its own cultural situation. It is self-validating.

The impossibility of a precise pinpointing in history of the 'organic rural community' has made some recent historians of culture dismiss the rural-urban differentiation as a romantic error. Because it is not possible to prove statistically the existence, at any point of time, of a village answering to all the attributes of the metaphorical village of the nineteenth-century rural conception, the rational historian concludes with faultless logic that rural society never had a fully differentiated sociological identity. If rural England was always an uneasy coexistence of conflicting interests, which it was in this view, the notion of the break-down of the rural community in the nineteenth century is indeed a myth. Though Raymond Williams, who is a proponent of this view, admits that in the period from George Eliot to Hardy the English countryside underwent radical changes, he seems more concerned with the economics of the change than with its emotional and psychological consequences.[1] We shall return to this view of rural history in the second half of this chapter.

There was what might be called an inner sociology of traditional rural communities which would not lend itself to the categories of chronological, linear history. In many such communities, for instance, the past persisted in the most irrational, historically unaccountable manner. Writing about oriental rural life Sir H. S. Maine observed: 'We find it to be

not wholly a conceit or a paradox to say that the distinction
between the Present and the Past disappears. Sometimes the
Past is the Present; more often it is removed from it by varying
distances, which, however, cannot be estimated or expressed
chronologically.'[2] Although this is said of the Indian village
the author believed that village communities in the East and
West were in all essentials identical: 'It does not appear to me
a hazardous proposition that the Indian and the ancient
European systems of enjoyment and tillage by men grouped in
village communities were in all essential particulars identical.'[3] This is a belief Hardy shared, as a diary entry of
1890 suggests: 'Mr. E. Clodd this morning gives an ex-
cellently neat answer to my question why the superstitions
of a remote Asiatic and a Dorset labourer are the same:
"The attitude of man", he says, "at corresponding levels of
culture before like phenomena, is pretty much the same." '[4]
The archetypal structure of rural life was progressively eroded
by the passage of time. One does not have to believe in the
English village as an earthly paradise to be able to comprehend
the rural-urban polarisation of feeling caused by the climactic
transformation of the countryside in the nineteenth century.
There is a compulsive quasi-metaphorical use of the rural
community in the writings of Cobbett, Clare, Jefferies, Sturt,
as well as in the passionately rural point of view of such rural
historians as Arthur Young, Joseph Arch, H. Rider Haggard,
to name only a few. The rural-urban 'dissociation of sensibility'
is reflected also in the Reports of Parliamentary Commissions
such as the one on the Employment of Children, Young Persons,
and Women in Agriculture which contains the testimony of
Reverend William Barnes of Dorset, friend of Hardy, to 'the
qualities of West English landfolk'.[5] The point I am trying to
make is that this metaphorical or quasi-metaphorical view of
rural life was not a literary stance but a habit of sociological
imagination that extends to the rural people themselves. We
can see this emotive view of rural life in the petition submitted
to the British Parliament by the people of Raunds in Northamp-
tonshire as early as 1797 against the impending enclosure of
their village.[6] The metaphor of community was exploited and
articulated by the literary imagination, but its roots went back
to the native soil of rural experience.

The rural-urban polarisation was not peculiar to England. In fact, it dominated the European sociological imagination of the nineteenth century. Tocqueville, Toennies, Weber, Durkheim, and Simmel all used, in new and unexpected ways, the commonplace opposition between the city and the village. In their metaphorical use of the rural community the sociologists were not creating fictions but only expressing the fictions inherent in the shapeless conduct of historical process. The symbolism of community in Toennies, for instance, resulted from his experience of the stable rural culture of his native province Schleswig-Holstein, but the historical form of his province is transformed in his master work into a universally applicable sociological metaphor.[7] Similarly, many of Durkheim's or Weber's insights into alienation were the consequence of their personal experience of fragmentation in specific historical contexts, but rather than offer the statistics of alienation in a particular city they created metaphors to communicate their sense of the correlation between alienation and the modern metropolis.

Whether or not the 'coherent and self-explanatory village' ever existed in history, the fact remains that there was a potent belief in the nineteenth century in its one-time existence. History is not complete unless it takes into account what men believe to be true in times of crisis as well as the objective truth. The later nineteenth century was an age of social experiment and innovation. It upset the traditional mind and necessitated a search for a 'substitute', for an ideological armour against the chaos of contemporary experience. The rural writer found his 'substitute' in atavistic memories, in the myth, as it was fast becoming, of a historically discredited and moribund social order. During the 1880s the sociologist Toennies was evolving a far-reaching sociological distinction between *Gemeinschaft* (community) and *Gesellschaft* (corporation) while the novelist Hardy was opposing the urban conception of life with his images of the lost rural community in England.

II

The rural-urban dialectic is the chief organising principle of Hardy's fiction. There is no major Hardy novel but involves a sustained opposition between community and the individual, the land and the city, the native and the alien. This has been noted earlier in Hardy criticism, but in terms scarcely adequate to Hardy's imaginings. To read the novels rigidly as a response to the economic and political events of the years 1870–1902 is to falsify their sociology, and to impose on them a reductive time-scale. It is Raymond Williams's argument[8] that the rural society of Hardy's times consisted not of the noble peasantry but of landowners, tenants, and farmers and that all Hardy's characters fall into this class structure. In strict socio-economic terms Tess is not a peasant, but the daughter of a life-holder; Grace Melbury is not a country girl, but the daughter of a timber merchant; Henchard is destroyed not by alien forces, but by the hazardous nature of his own trading. All this is true as far as it goes. But in this translation of Hardy's protagonists into their precise socio-economic stations one has somehow lost touch with their deeper motivations and responses, with everything that makes them somewhat anachronistic, historically and socially indeterminate, but nevertheless very real human beings. In examining the causes of the decline of Henchard's trading balance-sheet one has completely forgotten his personality. Williams's thesis that rural society was riven by the incompatibility of its different classes ignores the overriding sense of a collective moral and emotional identity that characterises members of a traditional community. It is precisely this sense in Hardy's world which cuts across class barriers. At highly significant moments, despite all their socio-economic disparities, there is a community of feeling between Michael Henchard and Abel Whittle, Grace Melbury and Giles Winterborne, landlady Bathsheba and shepherd Oak. Williams has nothing to say about Henchard's *character*, a focal point of Hardy's novel, or Tess's challenging purity of consciousness, or Oak's evident superiority despite his 'class'. He also ignores the parabolic quality of Hardy's idiom and the primitivism of his dramatic scenario which, in my view, symbolise Hardy's interest in the enduring structures of rural life. The Roman ruins and barrows and the pre-historic monuments in Hardy's landscape are visual symbols of his sense of the contemporaneity of the past. And if one is to come to terms with this sense of the continuing tribal past of Wessex, which relates to the heart of Hardy's sociological fiction, one should be prepared to go beyond the calendar of contemporary events.

Hardy was much exercised about views of history, about the different perceptual filters through which history is seen. He was aware that there are varieties of historical experience. 'We may say', he wrote in his journal, 'that three kinds of men write history: the gazeteer or annalist, the statesman, and the philosopher.'[9] He refused to write the gazeteer's or the annalist's history. When asked by the Dorchester Town Council to write an introduction to an official Guide to the town, he replied that he was not in a position to do so, adding that he had said all he needed to say about Dorchester under the pseudonym of 'Casterbridge' and that was it.[10]

Clearly, Hardy was averse to documentation and historical scientism. He had an historical vision, a feel of the place and its people, a tenacious memory of cultural idiosyncrasies. Hardy's approach to history cannot be explained better than in the following words of W. H. Auden:

> In grasping the character of a society, as in judging the character of an individual, no documents, statistics, 'objective' measurements can compete with the single intuitive glance. Intuition may err, for though its sound judgement is, as Pascal said, only a question of good eyesight, it must be good, for the principles are subtle and numerous, and the omission of one principle leads to error; but documentation, which is useless unless it is complete, must err in a field where completeness is impossible.[11]

It is also Auden's view that the advent in the nineteenth century of the new rationalist and analytic doctrines caused a final divorce between the historian and the poet in the human psyche and that this divorce led to a fractured sensibility in the literature that followed:

> The marriage in each of us whether as writers or readers, between the Historian and the Poet, first began to run into serious difficulties in the seventeenth century, but it is only in the industrialized societies of the last hundred and fifty years that, by the time most of us are twenty, the two have divorced.

The consequences are only too obvious. The primary world, as perceived by the divorced Historian, is a desacralized, depersonalised world where all facts are equally profane. Human history becomes a matter of statistics in which individual human beings are represented as faceless and anonymous puppets of impersonal forces. The characteristic virtue of the historian, his impartiality, which refrains from intruding his own moral values upon events, leaving that duty to the reader, becomes meaningless, for moral judgements can only be passed on personal deeds, and in the world he depicts, men are incapable of deeds and only exhibit social behaviour.

The divorced Poet, on the other hand, can find materials for building his secondary worlds only in his private subjectivity.[12]

In Hardy there is no such divorce between the Historian and the Poet. Social reality for him is not a matter of statistics but resides in the underlying rhythms of life-style, culture, and character. Nor does he build a private fictional world out of his own subjectivity. In fact, his narrative world repeatedly invokes communal rather than personal structures of feeling. His self-explanatory eloquent tableaux, his reliance on culturally sensitive material, his alignment of important psychological and emotional events in the novels with such common cultural landmarks as Christmas or May Dance, all speak of a narrative psychology attuned to a community sensibility. His is not a literature of personality. Despite a commanding authorial presence and the famous 'raids of philosophical speculation' his great stories leave a final impression of balladic simplicity and impersonality.

Hardy sees history as a drama of warring values. He cannot bring to his consciousness of history, therefore, the clinical detachment of the 'divorced' historian. Historical intelligence for him is inseparable from a capacity for a principle of moral choice, a point of view. He jotted down a comment on the moral and ideational centre of Carlyle's *French Revolution* from a contemporary article, with apparent approval: 'most perfect-epic-organic creation—"the central idea, the animating principle round which the matter gathers and develops into shape"...his historical workmanship is sound to the core.'[13] It was this kind of 'central idea' or 'animating principle' which gave to the nineteenth-century sociologists their ideal typology. Hardy was after the same animating principles of history and culture. In novel after novel he sought the sociologically submerged sources of feeling and action in a rural community rather than scratch the historical surface. He found Zola unbearable because of the latter's concentration on the gross phenomena, because, in one sense, of his historical materialism. 'You mistake in supposing I admire Zola. It is just what I don't do. I think him no artist and too material.'[14]

Hardy was neither a historiographer nor a pedlar of Erewhonian myths, but a novelist with an unerring sense of history. The Preface to *Far from the Madding Crowd* offers important clues to Hardy's understanding of rural history. Borrowing some of his terms from an anonymous article in *The Examiner* entitled 'The Wessex Labourer' he obliquely pleads guilty of 'the anachronism of imagining a Wessex population living under Queen Victoria...a modern Wessex...'. The point of the *Examiner* article was precisely to refute the charge of anachronism against Hardy's nineteenth-century Wessex communities, and assert the strange contemporaneity of the past in the region he was writing about: 'Time in Dorset has stood still; advancing civilization has given the labourer only lucifer matches and the penny post, and the clowns in *Hamlet* are no anachronism if placed in a West country village of our own day.'[15] The contiguity between the past and the present may not be, after all, a trick of Hardy's imagination but a sociological characteristic of certain isolated rural communities. However, Hardy takes complete responsibility for reducing the gap between the centuries. It is 'a partly real, partly dream country' he has created and he wants his readers 'to refuse steadfastly to believe that there are any inhabitants of a Victorian Wessex outside these volumes in which their lives and conversations are detailed.' But he ends the Preface by making the contrary claim that there had been in the recent past 'a sufficient reality to meet the descriptions both of background and personages'. It may be safely said, then, that while keeping clear of any responsibility for historical accuracy, Hardy would not have his novels read without the assurance that they are imaginative reconstructions of a lived pattern of life and society. The pattern may not always be corroborated by text-books of history, but it is authentic in the sense that it is inevitably led up to by the structure of experience in the novels, which are in Hardy's words 'circumstantial wholes which, when approached by events in real life, cause the observer to pause and reflect, and say, "what a striking history!" '[16] To Hardy the truth of fiction was more complete because it was based on a structural consistency often absent from life and history: 'It must always be borne in mind, despite the claims of realism, that the best fiction, like the highest artistic expression in other modes, is more true, so to put it, then [sic] history or nature can be.'[17] Fiction for Hardy was a criterion of truth. In life and history there are inevitable impediments to perception, 'hitches in the machinery of existence',[18] which it is the business of the artist to overcome. In the great works of imagination the missing clues are fully grasped so that fictions educate our notions of reality: 'what is called the idealization of characters is, in truth, the making of them too real to be possible.'[19] 'Attention to accessories',[20] in Hardy's view, was justified only to the extent that it led to 'the elucidation of higher things'.[21] Hardy's aesthetic of fiction rejects orthodox realism after conceding minor triumphs to it:

> To return for a moment to the theories of the scientific realists. Every friend to the novel should and must be in sympathy with their error, even while distinctly perceiving it. Though not true, it is well founded. To advance realism as complete copyism, to call the idle trade of story-telling a science, is the hyperbolic flight of an admirable enthusiasm, the exaggerated cry of an honest reaction from false, in which the truth has been impetuously approached and overleapt in fault of lighted on.[22]

But Hardy clearly and emphatically wants the novel to be a discovery of truth. In fact, the novelist's opportunity for getting at the whole truth is immense since 'the novel affords scope for getting nearer to the heart and meaning of things'.[23] An extended comment by Leslie Stephen on the question of historical truth in fiction, transcribed by Hardy in his note-book, is worth quoting because it so well sums up his own deepest convictions on the subject:

> The novelist, as Fielding often tells us, is the true historian of the time. He tries to show us the real moving forces in the great tragi-comedy of human life. He has to make the world intelligible to us, & the deeper & truer his insight, the greater his permanent power....He reveals to us certain aspects of the world in which we live & the men who live in it...truths capable of being proved by direct intuition...certain facts as they appear to him. If we are so constituted as to be unable to see what he sees, he can go no further....But, on the other hand, so far as we are in sympathy with him, the proof—if it be a proof—has all the cogency of direct vision. He has couched our dull eyes, drawn back the veil which hid from us the certain aspect of the world, & henceforward our views of life & the world will be more or less changed, because the bare scaffolding of fact which we previously saw will now be seen in the light of keener perceptions than our own.[24]

It was Hardy's belief that the novelist was better equipped to understand social reality than the historian. Nor was Hardy alone in this belief. The idea that the truth of poetry is superior to the truth of history, as we all know, goes back to Aristotle. And even formal historians have had to admit from time to time that poetry (meaning imaginative literature in general) was relevant to the concerns of history. F. M. Powicke observed in one of his lectures: 'The relation between poetry and historical material proper is close, for—although I should be the last to forget its immediate, its timeless, appeal to us—poetry, in the broadest sense of the word, comprehending much prose, is in itself a social expression.'[25] In the same lecture Powicke went on to assert that the 'historic sense' in Thomas Hardy was superbly developed: 'The only relief which he (Hardy) permits himself in his analysis of the plaything man is the pleasure of the historic sense.'[26]

Hardy's 'partly real, partly dream' Wessex was a product of sociological imagination. It was indeed a harvest of the closest observation of historical facts, but owed its total ambience to an imaginative response to those facts. Hardy's unwearying interest in local history cannot be denied. One has to see his *Commonplace Books* to believe how assiduous a student of local history and culture Hardy was. His fiction was a quest for the inherent but undiscovered forms of this history and culture. Wessex was a fictional world, no doubt, but a fictional world informed by Hardy's awareness of the fictional form of apprehended social reality. A true historian, Hardy is not only concerned with social data, with gross historical references, but with the elusive shape and rhythm of historical and social reality. Wessex is an emotive model for the discovery and communication of forms of social reality which are seldom acknowledged or felt by factful historians. It is true fiction which, as Michel Zeraffa points out in a recent study, need not be a contradiction in terms: 'Are life and the history of society simply the props of the forms of fiction? Or are these forms already present in society? Critical study of the novel too often wavers between these two questions, which constitute a false dilemma.'[27]

NOTES

1. See Raymond Williams, 'Literature and Rural Society', *The Listener* (16 November 1967).
2. Henry Summer Maine, *Village Communities in East and West* (London: John Murray, 1871), p. 7.
3. Ibid., p. 103.
4. See Florence Emily Hardy, *The Life of Thomas Hardy, 1840-1928*, p. 230.
5. 'Commission on the Employment of Children, Young Persons, and Women in Agriculture (1867)', *Parliamentary Papers (1868–69)*, p. 7.
6. See *Journal of The House of Commons*, Vol. 52 (19 June 1797), p. 661.
7. Ferdinand Toennies, *Community and Association (Gemeinschaft und Gesellschaft)*, 1887, tr., Charles P. Loomis (London: Routledge & Kegan Paul, 1955).
8. See Raymond Williams, 'Thomas Hardy'.
9. Thomas Hardy, *Commonplace Book* I, p. 270.
10. The letter is in the Dorset County Museum.
11. W. H. Auden, *The Dyer's Hand and Other Essays* (London: Faber & Faber 1963), p. 313.
12. W. H. Auden, *Secondary Worlds* (London: Faber & Faber, 1968), pp. 82–3.
13. Hardy, *Commonplace Book* I, pp. 189–90.
14. Hardy made this remark in a letter to Florence Henniker. See Evelyn Hardy and F. B. Pinion, eds., *One Rare Fair Woman* (London: Macmillan, 1972), p. 63.

15. *The Examiner*, No. 3572 (15 July 1876), p. 793.
16. Thomas Hardy, 'The Profitable Reading of Fiction', *Thomas Hardy's Personal Writings*, ed., Harold Orel, pp. 121–2.
17. Ibid., p. 117.
18. Ibid.
19. Ibid., p. 118.
20. Ibid., p. 119.
21. Ibid.
22. Thomas Hardy, 'The Science of Fiction', *Personal Writings*, p. 136.
23. Thomas Hardy, 'Why I Don't Write Plays', *Personal Writings*, p. 139.
24. Hardy, *Commonplace Book* I, pp. 157–9.
25. F. M. Powicke, *Three Lectures* (London: Oxford University Press, 1947), p. 62.
26. Ibid., p. 72.
27. Michel Zeraffa, *Fictions: The Novel and Social Reality* (Harmondsworth: Penguin, 1976), p. 7.

CHAPTER 2

Far from the Madding Crowd
(1874)

Many of its early reviewers were prone to judge
Far from the Madding Crowd in terms of its historical accuracy.
Some of them found its rural characters and situations un-
historical. Andrew Lang, for instance, wrote in his *Academy*
review: 'The country folk in the story have not heard of strikes,
or of Mr. Arch; they have, to all appearance, plenty to eat, and
warm clothes to wear, and when the sheep are shown in the
ancient barn of Weatherbury, the scene is one that Shakespeare
or that Chaucer might have watched. This immobile rural
existence is what the novelist has to paint.'[1] R. H. Hutton expressed a similar incredulity about the rural facts of the novel:
'The reader who has any general acquaintance with the civilization of the Wiltshire or Dorsetshire labourer, with his
average wages, and his average intelligence, will be disposed
to say at once that a more incredible picture than that of the
group of farm labourers as a whole which Mr. Hardy has given
us can hardly be conceived.'[2] But others made the opposite
claim that the novel was historically true. If that truth appeared
exaggerated to some, argued *The Examiner*, it was because they
were simply ignorant: 'Mr. Thomas Hardy's novels have been,
on the whole, favourably received, and many of their merits
recognized. Yet their most characteristic features have either
been passed over in silence, or pronounced exaggerated, simply
because very few of the readers are able to judge in those
matters of his workmanship.'[3] Horace Moule had earlier found
Under the Greenwood Tree 'remarkable for its fidelity to truth'.[4]
An article in *The Daily Telegraph* of April 30, 1872 described
Puddletown (the original of Weatherbury) as 'a model Dorsetshire village' where obtained many of the 'essentials of

Page references to *Far from the Madding Crowd* are to the New Wessex edition
(1974).

Arcadian felicity'.[5] Hardy's 'partly real, partly dream' novel strained separatist notions of reality and dream.

The majority of the contemporary reviewers tried to solve the problem by taking the novel as simply an idyll, although some did not fail to notice that idyllicism could not account for the novel in its entirety. *The Times* said: 'there is...evidence of his possessing a certain vein of original thought, and a delicate perceptive faculty, which transforms, with skilful touch, the matter-of-fact prosaic details of everyday life into an idyll or a pastoral poem.'[6] *The Guardian*, while accepting the novel as 'purely pastoral', argued that it was pastoral with a difference: 'It is in truth a purely pastoral idyll, in which, however, the shepherds and shepherdesses are of a very different strain from the Corydon and Phyllis of conventional poetry.'[7] Hardy himself, in his very first reference to the novel, described it as 'a pastoral tale'.[8] However, as has been pointed out in the *Guardian* review and more recently by Michael Squires, the pastoral in *Far from the Madding Crowd* is fruitfully adjusted to the realistic and dramatic conventions of the mid-Victorian novel. While it may be called a novel deeply pastoral in feeling, there is little doubt that 'the falsification and artificiality of traditional pastoral have been rigorously excluded from Hardy's account.'[9] Hence the title of Squires's article: '*Far from the Madding Crowd* as Modified Pastoral'. Although I would entirely agree with the view that Hardy is a celebrant of the rural way of life and that its detailed and unwearied perception provides the staple of his great fiction, the use of the term 'pastoral' calls up somewhat alien associations, that is, alien to the true shape of experience in this novel. That may be the reason why there has been so much protest against and denial of even the most positive and least ambiguously pastoral elements of the novel. It has, for instance, been claimed that far from being even remotely pastoral in intention, this novel is actually 'a fable of the barrenness and death of the pastoral world'.[10] Or, in the challenging words of Ian Gregor: 'If Hardy is celebrating pastoral life in his novel, it must surely be in the spirit of Samuel Beckett.'[11] Although *Far from the Madding Crowd* has a shepherd hero, he is quite clearly not the conventional, piping, moonstruck shepherd. He is sufficiently deromanticised to authenticate himself as a credible human character. As if to ward off any false romantic glamour attaching to his image Hardy presents him in the beginning in a comic-realistic perspective: 'His Christian name was Gabriel, and on working days he was a young man of sound judgment, easy motions, proper dress, and general good character.' (p. 41) This is a view of character which strikes one, in isolation, as nearer to the manner of Jane Austen than to that of Thomas Hardy. Gabriel does not live in Arcadia, but in a world of modern pressures: 'to state his character as it stood in the scale of public opinion, when his friends and critics were in tantrums, he was considered rather a bad man; when they were pleased, he was rather a good man; when they were neither, he was a man whose moral colour was a kind of pepper-and-salt mixture.' (p. 41) He is made to appear ordinary, even ridiculous, in his dress and manners and worldly possessions. The initial picture is that of a man singularly unprepossessing. The description of his watch, which Henry James thought irrelevant and facetious,[12] seems to me to be part of the process of deliberate comic deflation to which Hardy initially subjects the character of Gabriel Oak. But before this first comic chapter comes to a close Gabriel is, subtly and with a seeming lack of design, invested with an irrefutable moral authority. Bathsheba's waggon held by the gate-keeper at the toll-bar provides the occasion for Gabriel's sudden transformation from an awkward bumpkin to a man of understanding and culture, capable of articulating his values and not failing, in Lawrence's phrase, 'to produce' himself when the occasion demands it. The brisk conversation between Gabriel and the gate-keeper following Bathsheba's departure, whom Gabriel has treated with an almost contemptuous chivalry (p. 45), at once lifts him to a superior moral plane. His simple remark that 'vanity' is the most outstanding trait of Bathsheba's personality introduces the central theme of the novel and adumbrates his own role in the exploration of that theme. Gabriel has already seen Bathsheba admire her image in the mirror—'She blushed at herself, and seeing her reflection blush, blushed the more' (p. 44)—so that his remark to the gate-keeper has the authority of truth.

In likening Gabriel's hut to Noah's Ark in the next chapter Hardy is further stressing Gabriel's role as a protector and his relative invulnerability, although still at this point the comic note intermingles with the premonitory metaphor of Noah's Ark: 'The image as a whole was that of a small Noah's Ark on a small Ararat, allowing the traditionary outlines and general form of the Ark which are followed by toy-makers—and by these means are established in men's imaginations among their firmest, because earliest impressions—to pass as an approximate pattern.' (p. 48) The miniature Noah's Ark carries a suggestion of comic diminution but there is no reversal of meaning, no ironic intention in the patterning of the mythic image. A funny Noah's Ark is still a Noah's Ark. As if to sustain our credulity Hardy describes the interior of the hut in down-to-earth realistic detail:

> The inside of the hut...was cosy and alluring.... In the corner stood the sheep-crook, and along a shelf at one side were ranged bottles and canisters of the simple preparations pertaining to ovine surgery and physic; spirits of wine, turpentine, tar, magnesia, ginger, and castor-oil being the chief. On a triangular shelf across the corner stood bread, bacon, cheese, and a cup for ale or cider, which was supplied from a flagon beneath. (p. 49)

All this forms part of the perspective in which Gabriel Oak is presented in the novel. The details woven round his daily existence are as far removed from the texture of existence of a 'literary' shepherd as is the suggestion that he stands for an ideal of character which is the reverse of pastoral. In his romance with Bathsheba, Gabriel's innate goodness and purity are accompanied by an embarrassing lack of tact. Faintly echoing Cordelia's failure of communication he tells Bathsheba that he cannot match her in 'mapping out my mind upon my tongue'. (p. 59) He knows not the art of amorous conversation to advantage:

> 'I am sorry,' he said the instant after.
> 'What for?'
> 'Letting your hand go so quick.'
> 'You may have it again if you like; there it is.' She gave him her hand again.

Oak held it longer this time—indeed, curiously long.

'How soft it is—being winter time, too—not chapped or rough, or anything!' he said.

'There—that's long enough,' said she, though without pulling it away. 'But I suppose you are thinking you would like to kiss it? You may if you want to.'

'I wasn't thinking of any such thing,' said Gabriel simply; but I will—'

'That you won't!' She snatched back her hand. Gabriel felt himself guilty of another want of tact. (pp. 59–60)

Gabriel continues to be viewed unromantically against the pert and vivacious and seemingly unconquerable Bathsheba. But already in their first meeting a special and thematically significant bond seems to have been suggested between them. Bathsheba, still largely unknown by Oak, comes to him at a time of disaster and saves him from death. The pastoral paradigm of the milkmaid and the shepherd being mutually vital and protective is held in check only by the comic-realistic slant of the sequence. Nevertheless, Bathsheba's life-saving intervention, her bringing the unconscious Gabriel back to life by throwing milk over him (p. 58) releases quite another dimension of meaning. It establishes the basic milkmaid-shepherd compact between Bathsheba and Gabriel, and makes their failure to communicate verbally a delaying tactic, an element of the comic plot rather than of the essential theme. Thematically, Gabriel and Bathsheba are closely aligned. Their unity is not the easily perceivable unity of external forms, but an intuitive, imperceptible unity of feeling and cultural psychology. This unity is clouded over by the plot which requires Bathsheba often to act in violation of her cultural sensibility and values. The action of the novel does not take the shape so much of the taming of Bathsheba by Gabriel Oak[13] as that of the slow emergence of a cultural, communal basis for human action amidst the chaos of warring egos and disorientated personalities. Bathsheba's unconventionality is a pose which the action of the novel will soon dissolve. Her sauciness and prankishness have been unjustifiably overinterpreted as symptoms of an emotional and intellectual urgency met in latter-day heroines like Ursula Brangwen. Her misogamistic declarations are superbly placed against Gabriel's comically distended and insistent conventionality, but it is no more menacing or meaningful than that familiar exercise of female intransigence in the face of male ardour. Statements like 'I *hate* to be thought men's property in that way, though possibly I shall be had some day' (p. 66) or 'I shouldn't mind being a bride at a wedding, if I could be one without having a husband' (p. 67) recall Shakespearean wenches as much as any latter-day heroines. They are not parts of a larger structure of meaning, but seem designed to stress the comic piquancy of Mr Oak's, as Hardy honorifically addresses him during this sequence, predicament. Oak's idea of marriage is hopelessly conventional:

> 'And when the wedding was over, we'd have it put in the newspaper list of marriages.'
> 'Dearly I should like that!'
> 'And the babies in the births—every man jack o' em! And at home by the fire, whenever you look up, there I shall be—and whenever I look up, there will be you.'
> (p. 66)

When Bathsheba tells him that he would soon get to despise her: ' "Never," said Mr Oak, so earnestly that he seemed to be coming, by the force of his words, straight through the bush and into her arms. "I shall do one thing in this life—one thing certain—that is, love you, and long for you, and *keep wanting you* till I die." ' (p. 68) To Bathsheba's suggestion that he ought, in common prudence, to marry a woman with more money than herself he replies: 'That's the very thing I had been thinking myself!', upon which Hardy's comment is: 'Farmer Oak had one-and-a-half Christian characteristics too many to succeed with Bathsheba: his humility, and a superfluous moeity of honesty. Bathsheba was decidedly disconcerted.' (p. 68) Oak's disappointment in love is viewed comically: 'No man likes to see his emotions the sport of a merry-go-round of skittishness. "Very well," said Oak firmly, with the bearing of one who was going to give his days and nights to Ecclesiastes for ever. "Then I'll ask you no more." '

(p. 69) Oak's comic conventionality is opposed to Bathsheba's youthful hauteur. What is happening is that the comic bearings of Oak's character have been isolated from his totally conceived personality. In like manner Bathsheba's haughtiness and sexual arrogance have been isolated and heightened. Oak— the comic victim—is brought into a violent, almost Pickwickian collision with Bathsheba—the intractable. The result is a comic *tour de force* which seems to run away with the novel. It expresses Hardy's sense of the ridiculous even in his most serious characters. He is laughing at Oak and is not at all distressed by Bathsheba's flashing temper. But the novel has not begun yet. The comedy of these two incongruous characters is a mere prelude to the story that follows. Viewed only in terms of their distorting egos and isolated quirks and fancies they may even be judged, as they indeed have been, as not quite out of place in the world of the absurd where unrelatedness is a philosophical necessity. *Far from the Madding Crowd*, however, is concerned with the exploration of a communal and cultural basis of personality and human relationship. After the preliminary comedy of their exacerbated, unaccommodated selves the story goes on to establish the characters of Oak and Bathsheba in terms of their total response to life accenting their relationship with the impersonal world of nature and the immemorial cultural routine of the life they live. Already, as we have seen, a deeper unity between Oak and Bathsheba has been suggested.

The chapter describing the tragic incident of Gabriel's loss of his sheep begins to shape his character as distinct from his somewhat quaint and comical personality. Two aspects of his character which receive special emphasis are his compassion and *sang froid*. His first feeling at the sight of his dead ewes is not that of what he has lost by way of property, but a feeling only of profound compassion for the suffering of his dumb flock:

> Oak was an intensely humane man: indeed, his humanity often tore in pieces any politic intentions of his which bordered on strategy, and carried him on as by gravitation. A shadow in his life had always been that his flock ended in mutton—that a day came and found every shepherd an arrant traitor to his defenceless sheep. (p. 73)

Gabriel's feeling is infused with a typically Hardyan awareness of cosmic cruelty. The occasion provides an opportunity for the tragic imagination to suggest, as Hardy put it in his last novel, that 'Nature's law be mutual butchery'. The tragic awareness has encompassed more than the facts of the present episode. It has gone on to point out the inevitable treachery of circumstance which turns the kindest intention to positive cruelty: 'a day came and found every shepherd an arrant traitor to his defenceless sheep.' The tragic surge of feeling is unmistakable. But it does not cancel out Oak's compassion. Within the tragic context the statement that 'Oak was an intensely humane man' is still not meant to convey any ironic ambiguity. The other salience is Oak's ability to face up to the crises of his life, to have a larger tragic awareness which makes personal losses bearable and less completely destructive of human integrity. This ability of Oak's to stand fully cognisant of the tragic nature of life is conveyed brilliantly in the evocation of a deathly atmosphere around the bare facts of his own loss:

> Oak raised his head, and wondering what he could do, listlessly surveyed the scene. By the outer margin of the pit was an oval pond, and over it hung the attenuated skeleton of a chrome-yellow moon, which had only a few days to last—the morning star dogging her on the left hand. The pool glittered like a dead man's eye, and as the world awoke a breeze blew, shaking and elongating the reflection of the moon without breaking it, and turning the image of the star to a phosphoric streak upon the water. All this Oak saw and remembered. (p. 73)

This is not mere pathetic fallacy, but a token of tragic perception. The world around Gabriel Oak is a story of endless desolation, as brought home so vividly in the minute particulars of the above scene, but the fact only adds a fresh urgency to human endeavour and human courage of which Gabriel is so supreme an exemplar. 'All this Oak saw and remembered.' The imagery does not only register Gabriel's profound dismay and helplessness in the face of his immediate disaster but evinces his tragic comprehension of life which is the source in his character of what Virginia Woolf described as his 'open-eyed endurance without flinching'.[14] Adversity, in Hardy's fiction, has its uses:

> He had passed through an ordeal of wretchedness which had given him more than it had taken away. He had sunk from his modest elevation as pastoral king into the very slime-pits of Siddim; but there was left to him a dignified calm he had never before known, and that indifference to fate which, though it often makes a villain of a man, is the basis of his sublimity when it does not. And thus the abasement had been exaltation, and the loss gain. (p. 75)

This 'positive' effect of suffering on the Hardyan ideal of character, what Philip Larkin describes as the association in Hardy of 'awareness of the causes of pain with superior spiritual character',[15] is nowhere more evident than in Gabriel Oak's responses.

Fortified by the experience of loss and pain and well initiated into the central life of the novel Gabriel will now be put through a succession of situations which bring out his solidarity with the community, his intense tragic awareness, and his native intelligence and resourcefulness. All this is inextricably bound up with the romantic drama of his unrequited love for Bathsheba.

It is significant that the first thing Gabriel does as he enters Weatherbury in search of employment is to save Bathsheba's ricks from burning without really knowing that they belong to her. Earlier, while still in the waggon which is taking him to Weatherbury, he hears fellow-passengers discussing a lady whom they characterise as very vain: 'She's a very vain feymell— so 'tis said here and there.' They also know the basis for this report of her vanity: 'Yes—she's very vain. 'Tis said that every night at going to bed she looks in the glass to put on her nightcap properly.' (p. 79) This perfectly plausible dramatic device of introducing anonymous people talking about an anonymous subject economically establishes Gabriel's continuity of feeling and moral judgement with the anonymous community. His timely rescue of Bathsheba's property recalls Bathsheba's rescue of his life in the first phase of their life at

Norcombe and becomes an almost symbolic reminder of the pattern of interdependence and mutual protectiveness between Gabriel and Bathsheba that lies at the imaginative centre of the novel. This true and involuntary relationship asserts itself amidst all the reversal and denial and wilful separation which baulks their lives and provides so much of the painful and discordant material of the novel. The peculiar sense of menace and cosmic hostility, apparent as early as Chapter Five ('Departure of Bathsheba—A Pastoral Tragedy') continues to add for a few moments a vague, Kafkaesque element of undefined horror to some of the scenes and incidents. An early instance of the bizarre is the rendering of Gabriel's impression of Bathsheba's burning ricks:

> Individual straws in the foreground were consumed in a creeping movement of ruddy heat, as if they were knots of red worms, and above shone imaginary fiery faces, tongues hanging from lips, glaring eyes and other impish forms, from which at intervals sparks flew in clusters like birds from a nest. (p. 81)

Some have argued that the novel is marred by such 'flurries of gratuitous gothic imagery'. To me it seems much more functional in that it extends the impression of horror and external threat which is never absent from Hardy's message. But to base a reading of the novel solely on such occasional flourishes would be no less mistaken. The gothic is part of the context of the novel, but not its final meaning. To read *Far from the Madding Crowd* as a displacement of any other meaning by grotesque impressionism and fragmentariness is to translate the novel out of its felt condition. However, the dread and darkness natural to Hardy's vision are effectively communicated through the grotesque images. What is significant is how these images relate to the perception of character and human identity in the novel. The horrific here is a narrational stance rather than a philosophical or symbolic vortex of meaning. The element of horror in Gabriel's experience of the fire does not rule out the possibility of action or normal human resistance. It does not even rule out the possibility of heroism and distinctive human triumph in limited situations. The grotesquely menacing, anthropomorphising imagination, as well as the undaunted and often successful struggle against forces that menace, is part perhaps of a countryman's mind, of his internalised culture, of which Hardy is the sure delineator. The chapter significantly called 'The Storm—The Two Together' is, structurally, one of the central chapters of the novel. It brings together the two central characters against a background of cosmic disturbance and devilry coupled with social malaise. But the storm does not subdue them to passivity. It calls forth fresh forms of action:

> Manoeuvres of a most extraordinary kind were going on in the vast firmamental hollows overhead. The lightning now was the colour of silver, and gleamed in the heavens like a mailed army. Rumbles became rattles. Gabriel from his elevated position could see over the landscape at least half-a-dozen miles in front. Every hedge, bush, and tree was distinct as in a line engraving....Then the picture vanished leaving the darkness so intense that Gabriel worked entirely by feeling with his hands. (p. 277)

Gabriel and Bathsheba are united in this crisis through their deeply ingrained habits of work and of meeting cataclysmic emergencies. Their union here is abrupt, unplanned, socially awkward in view of the fact that Bathsheba has only just married her soldier-hero whose infectious recklessness is partly the reason why the crop had not been sufficiently protected against the threatening weather, but the brief relationship is nevertheless genuine in the articulateness of work and instinctive interdependence. This emergent community of working and feeling between Gabriel and Bathsheba is vividly present in the chapter, although the rhetoric of horror often throws it in tension with an apocalyptic negativeness and nescience of which the raging storm is so apt a dramatic correlative:

> The forms of skeletons appeared in the air, shaped with blue fire for bones—dancing, leaping, striding, racing around, and mingling altogether in unparalleled confusion. With these were intertwined undulating snakes of green, and

behind these was a broad mass of lesser light. Simultaneously came from every part of the tumbling sky what may be called a shout; since, though no shout ever came near it, it was more of the nature of a shout than of anything else earthly. In the meantime one of the grisly forms had alighted upon the point of Gabriel's rod, to run invisibly down it, down the chain, and into the earth. Gabriel was almost blinded, and he could feel Bathsheba's warm arm tremble in his hand—a sensation novel and thrilling enough; but love, life, everything human, seemed small and trifling in such close juxtaposition with an infuriated universe. (p. 279)

Carl J. Weber declared in a 1940 article that Hardy had almost bodily lifted the entire 'storm' chapter out of Harrison Ainsworth's *Rookwood*. 'It went undetected', said Weber with an air of self-congratulation 'for sixty-seven years.'[16] The similarity of phrasing between Hardy's storm and that in *Rookwood* of course meant for Weber that the whole thing had been artificially inducted into the novel and was, therefore, no part of its authentic creation. Recently, Ian Gregor, though expressing his disapproval of Weber's tone in debunking Hardy, has accepted his essential argument that the storm is a set-piece, an attempt 'to shift gear, to give the novel a new tragic dimension'.[17] Gregor further argues: 'In itself, the episode is admirable; in the context of the novel, it fails to find an adequate supporting structure.'[18] It is perhaps arguable that in itself the episode may seem artificially stimulated, overtly portentous, and reminiscent of Harrison Ainsworth. Weber's finding after all has a basis in fact. In vocabulary and rhetoric the scene is not very different from the Ainsworth parallel. After setting the pertinent parts from the two books side by side, Weber comments:

In both passages the sequence of events is the same: the sultry weather, the confused activity of the animals, the calm, the vivid flash of lightning, the crash of thunder, the black sky, the torrent of rain. All this Hardy might have learnt directly from nature herself; but only Ainsworth supplied him with the long list of identical words: sultry, lurid, metallic look, night, rooks, lightning, flash, peal—

a list that would have been multiplied but for the skilful way in which Hardy paraphrased Ainsworth, turning 'kine' into 'sheep', 'deer' into 'heifers', 'the grave' into 'a death', 'hazy vapour' into 'hot breeze', 'sighing wind' into 'expiration of air from heaven', 'highest branches' into 'summits of lofty objects', 'pitch dark' into 'black sky', etc.... Thomas Hardy soon outdistanced his teacher but it was Ainsworth who taught him how to describe a storm.[19]

The words used to describe the storm may appear too literary and, on the above evidence, even have an Ainsworthian echo. But the chapter as a whole is not an excursion into meaningless word-painting or word-poaching. First of all, it is perceptually continuous with earlier episodes in the novel. The lurid, grotesque atmosphere evoked here has been felt earlier in Gabriel's first disaster and in his reaction to the burning ricks. Here the same imagery is developed on a larger scale to evoke a greater atmospheric disturbance. Besides, the storm provides a very subtle context for Hardy to bring Oak and Bathsheba together and show that there exists between them an unconscious magnetism. And here the chapter holds an important key to the thematic structure of the novel which relates to the innerness and inevitability of a communal relationship between Oak and Bathsheba, away from the distortions and deceptions of romance. Hardy deliberately involves Bathsheba in two different planes of action in the novel—the romantic, and the moral. Bathsheba is both the dazzling, infernally coquettish heroine of popular romantic fiction and the embodiment of a community sensibility and culture. It is in the latter role that she can comprehend and be responsive to Oak, while her romantic inclinations mock and resist him and reduce him to the level of a comic survival from an antediluvian world. The novel is so structured as to dissipate Bathsheba's romantic self and show the validity of her allegiance to the communal ethic. The storm provides a brilliant focus for the articulation of this allegiance. In laying bare to Gabriel her motives in marrying Troy she evinces a kind of intuitive trust in him and a willing subjection to the way of life so crassly contravened by Troy. It is not only her regretful admission that 'between jealousy and distraction, I married him!' (p. 282) but the mood released by the whole episode, with its rhythm of impersonal toil and shared impulses against a background of natural disaster, which brings home the essential unity between the characters of Oak and Bathsheba which to me is the central theme of the novel. The storm scene, therefore, is not a literary excrescence or an irrelevant importation from an alien source. Its similarity of vocabulary and phrasing with a less reputable parallel may be the result of Hardy's acquaintance with the earlier novel or may be purely coincidental, but its function in the human drama of Hardy's novel is as much of Hardy's genius as are the characters of Oak and Bathsheba. To think of the storm is to think of them thatching and rescuing the corn with a piety and trustful interdependence which lie at the heart of Hardy's vision of community.

Bathsheba's relationship with Oak is an index of her initiation into the community. The fact that she instinctively turns to Oak in moments of crisis and difficulty is indicative of her undamaged susceptibility to the communal ethic of which Oak is the chief protagonist. 'DO NOT DESERT ME GABRIEL' has the ring of supplication. Not only does Bathsheba turn to Gabriel for material help but depends on him in matters moral and emotional as well. No matter how complete the dissolution and dismay, the action of the community never ceases. Thus, when, after the sad exposure of Fanny's and her child's corpses which brings untold miseries upon Bathsheba, she travels through the swamp, the swamp may well be regarded as a symbol of spiritual sickness and of the impossibility of redemption. But Bathsheba's consciousness of the ordinary processes of life in nature and in the human community is still intact, still active through the negatives of her situation. In more than a literal sense she does not sink in the swamp:

'O, ma'am! I am so glad I have found you,' said the girl, as soon as she saw Bathsheba.

'You can't come across,' Bathsheba said in a whisper, which she vainly endeavoured to make loud enough to reach Liddy's ears. Liddy, not knowing this, stepped down upon the swamp, saying, as she did so, 'It will bear me up, I think.'

Bathsheba never forgot that transient little picture of Liddy crossing the swamp to her there in the morning light.

Iridescent bubbles of dank subterranean breath rose from
the sweating sod beside the waiting-maid's feet as she trod,
hissing as they burst and expanded away to join the vapoury
firmament above. Liddy did not sink, as Bathsheba had
anticipated. (p. 330)

The storms and the swamps, howsoever they circumscribe and
infect the human spirit, do not pose an impassable barrier to
interpersonal relationships. This is superbly illustrated by this
whole episode of Bathsheba's way through the swamp to the
confluence of personalities and the reawakening of old indestructible bonds between members of the community.
Bathsheba's essential harmony with the folk is explicitly
stated by the narrator. Putting her character in perspective
against her out-of-character, whimsical involvement with Troy,
Hardy says:

Though in one sense a woman of the world, it was, after all,
that world of daylight coteries and green carpets wherein
cattle form the passing crowd and winds the busy hum;
where a quiet family of rabbits or hares lives on the other
side of your party-wall, where your neighbour is everybody
in the tything, and where calculation is confined to market-
days. (p. 219)

Her place in the community is never questioned and all her
offences against it, in the total perspective of the novel, seem
to be a part of the trial of her basic character. That it withstands
all the terrible consequences of her capriciousness and her ill-
fortune and learns from those experiences a new fortitude and
wisdom is a measure of Hardy's confidence in the traditional
order. For Bathsheba to be fully reconciled to the community
she must have adequate relationship with Gabriel Oak who is
the community's 'best self, its point of articulateness'. She has
always felt an essential bond with Oak without external props
and symbols. The ritualisation of this relationship in their
marriage at the end of the novel is hardly necessary. It may well
be that Hardy adopted this novelistic cliche to hoodwink the
Victorian reader like Charles Darwin who childishly demanded
a happy ending. There is something incongruous about

Bathsheba's image as a subdued, beaten-down, middle-aged bride after having been visualised as a poetically superior individuality:

> Deeds of endurance which seem ordinary in philosophy are rare in conduct, and Bathsheba was astonishing all around her now, for her philosophy was her conduct, and she seldom thought practicable what she did not practise. She was of the stuff of which great men's mothers are made. She was indispensable to high generation, hated at tea parties, feared in shops, and loved at crises. (pp. 402–3)

Their marriage, however, does not blunt the keenness of the perception of their actual, self-forming relationship which excludes externality and stands independent of conventional formulation:

> They spoke very little of their mutual feelings; pretty phrases and warm expressions being probably unnecessary between such tried friends. Theirs was that substantial affection which arises (if any arises at all) when the two who are thrown together begin first by knowing the rougher sides of each other's character, and not the best till further on, the romance growing up in the interstices of a mass of hard prosaic reality. This good-fellowship—*camaraderie*—usually occurring through similarity of pursuits, is unfortunately seldom superadded to love between the sexes, because men and women associate, not in their labours, but in their pleasures merely. Where, however, happy circumstance permits its development, the compounded feeling proves itself to be the only love which is strong as death—that love which many waters cannot quench, nor the floods drown, beside which the passion usually called by the name is evanescent as steam. (p. 419)

A passage like this only proves the aptness of John Bayley's remark that Hardy leaves little for his critics. But rhetorical exposition in Hardy, as in this instance, is usually supported by irrefutable dramatic perception. In spite of the overinsistent rhetoric, in spite of their marriage, the whole novel seems to say that the bond between Gabriel and Bathsheba is 'strong as death'.

The relationship between Gabriel and Bathsheba is not viewed in isolation, but within the larger movement of the community, which is an ancient agrarian community presented dynamically with all the tensions and difficulties and contradictions inherent in any living organism. No idealising glamour is cast over the lives and deeds of the rustics who constitute the world of the novel. They are a mixed lot— noble, wicked, intelligent, stupid, fatuous, witty. Occupationally, they range from the bailiff to the house-maid. There is no attempt to put them too strictly in any one class or social bracket. What unites them is their relationship with their environment and their collective ubiquity through the vicissitudes of the central action. A marked peculiarity of their culture is their slowness to change:

> In comparison with cities, Weatherbury was immutable. The citizen's *Then* is the rustic's *Now*. In London, twenty or thirty years ago are old times; in Paris ten years, or five; in Weatherbury three or four score years were included in the mere present, and nothing less than a century set a mark on its face or tone. Five decades hardly modified the cut of a gaiter, the embroidery of a smock-frock, by the breadth of a hair. Ten generations failed to alter the turn of a single phrase. In these Wessex nooks the busy outsider's ancient times are only old; his old times are still new; his present is futurity.
> So the barn was natural to the shearers, and the shearers were in harmony with the barn. (p. 177)

Ian Gregor suggests that the last sentence of this passage has a tongue-in-cheek quality. He says: 'a sentence like "the barn was natural to the shearers, and the shearers were in harmony with the barn" may be true to a mood in *Far from the Madding Crowd*, but the form the novel finally takes will reveal it as a sentiment lying only on the edge of Hardy's concern.'[20] This reading of the barn and its relationship with the people who work in it seems to me very subjective. Ian Gregor himself comments that: 'It is the impersonality of work, together with the support of the human community it necessarily requires, which Hardy uses as a counterpoint to the isolating self-absorption of passion.'[21] Given this structure of feeling the barn can scarcely be interpreted as an indulgence in passing sentimentality. It symbolises the solidity and the social strength of the community. Of course, it is true that here Hardy emphasises the positive, beneficent aspects of the community. But he is in all seriousness a celebrant, not an ironic questioner, of the more positive aspects of the rural ethos: 'Every green was young, every pore was open, and every stalk was swollen with racing currents of juice. God was palpably present in the country, and the devil had gone with the world to town.' (p. 175) The sensuousness and the pastoral vein in Hardy's imagination are not a matter of literary parody or pastiche, but are directly rooted in his moral apprehension of life. If the word 'pastoral' does not seem adequate for Hardy's imagined world, it is not because there is any deliberate undermining of the pastoral or its marked absence, but only because the pastoral becomes implicit in his evocation of an authentic way of life, so that it does not require consideration as a literary motif. It is implicit and authentic; in John Bayley's words, 'a law of life, not a literary method'.[22]

Hardy diversifies his picture of the moral community with a comic, ironic individuation of some of its members. This has led some critics to think that Hardy's faith in the community was half-hearted, that he made the pastoral aspects of this community the butt of his ironic and sceptical imagination. Hence, to these critics the deviant action and conversation of some of the rustics in Buck's Head or in The Malt House is nearer to truth than their more fundamental and more productive role in the community. Joseph Poorgrass's callousness in regard to Fanny's corpse has often been cited as an instance of apathy and immorality in the community. But the total perspective of the chapter does not warrant such a reading. On his way from the Casterbridge Workhouse, where he has picked up Fanny's coffin, Poorgrass decides to stop at Buck's Head for a drink and is so drawn into conversation with Mark Clark that he becomes inebriated and unmindful of his sad charge. Hardy gives the whole episode a comic orientation:

These owners of the two most appreciative throats in the neighbourhood, within the pale of respectability, were now sitting face to face over a three-legged circular table, having an iron rim to keep cups and pots from being accidentally elbowed off; they might have been said to resemble the setting sun and the full moon shining *vis-a-vis* across the globe. (p. 312)

There is no suggestion here of a pernicious and violent deviation from the communal ethic as, for instance, there is in Troy's drinking bout, nor any trace of the anger and perplexity which characterise Hardy's exposure of the latter. The reference to Fanny's death, in the conversation at Buck's Head, is unsentimental but respectful and realistic: ' Ay—I've heard of it. And so she's nailed up in parish boards after all, and nobody to pay the bell shilling and the grave half-crown.' (p. 312) Rather than undermine communal strength and loyalties, the episode provides yet another occasion for Hardy to clinch the communal argument. Coggan's reasons for clinging to the church against the chapel are aggressively communal and anti-theological. Hardy makes his argument stand out vividly as a gesture of communal solidarity:

'Yes,' said Coggan. 'We know very well that if anybody do go to heaven, they will. They've worked hard for it, and they deserve to have it, such as 'tis. I bain't such a fool as to pretend that we who stick to the church have the same chance as they, because we know we have not. But I hate a feller who'll change his old ancient doctrines for the sake of getting to heaven. I'd as soon turn king's-evidence for the few pounds you get. Why, neighbours, when every one of my taties were frosted, our Pa'son Thirdly were the man who gave me a sack for seed, though he hardly had one for his own use, and no money to buy 'em. If it hadn't been for him, I shouldn't hae had a tatie to put in my garden. D'ye think I'd turn after that? No, I'll stick to my side; and if we be in the wrong, so be it: I'll fall with the fallen!' (p. 314)

Poorgrass's weakness for liquor is treated with amused irony, but it does not seriously jeopardise the moral basis of the community. The rural folk's respect for the dead goes beyond external proprieties and funereal solemnity. What may seem like a brutal callousness towards the dead is redeemed by a consciousness, a typically folk consciousness, that the dead and the living share a common destiny of suffering and mortality: ' "Nobody can hurt a dead woman," at length said Coggan, with the precision of a machine. "All that could be done for her is done—she's beyond us...she's dead, and no speed of ours will bring her to life....Drink, shepherd, and be friends, for to-morrow we may be like her." ' (p. 315) For all the negligence and unscrupulousness of the temporarily aberrant individual, the genuine sources of compassion and right action in the community are never atrophied. The chapter, which takes the merry rustics to task for their all too human weaknesses, ends with Gabriel's undemonstrative but profound commiseration towards the dead Fanny and his poignant effort to save Bathsheba the pain of discovering the fact of Fanny's involvement with Troy. Gabriel's compassion casts a retrospective benignity over the preceding events of the chapter and though it does not exonerate the individuals at Buck's Head, it nevertheless magically subdues their actions to Gabriel's dominant sensibility. There is no ironic dissonance between the good and the less good elements of the community. Of course the comic perspective through which the community is seen rules out pastoral simplification. It includes the possibility of tonal variance within the whole image, but no scepticism need be associated with the slightly mocking, amused tone of Hardy's treatment of some of his rustics. If there is no paradisal harmony in the community, there is no evidence of any tragic disjunction either. The rustics are sufficiently individualised, sometimes in the rather comic terms of external characteristics such as oddities of speech or dress and manner, but together they constitute, in Virginia Woolf's phrase, 'a pool of common wisdom'[23] which is nothing more special than their capacity for endurance and an almost involuntary submission to the cultural memory exemplified in their daily round of work and manner of relating to one another.

It has been argued that Gabriel and Bathsheba, the two most finely articulated members of the community, are actually outsiders to Weatherbury while Troy and Boldwood, who wreak havoc on the community, are 'insiders',[24] for they are both local Weatherbury men. In terms of a census of local men they are indeed 'insiders' but in terms of the structure of community in the novel they stand in stark isolation from everything which makes Weatherbury a stable agricultural community. Troy is quite clearly a negation of the rural ethic and way of life. His antagonism to the community is best seen in his attitude to time and memory:

> He was a man to whom memories were an incumbrance, and anticipations a superfluity. Simply feeling, considering, and caring for what was before his eyes, he was vulnerable only in the present. His outlook upon time was as a transient flash of the eye now and then: that projection of consciousness into days gone by and to come, which makes the past a synonym for the pathetic and the future a word for circumspection, was foreign to Troy. With him the past was yesterday; the future, to-morrow; never, the day after. (p. 197)

His education and all the characteristics that flow from it also set him apart from the communal man—Gabriel Oak, for instance—whose basic attitudes are governed by character rather than education. Troy's accomplishments are seen satirically as denominators of a striking absence of integrity: 'He was a fairly well-educated man for one of middle class—exceptionally well educated for a common soldier. He spoke fluently and unceasingly. He could in this way be one thing and seem another; for instance, he could speak of love and think of dinner; call on the husband to look at the wife; be eager to pay and intend to owe.' (p. 198) He, even more than the stupidest of rustics, seems to be 'morally stunted'.[25] The bases of moral action in his personality remain permanent hypotheses: 'He had a quick comprehension and considerable force of character; but, being without the power to combine them, the comprehension became engaged with trivialities whilst waiting for the will to direct it, and the force wasted itself in useless grooves through unheeding the comprehension.' (p. 198) But Troy is endowed with a desperate energy and brilliance. His chief weapon is his sexual charm and a certain male vividness. This is pointedly

conveyed in the chapter 'The Hollow amid the Ferns' acknowledged by many as a masterpiece of sexual symbolism. Troy's
fantastic sword play, which brings Bathsheba under his sway, is
incontestably a projection of the Sergeant's aggressive sexuality.
The skill and rapidity with which Troy administers the cuts
have an appeal to Bathsheba as well as to the narrator. The
proceedings are described with a kind of rapt amazement which
isolates the chapter from the relaxed, unhurried atmosphere of
the rest of the narrative. The whole chapter has a Lawrentian
beat and colour. It would be mistaken, however, to regard the
uninhibited play of sexual energy and wizardry in this chapter
as offering a new point of moral assessment. The brilliance of
Troy's actions here does little to redeem his character from
pettiness and unprincipled opportunism. He is a thoroughly
'acculturated' Don Juan figure standing at the head of a whole
line of such outsiders in Hardy's novels—outsiders who are
used to counterpoint the structure of life in the community.
Troy's sword-happy swagger, no less than his characteristically
romantic grief at the pathetic death of Fanny and his foolish
attempts to make amends for the irreparable wrongs he did a
living Fanny by decking her grave with flowers and memorial
tablets, is a measure of his isolation from the community to
which, in the form of Fanny or Bathsheba or Oak or the lesser
rustics whom he temporarily forces into a state of drunken
stupor, he is a constant menace. The total image of life and
community in the novel makes it impossible to read Troy's
rootless individualism more positively. So, although Troy is a
local lad he is so thoroughly deracinated that he can be quite
naturally imagined as 'Professor of Gymnastics, Sword Exercise,
Fencing, and Pugilism in various towns in America'. (p. 364)
In giving him a half-French parentage and an irregular birth
and, of course, an alienating military career, Hardy accentuates
his dissociation from the community at the very outset. All that
remains for him to do, therefore, is to engage actively in subvert-
ing and denying the best-loved and most necessary ideals and
forms of popular life in the novel and, in the process, radiate a
false brilliance of brass and scarlet hiding an inner vacuity.
There may be many weaknesses and blind spots in the community as well but Troy's deficiencies are of an entirely different
order. It is not that Troy is the only villain in a community of

saints. His relevance in the novel consists in his insensitiveness to an active traditional culture, not in any inherent viciousness. That is why the authorial attitude towards him wavers between that of amused tolerance and outright contempt. But given the certainty of Troy's relationship with the world in which he is an anomaly, Hardy can afford to treat him with occasional kindness.

Boldwood is the victim of a particular 'humour' and is best understood as a 'humorous' character. He is an element of the plot rather than a fully achieved character on the total imaginative scale of the book. He is so dominated by a single 'humour' that he seems a kind of pasteboard figure of sexual obsession unable by definition to attain full tragic stature while carrying about him a portentous air of tragedy. His presence in the Weatherbury community gives Hardy another negative point of cultural definition. His passion and recklessness and masochism do not affect the validity of the communal ethic except as they lend it a fresh urgency and point as, indeed, does the entire plot of the novel. Boldwood is that necessary aberration in a culture without which it will lack sufficient self-awareness. Both Troy and Boldwood remain exiles for all their ostensible connections with Weatherbury.

In bringing his comic imagination to play upon the content of a pastoral community and in opposing it with a tragic vision of the universe and with aberrant and disinherited individuals Hardy creates the particular fictional context most suited to his imaginative needs and commitments. Havelock Ellis[26] and, more recently, John Bayley[27] have seen the centrality of the comic impulse in Hardy. *Far from the Madding Crowd* owes much of its freshness and authenticity to this exploratory, comic treatment of a basically pastoral society. That explains why Hardy seems to be working in 'a convention far more basically realistic than Renaissance pastoral',[28] although there is no attempt in the Wessex novels to deny or distort the pastoral elements inherent in the total experience. No matter how intellectual fashions may deny it Hardy's identification with people like Gabriel Oak and the culture of which he is a product remains unquestionable.

Far from the Madding Crowd was written for an urban readership under the constant editorial nagging of a distinguished man of letters. There is much in the novel which is an accretion from the great tradition of English literature, which is perhaps the result of Hardy's literary memories or of his anxiety to be acceptable to the world of literature and culture represented by his wife Emma or his great editor Leslie Stephen. But the novel's uniqueness and 'innerness' consists in its instinctive identifications and urges, in its ecology of ethical and cultural provincialism. Commenting on Matthew Arnold's strictures against provincialism, Hardy said: 'Arnold is wrong about provincialism, if he means anything more than a provincialism of style and manner in expression. A certain provincialism of feeling is invaluable.'[29] It is perhaps this 'provincialism of feeling' which made Emma say of *Far from the Madding Crowd*, 'your novel sometimes seems like a child, all your own and none of me.'[30] She could not be more right.

NOTES

1. Reprinted in R. G. Cox, ed., *Thomas Hardy: The Critical Heritage*, p. 35.
2. See ibid., p. 22.
3. 'The Wessex Labourer' in *The Examiner* (15 July 1876), p. 793.
4. Horace Moule, in his adulatory review of the novel, particularly drew attention to its masterly depiction of 'the inner life of a rural parish'. He called it 'a prose idyll' but one that was remarkable for its fidelity to truth. 'Anyone who knows tolerably well', he wrote, 'the remoter parts of the South-Western counties of England will be able to judge for himself of the power and truthfulness shown in these studies of the better class of rustics.' *Saturday Review* (28 September 1872), pp. 417–18.
5. Quoted in Michael Millgate, *Thomas Hardy: His Career as a Novelist*, p. 101.
6. See Laurence Lerner and John Holmstorm, eds., *Thomas Hardy and His Readers: A Selection of Contemporary Reviews*, p. 38.
7. *Supplement to The Guardian*, No. 1525 (24 February 1875), p. 243.
8. See Florence Emily Hardy, *The Life of Thomas Hardy, 1840–1928*, p. 95.
9. Michael Squires, '*Far from the Madding Crowd* as Modified Pastoral', pp. 299–326.
10. Charles E. May, '*Far from the Madding Crowd* and *The Woodlanders*: Hardy's Grotesque Pastorals', pp. 147–58.
11. Ian Gregor, *The Great Web: The Form of Hardy's Major Fiction*, p. 49.
12. Henry James, *Literary Reviews and Essays on American, English, and French Literature*, ed., Albert Mordell (New York: Twayne Publishers, 1957), p. 294.
13. Alan Friedman in *The Turn of the Novel* (New York: Oxford University Press, 1966), p. 39, argues that the novel takes the form of the taming of the shrew.

14. Virginia Woolf, *The Common Reader*, Second Series (1932; London: The Hogarth Press, 1948), p. 251.
15. Philip Larkin, 'Wanted: Good Hardy Critic'.
16. Carl J. Weber, 'Ainsworth and Thomas Hardy'.
17. Gregor, *The Great Web*, p. 70.
18. Ibid.
19. Weber, 'Ainsworth and Thomas Hardy'.
20. Gregor, *The Great Web*, p. 69.
21. Ibid., p. 56.
22. John Bayley, Introduction to *Far from the Madding Crowd* (New Wessex edition, 1974), p. 11.
23. Woolf, *The Common Reader*, Second Series, p. 249.
24. Gregor, *The Great Web*, p. 57.
25. Laurence Lerner thinks that the rustics in this novel are 'morally stunted'. See his *Thomas Hardy's* The Mayor of Casterbridge: *Tragedy or Social History?*, p. 91.
26. See Havelock Ellis, 'Thomas Hardy's Novels', *Westminster Review* (April 1883). Reprinted in Cox, ed., *The Critical Heritage*, pp. 103–32.
27. Bayley, Introduction to *Far from the Madding Crowd*.
28. Arnold Kettle, *Hardy the Novelist: A Reconsideration*, The W. D. Thomas Memorial Lecture (Swansea: University College, 1966), p. 10.
29. Florence Emily Hardy, *Life of Thomas Hardy*, pp. 146–7.
30. Quoted in Robert Gittings, *Young Thomas Hardy*, p. 193.

CHAPTER 3

The Return of the Native
(1878)

There has been a marked tendency in some
recent criticism of *The Return of the Native* to regard this novel
as an expression basically of Hardy's philosophical incertitude,
of his refusal to find any social or moral continuity in his
imagined world. It is read as a testimony to the exile rather
than the return of the native. The two central characters—
Clym and Eustacia—become: 'figures in an allegory of flesh
and spirit, like the abstractly patterned interplay of flesh and
spirit (or perverse spirit) in *Jude the Obscure*.'[1] Although it
belongs to Hardy's middle period and is separated from *Far
from the Madding Crowd* only by *The Hand of Ethelberta*, it is held
to be a radically different kind of book. Concluding his analysis
of the novel Richard Benvenuto says: 'Clym is left precisely
where Hardy's original conception required him to be; in an
indifferent and ambiguous world, searching to no apparent
avail for what it is to do well.'[2] The human reality of the
characters has been subordinated to metaphoric or metaphysical functions. Eustacia is represented either as an embodiment of preternatural diabolism—a witch, a temptress, an
'immemorial antagonist of the Christian faith'[3]—or, conversely, she is regarded as an archangel ruined, an almost
sexless symbol of some undefined purity and excellence. Some
see her character as sustained only by the co-presence of
two mutually opposed literary conventions in which she is
presented:

This romantic heroine is both a goddess and a mortal
walking on stilts.... Thus Hardy uses two complementary

Page references to *The Return of the Native* are to the New Wessex edition
(1974).

sets of metaphors to describe the double nature of such heroism: the tragic metaphors of classical myth and folklore and the satiric or mock-heroic metaphors of a debased and bungled courtly love.[4]

The woman who exists in the novel and desperately pursues such familiar human ends as love, marriage, wifehood, death, has been interpreted out of existence. The details of her life are left out of most accounts of the novel. In fact, these are even said to be irrelevant: 'it is in that unformulated drive that Eustacia claims epic status, not in "the dark splendour" of her beauty, and certainly not in the details of her behaviour.'[5] All in all, *The Return of the Native* has been regarded as far too philosophical to be easily susceptible to the ordinary categories of novel criticism. It becomes a cryptograph and ceases to be a novel:

> What we have in *The Return of the Native* is less a 'realistic' novel in the tradition, say, of *Madame Bovary* or *Anna Karenina* than a broadly symbolic vision of, or metaphysical statement about, human existence as a whole in its fundamental absurdity....Almost literally, *The Return of the Native* is a 'tale told by an idiot'.[6]

For others, equally unwilling to accept it as a human document, it becomes a feat of stylistic manipulation, a novel about a novel, 'a tale illustrating high aesthetic problems.'[7] It has no meaning other than that inherent in the vibrations of its poetics. It is 'the apotheosis of Hardy's theories on the art of the novel'.[8] Its action is regarded as highly stylised, self-enclosed, emblematic. The effect of this on the reader, remarks Ian Gregor, is:

> that he takes the tragedy of the novel persistently at one remove from his own situation. When Wildeve and Venn gamble on the Heath for instance, there are considerable issues at stake, but we feel that these are rooted only in the exigencies of the story. Memorable as the episode is, it is 'self-enclosed' taking place in a never-never land. In the novels to come Hardy will make sure that risks of fortune

will be illuminated not by the light of glow worms, but by
those of the market place.[9]

The uneasiness about glow worms, I think, is symptomatic of
a general uneasiness about the defining particularities of
Hardy's fictional environment and of a pervasive desire to see
those particularities as either obstructive accessories or figura-
tive notations of some abstract philosophical position. Such
readings invite comparison with the way in which Clym, standing on an illusory pedestal, preaching airy enlightenment to
mankind, negates much of the warm, sensuous, immediate life
that he leads as a son, a lover, and a husband or even as an
inhabitant of Egdon, a common labourer in touch with the
primary condition of life. The success of *The Return of the Native*
depends largely on its ability to keep the peculiar rhythm of
life on the heath going through all the malignancy of the
universe and crises of individual ambition and enterprise. In
concentrating on the philosophical superficies in the novel
many critics have lost sight of the profound assurance with
which it celebrates 'the diurnal visible microcosm of Wessex'.[10]
In clinging so tenaciously to the cultural imprint of the past,
in its creative nostalgia, its feeling for place and people, and
its unerring sense of the significance of cultural continuity, the
Hardyan narrative challenges its own intellectual despair and
counterpoints the mechanical inexorableness of its plotting.
It seems to me that Hardy's art succeeds not because of its
contemplative vacancies or its discovery of the operation of
great irrational forces, but in spite of them. Even those most
inclined to judge him in terms of the more obvious, the more
stylised, aspects of his work have not altogether escaped coming
under a totally unexpected sort of influence. John Paterson,
who has had much more to say about *The Return of the Native*
than perhaps anyone else, asks himself what the source of
greatness in this novel is. When he has gone over the mechanics
of its plot and the tragic nature of the world it exhibits, he
rightly concludes that it seems little more than 'the applied
will or wilfulness of the author', and thus deficient in 'the
terrific and terrifying logic of cause and effect that marks the
plots of the greatest exercises in this line'.[11] It is lacking, in
other words, in the requisite tragic necessity. But to say that

is only to begin thinking about the novel for it is 'better than its defects': 'In spite of the many excellent and obvious reasons for not believing in the experience of the novel, we do in the end believe in it because Hardy himself did. He wins our consent because what he records has both been closely observed and deeply felt.'[12] By 'closely observed and deeply felt' Paterson means something subtler than mere picturesqueness and emotional vehemence:

> At the very last, however, the source of the novel's 'felt' life or power is much more elusive, less accessible, than the chemistry of its language and imagery . . . . It may be difficult to accept, to believe in, the novel's rickety and arbitrarily directed plot; but it is not at all difficult to accept and believe in its 'action', the curve of the emotion that animates it and is the true shape of its 'felt' life.[13]

At this point, however, Paterson loses his critical perspicacity and his hitherto fine discrimination is suddenly blurred by his attribution of what he has called 'the true shape of its "felt" life' to an 'ambience of poetic beauty and wonder'.[14] Just when he seems to have got under the skin of the novel he withdraws into easy generalisation and can think of nothing better to characterise Hardy's elusive genius than 'the magic of [his] incandescent imagination'.[15] The phrase is redolent of what Q. D. Leavis called the 'belletristic' approach of the earlier critics of Hardy. But Paterson is on the whole saying something of real value. In claiming that *The Return of the Native* has a power and merit distinguishable from its plot and surface action, a distinct quality in its 'felt' life, he is offering a challenge to the most predominant readings of the novel. A closer consideration of this sensitive inner movement may prove more rewarding than all the familiar ways in which the novel has been seen and judged.

Egdon Heath has been more of a stumbling block in the reading of the novel than anything else. It occupies a prominent place in the story and is a major determinant of the book's atmosphere, but to regard it as a blanket symbol of some governing metaphysical principle is to set upon it a seal of distinction it is not meant to possess. Part of the reason why

Egdon has encouraged symbolic readings lies of course in the metaphorical language in which it is presented. It is described as 'a near relation of night'. (p. 23) Then it becomes 'the home of strange phantoms; and... the hitherto unrecognized original of those wild regions of obscurity which are vaguely felt to be compassing us about in midnight dreams of flight and disaster....' (p. 35) Furthermore, Hardy's anthropomorphic imagination invests it with human attributes. 'It had a lonely face, suggesting tragical possibilities.' But, for all the seriousness and singularity with which this transfiguration of the heath in the opening chapter of the novel has come to be regarded, Egdon as a metaphor does not seem to me to be wholly convincing. If Egdon remains an intrinsic part of our experience of life in the novel and if it seems to be acting upon that experience incessantly, that is owing not to the brilliance of its metaphorical conception but to the fact of its solidity, its total integration with the human experience of the story revealed in such bare literalness as this:

> He walked along towards home without attending to paths. If any one knew the heath well it was Clym. He was permeated with its scenes, with its substance, and with its odours. He might be said to be its product. His eyes had first opened thereon; with its appearance all the first images of his memory were mingled; his estimate of life had been coloured by it; his toys had been the flint knives and arrowheads which he found there, wondering why stones should 'grow' to such odd shapes; his flowers, the purple bells and yellow furze; his animal kingdom, the snakes and croppers; his society, its human haunters. (p. 197)

Clearly, the heath has a reality measurable in the precise and unmistakable terms used to describe its impact upon childhood. There is a continuous suggestion that the heath is a tract of land, a geophysical entity resistant to change and civilisation ('civilisation was its enemy', p. 35). Thomasin's down-to-earth attitude towards the heath—'To her there were not, as to Eustacia, demons in the air, and malice in every bush and bough. The drops which lashed her face were not scorpions, but prosy rain; Egdon in the mass was no monster whatever, but impersonal open ground' (p. 380) —is a reminder that there has been a great deal of philosophical trespassing upon the heath. The unmediated immediacy of life on the heath comes through in the chapter describing Clym's daily toils microscopically (Book IV, Chapter 2). Viewed through Eustacia's telescope, from a safe psychological distance, the heath is denatured into a vast monstrosity. Its features become blurred and indistinct, its natural sounds strangely portentous, and the richly particularised heath country shades off into 'Homer's Cimmerian Land' gathering to itself vague suggestions of a generalised cosmic hostility. George Wing's remark that 'when Eustacia struggles against the hostility of the heath, she is boxing shadows'[16] has a particular force not because, as he argues, the heath is a pasteboard landscape menacing from outside the artistic action of the story, but precisely because the heath is an inextricable part of the total fabric of life presented by the novel. It is only in interaction with the heath that the humans of the story acquire their cultural definition. Eustacia is the rank outsider. She is separated from the heath by a gulf of incomprehension. Nor is this left to inference or interpretation. Where essential questions are involved, Hardy leaves nothing to chance. He is explicit: 'To dwell on a heath without studying its meanings was like wedding a foreigner without learning his tongue. The subtle beauties of the heath were lost to Eustacia; she only caught its vapours.' (p. 97) Almost literally she weds Egdon without learning its language. That Hardy is anxious to establish the historical reality of Egdon becomes evident even in the celebrated first chapter in spite of its generally misleading vocabulary:

This obscure, obsolete, superseded country figures in Domesday. Its condition is recorded therein as that of heathy, furzy, briary wilderness—'Bruaria'. Then follows the length and breadth in leagues; and, though some uncertainty exists as to the exact extent of this ancient lineal measure, it appears from the figures that the area of Egdon down to the present day has but little diminished. 'Turbaria Bruaria'—the right of cutting heath-turf—occurs in charters relating to the district. 'Overgrown with heth and mosse', says Leland of the same dark sweep of country. (p. 35)

However, it must be admitted that in the introductory chapter at least this concreteness is for the most part overlaid by the philosophical rhetoric. There is everywhere in Hardy an excess of feeling—what Eliot thought a decadent emotionalism—which sometimes strains his fictional resources to the breaking point. One remembers Hardy's unease with the form of fiction. But the remarkable thing about Hardy is that this poetic rebellion against the crampedness of his medium resolves itself within that medium itself. The introductory chapter on Egdon is a supreme example of the non-narrational or poetic resources of Hardy's novels. What needs special recognition, however, is the fact that this poetic ambience is not entirely unrelated to the total experience of the novel. Critics have usually found a dichotomy between the poet and the novelist in Hardy. The classic expression of this view is Forster's. After having found most details of the Wessex novels hopelessly contrived and wanting in the artistic power to persuade, Forster concludes that 'Hardy seems to me essentially a poet who conceives of his novels from an enormous height.'[17] Paterson roundly calls the Egdon chapter a 'ceremonial' chapter.[18] To me it seems much more functional in mobilising the world of the novel. The mythologisation of the heath in this chapter is essential to Hardy's creation of a cultural arte-fact. Through the mythic character of the heath he is able to elevate his tale of the primitive rural community out of the narrow limits of fictional realism. What Hardy achieves in his elaborate delineation of the heath is not a stationary picture but a dynamic quality which enters into our total response to the novel. The heath remains a masterpiece of superbly detailed landscape but it also validates and makes acceptable the emotional climate of the story. I entirely agree with Walter Allen that without it 'the novel would be unimaginable, for the heath provides it with the especial dimension in which it has its being.'[19] The novel would be unimaginable without it not only because, as Allen and others have argued, it helps to make the novel a fable of the tragic human situation, but also because it enriches and completes the life of the community with which the novel is engaged and gives it an epic dimension. It is in this sense that Egdon can be said to have a poetic function. The grand style used in the first chapter has contributed to the general misunderstanding about Egdon. The poetic centrality of the heath in the felt life of the novel, however, survives the stylistic ineptitudes of the first chapter, is in fact active even through those ineptitudes. The turgidity and heavy-footedness of Hardy's general style are too well-known to need illustration. The chapter on Egdon takes its share of those faults: it is marked by a funereal sombreness, and there is a good deal of artiness and overwriting in it. But, whatever the stylistic flaws, the quintessential Egdon has been created already in this chapter. 'It was a spot which returned upon the memory of those who loved it with an aspect of peculiar and kindly congruity.' (p. 34) It does return upon the memory like an inevitable condition of the story's vital structure of feeling.

Most criticism of *The Return of the Native* has taken the form of a partisanship either of Clym or Eustacia. Clym is seen both as 'the noblest character in the book'[20] and as 'a dull dog'.[21] Eustacia similarly is either 'a romantic light-weight',[22] an 'inauthentic personality',[23] or, conversely, she becomes the chief enactress of the novel's moral theme, its 'imaginative centrality'.[24] John Paterson sees two distinct and warring tendencies in Hardy:

> As a Londoner, as a man of his century, Hardy sympathized with the violent humanism of the romantic movement.... He was not, however, altogether the Londoner, the man of his time; he was more particularly a product of the province of Dorset and, as such, the inheritor of a traditional moral wisdom older and more durable than the wisdom of romantic philosophy and profoundly skeptical of it.[25]

In *The Return of the Native*, Paterson argues, the Londoner triumphs over the Dorset peasant and Eustacia Vye is the special fictional token of that triumph. Paterson at least recognises the presence of a shaping matrix in the novel, but to some others the novel is a repudiation of any such matrix; it is merely existentialist: 'But there is no basis by which to compare the rightness of Thomasin's vision with Eustacia's or that of either with Clym's. Their different views coexist and are as independent as the personalities they reveal.' I do not think that any of these views does justice to the novel. No novel written on purpose to justify or repudiate a given position can be a successful novel. Nor can a novelist afford to be a partisan of this or that character he has created. Such moral approval as he may accord to a character has to inhere in the dramatic life of that character, and not remain recognisable, therefore, as moral approval. To say that *The Return of the Native* is written to justify Eustacia or Clym is to go against the grain of the narrative. But it might be said with greater justice that the novel is an examination of the moral quality of their life and action, subordinating their individual lives to certain primordial rhythms and rightnesses in which it instinctively believes. In Hardy the norm rests in the rural community. This is not to say that the peasant leads a nobler or better life than the Londoner or that Wessex is the repository of all purity and wisdom. Wessex is not paradise, and even the noblest of the rustics have their peculiar limitations. They are not by any means idealised. But they are open to the redemptive influences of cultural memory and responsive to the world beyond the narrow limits of their own egos. Thus, in terms strictly of the novel's fundamental creative bias, these rustics acquire a strange kind of sufficiency while all the high-minded nobility of romantic rebels remains a permanent assumption. Rusticity is not a condition of moral life, but it is a major compulsion behind the instinctive movement of Hardy's imagination.

The rhetoric of the 'Queen of Night' chapter has been the subject of much critical debate and controversy. Some think that it is mere romantic bravura trying to elevate a selfish, immature, incurably romantic girl into a 'model goddess'. Paterson calls this chapter, as well as the opening Egdon chapter, as I have noted earlier, merely 'ceremonial'. Others think that Hardy could not be so naive as to really mean what he says about Eustacia. They find ironic ambiguity at work behind the high-falutin rhetoric. Their argument is that Hardy resolves his basic ambivalence towards Eustacia by using a kind of bifocal perspective, by presenting her simultaneously 'as the tragic Queen of Night and as the comic and morbid courtly pretender'. To me the chapter seems a much more straightforward kind of portrait. It is basically concerned with Eustacia's unusual physical attractiveness: 'She was in person full-limbed and somewhat heavy; without ruddiness, as without pallor; and soft to the touch as a cloud. To see her hair was to fancy that a whole winter did not contain darkness enough to form its shadow ....' (p. 93) In fact, the novelist quite frankly delights in bringing together his portrait of a beauty:

> She had Pagan eyes, full of nocturnal mysteries, and their light, as it came and went, and came again, was partially hampered by their oppressive lids and lashes; and of these the under lid was much fuller than it usually is with English women.... The mouth seemed formed less to speak than to quiver, less to quiver than to kiss. (pp. 93-4)

It is true that as the chapter develops Hardy attempts some kind of a spiritual biography as well. But even the analysis of the inner woman in Eustacia falls into fairly straightforward and conventional lines. She is dreamy, ambitious, and empty-headed:

> Thus it happened that in Eustacia's brain were juxtaposed the strangest assortment of ideas, from old time and from new. There was no middle distance in her perspective: romantic recollections of sunny afternoons on an esplanade, with military bands, officers, and gallants around, stood like gilded letters upon the dark tablet of surrounding Egdon. (p. 95)

The very fact that Hardy can talk about her with such authoritative gusto means that she does not engage him at any deeper level of exploration and analysis. He can convey his full sense of her personality in stock poetical images: 'Her presence brought memories of such things as Bourbon roses, rubies, and tropical midnights; her moods recalled lotus-eaters and the march in "Athalie"; her motions, the ebb and flow of the sea; her voice, the viola.' (p. 94) She is treated sympathetically and even with a measure of respect, but she remains too much of a performing heroine—deprived by definition of the cultural identity which is the novel's central moral criterion. The 'Queen of Night' chapter only rehearses the romantic pampering which she will need throughout the novel to be able to perform her role. Her dream in Chapter III, Book

Second, reflects the deep-seated romanticism and psychological disengagement of her basic character:

> the heath dimly appeared behind the general brilliancy of the action. She was dancing to wondrous music, and her partner was the man in silver armour who had accompanied her through the previous fantastic changes, the visor of his helmet being closed. The mazes of the dance were ecstatic. Soft whispering came into her ear from under the radiant helmet, and she felt like a woman in Paradise. (p. 142)

Temperamentally Eustacia is averse to action, to commitment, to cultural identification. She can feel intensely only about an absence—Paris, or some other glittering city of the mind, and non-existent heroes can stir her imagination to a feverish pitch of activity. It is worth remarking that while describing Eustacia's attitude towards mummers and mumming Hardy dismisses her distaste for such practices in one sentence and offers a rather shrewd psychological differentiation between the real and the spurious forms of traditional rituals:

> For mummers and mumming Eustacia had the greatest contempt. The mummers themselves were not afflicted with any such feeling for their art, though at the same time they were not enthusiastic. A traditional pastime is to be distinguished from a mere revival in no more striking feature than in this, that while in the revival all is excitement and fervour, the survival is carried on with a stolidity and absence of stir which sets one wondering why a thing that is done so perfunctorily should be kept up at all. Like Balaam and other unwilling prophets, the agents seem moved by an inner compulsion to say and do their allotted parts whether they will or no. This unweeting manner of performance is the true ring by which, in this refurbishing age, a fossilized survival may be known from a spurious reproduction. (p. 147)

This extended analysis of the psychology of a traditional pastime further exposes the failure of cultural motivation in Eustacia, which, in the value-system of the novel, means a total paralysis of moral imagination. Hardy does not ascribe any deliberate wickedness to Eustacia. Even in situations where she might easily be held culpable, he seems to give her the benefit of the doubt. Hardy's was too gentle an imagination to conceive of anyone as entirely guilty. He is too solicitous of human happiness to afford moral scrupulosity. But it is not in the nature of his art to refrain from pointing out in purely dramatic, non-accusatory terms certain kinds of deficiencies and human failures. Driven by this fundamental habit of imagination, he shows how Eustacia fails, at some very crucial moments, to act from inner compulsion. 'The Closed Door' episode (Chapter VI, Book Fourth), which is a major turning-point of the story, illustrates just that kind of withdrawal in Eustacia. When she hears the knock at the door, there is nothing in the physical circumstances at the moment to prevent her letting the visitor in, at least not for all she cares. She would not have Wildeve hide himself for the sake of propriety: ' "No," she said, "We won't have any of this. If she comes in she must see you—and think if she likes there's something wrong! But how can I open the door to her, when she dislikes me—wishes to see not me, but her son? I won't open the door!" ' (p. 304) It is interesting how she feels challenged to open the door even if it is with no other intention than to affront Mrs Yeobright, and yet remains quite firmly determined not to open it. What appears to be utter lack of deceit in her ('We won't have any of this') is at bottom an empty verbal posture concealing her basic inability to act morally one way or the other. 'I won't open the door' is an expression of her refusal to meet the consequences of her life and action. She waits for others to answer knocks at the door ('Her knocking will, in all likelihood, awaken him,' continued Eustacia; 'and then he will let her in himself. Ah—listen.') This seems to me a very telling instance of Eustacia's pathological moral hesitancy, of her inability to share in the culturally accredited sanctions of the novel. In other words she is at odds with her environment without having a moral alternative to it. Susan Nunsuch's burning of Eustacia's wax effigy is, I think, at the level of the comical and the absurd, a ritualistic re-enactment of her rejection by the entire native community. I am not suggesting that Hardy intended this bizarre episode to be symbolic. It is to be taken quite literally, but it does exert a particular pressure on the scheme of character valuation in the novel. In his recent introduction to *Far from the Madding Crowd* John Bayley sees Hardy's art as 'embodying irony with the calm inevitability of the age-old rural processes themselves, not intruding it as an obvious part of the author's intention.' I see the importance of superstition in the novels falling into a somewhat similar pattern. Superstition is not just so much local colour or grotesquerie thrown into his narrative, but is for Hardy an important structural device in creating the ethology of his novels. It expresses, on the one hand, the native shock of feeling which the language of rational behaviour has no power to express, and serves, on the other, as an important sociological strand in the novels. It might be called a dialect of feeling. For the emotions expressed through superstitious beliefs and practices are basically the same primary emotions; it is only the form of their expression which has changed and become twisted. As exemplified by Susan Nunsuch's burning of Eustacia's effigy, superstition does become a useful device in the modulation of feeling in Hardy's novels. When we remember that the final breach between Eustacia and Clym is caused by the revelation of the circumstances of his mother's death brought to Clym by Susan's boy Johnny, our reaction to Susan's grotesque act on Eustacia becomes inseparable from that intelligence. And Susan has her reasons, no matter how irrational they are: 'Susan's sight of her (Eustacia's) passing figure earlier in the evening, not five minutes after the sick boy's exclamation, "Mother, I do feel so bad!" persuaded the matron that an evil influence was certainly exercised by Eustacia's propinquity.' (p. 372) Her reasons, in any case, are no more irrational than our emotional belief that her burning of a wax image did in some mysterious way bring 'powerlessness, atrophy, and annihilation' to Eustacia. The point is that there is an alignment of feeling which does not always obey the dictates of rational judgement. And Hardy exploits that other kind of reason in his attempt to apprehend the whole truth. In many different ways Hardy expresses his recognition of Eustacia's incompatibility with Egdon.

Clym, the controversial hero of the novel, is presented as a

basically incorruptible 'native'. He is a son of the soil. 'If anyone knew the heath well it was Clym.' (p. 197) All his values are
derived from the community to which he belongs, and more
particularly from his mother. His attachment to his mother is
treated much more seriously than as a matter of passing filial
sentimentality. The stress falls on the inevitability of that
relationship:

> His theory and his wishes...had made an impression on
> Mrs Yeobright. Indeed, how could it be otherwise when he
> was a part of her—when their discourses were as if carried
> on between the right and the left hands of the same body?
> He had despaired of reaching her by argument; and it was
> almost as a discovery to him that he could reach her by a
> magnetism which was as superior to words as words are to
> yells. (p. 212)

A similar kind of magnetism draws him to the heath. He is
'inwoven' with it, and looks upon it as his natural home: 'To
my mind it is most exhilarating, and strengthening, and
soothing. I would rather live on these hills than anywhere else
in the world.' (p. 209) His identification with the physical
surroundings of the heath and his increasing absorption in it
become a psychological fugue. As a child he is said to have
romped about the heath and known no other toys than its
'flint knives' and 'arrow-heads'. Later, after his many dis-
appointments in the outside world or even at home, he finds
physical contact with the heath very comforting. He is scarcely
distinguishable from the natural forms of life on the heath. To
his own mother he appears 'not more distinguishable from the
scene around him than the green caterpillar from the leaf it
feeds on.' (p. 297) Clym's character, too, seems to be an emanation from the heath. Even his reformist tendencies do not
create any real barriers between himself and the community.
He remains within the fold to the very end. He not only stands
for a certain kind of life but lives it. For all the alleged
modernity of his ideals he remains firmly committed to his
cultural inheritance. He has a concrete historical imagination:

He frequently walked the heath alone, when the past seized

upon him with its shadowy hand, and held him there to listen to its tale. His imagination would then people the spot with its ancient inhabitants: forgotten Celtic tribes trod their tracks about him, and he could almost live among them, look in their faces, and see them standing beside the barrows which swelled around, untouched and perfect as at the time of their erection. (p. 399)

Egdon becomes a tablet of hieroglyphs for Clym. His involvement with Egdon in all its ramifications is the only basis of his fictional existence.

The problem about Clym, however, is that he appears on the scene rather late. It is not until Chapter II, Book Third, that he really makes his presence felt. And when he comes into his own as a psychologically viable character, one has a feeling that all those preceding introductory accounts of him have very little to do with his action in the novel. They even appear gratuitous and misleading in retrospect. He is not the abstracted, cerebral, perusing animal that we have been led to expect. He is, by hearsay, a perusing sort of person, and he is for ever setting up his study, but his bibliomania remains largely a matter of conjecture. His vague idealism and desire to teach his fellowmen 'how to breast the misery they are born to' can as easily be seen to derive from his somewhat emotional response to life as from any ingrained habit of contemplation or obsession with books. His first defining choices in the novel—romantic infatuation and, consequently, marriage with Eustacia and estrangement from his mother—are again understandable in terms of ordinary human psychology. His 'wearing habit of meditation' (p. 162), his cynical 'view of life as a thing to be put up with' (p. 191), and his alleged asceticism seem in no way to characterise his living conduct in the novel. His powerful and haunting human identity in the novel consists entirely in his native resources. He takes his reality from such actions as carrying his dying mother across the heath 'like Aeneas with his father; the bats circling round his head, nightjars flapping their wings within a yard of his face, and not a human being within call' (p. 313), or, his accusation of Eustacia: 'You shut the door—you looked out of the window upon her—you had a man in the house with

you— you sent her away to die. The inhumanity—the treachery—I will not touch you—stand away from me—and confess
every word!' (p. 345) To some people it seems entirely un-
reasonable for Clym to address such words to Eustacia and they
take his passionate rebuke as a final proof of his callousness
towards his once-loved wife. But before Eustacia has gone away
from Clym, following their quarrel, there comes a moment of
angelic rectitude; a stroke of genius:

> She hastily dressed herself, Yeobright moodily walking up
> and down the room the whole of the time. At last all her
> things were on. Her little hands quivered so violently as
> she held them to her chin to fasten her bonnet that she could
> not tie the strings, and after a few moments she relinquished
> the attempt. Seeing this he moved forward and said, 'Let me
> tie them.'
>   She assented in silence, and lifted her chin. For once at
> least in her life she was totally oblivious of the charm of her
> attitude. But he was not, and he turned his eyes aside, that
> he might not be tempted to softness. (p. 349)

Later when he has moved to Blooms-End, the poignancy of his
strange expectation of Eustacia is communicated thus:

> When a leaf floated to the earth he turned his head, thinking
> it might be her footfall. A bird searching for worms in the
> mould of the flower-beds sounded like her hand on the latch
> of the gate; and at dusk, when soft, strange ventriloquisms
> came from holes in the ground, hollow stalks, curled dead
> leaves, and other crannies wherein breezes, worms, and
> insects can work their will, he fancied that they were Eustacia,
> standing without and breathing wishes of reconciliation.
> (p. 361)

Clym's manifest character in the novel totally denies the
conceptual image in which he is presented in the introductory
chapters. Perhaps Hardy tried to create a living human being
out of the hypotheses of his prefatory remarks, and failed.
But Clym's, nevertheless, is a fully achieved character. It illustrates the supremacy of the habitual movement of Hardy's

imagination. The history of Clym's character is the history of
the triumph of the Dorset peasant over the Darwinian philosopher. Because of the abortive blueprint with which Hardy
begins to set him up, most critics have regarded Clym as an intol-
erable prig, a pseudo-idealist, and an inauthentic personality.
Hardy, as I have said, is partly responsible for this misunderstanding. What has created further confusion about the meaning
of the novel, and particularly about Clym, is Book Sixth which
was a later addition to the story, according to an authorial
footnote in the text (see p. 413). But Book Sixth is not just
about the marriage between Thomasin and Venn. It also tries
to modify Clym's image by attributing to him what has
been called 'negative and sterile behavioural modes'.[26] Clym
again seems to be hardening into the philosophical model of
the introductory chapters:

> He did sometimes think he had been ill-used by fortune, so
> far as to say that to be born is a palpable dilemma, and that
> instead of men aiming to advance in life with glory they
> should calculate how to retreat out of it without shame. But
> that he and his had been sarcastically and pitilessly handled
> in having such irons thrust into their souls he did not main-
> tain long. (p. 398)

He is subjected to some damaging irony as he sits over 'books
of an exceptionally large type', divided by a wood partition
from the bustling life of 'his sweet cousin'. The irony is obvious
and has been treated as a clue to Hardy's entire character-image
of Clym. But I think there is a kind of counter-irony in the
perfunctoriness with which Clym sits over his books, all the
while listening to and visualising slight noises about the
house:

> his ear became at last so accustomed to these slight noises
> from the other part of the house that he almost could
> witness the scenes they signified. A faint beat of half-seconds
> conjured up Thomasin rocking the cradle, a wavering hum
> meant that she was singing the baby to sleep, a crunching of
> sand as between millstones raised the picture of Humphrey's,
> Fairway's, or Sam's heavy feet crossing the stone floor of the

kitchen; a light boyish step, and a gay tune in a high key, betokened a visit from Grandfer Cantle.... (p. 399)

Clym's 'ideas' about life are not manifest in his concrete behaviour in the novel. They are something we take on trust from the novelist. Admittedly Clym's image is considerably deflated in Book Sixth, but 'the ironies which attend Clym's presence in the last chapters are Hardy's distress signals about a character who has outstayed his welcome'[27] and, one might add, his artistic *raison d'etre*.

No discussion of *The Return of the Native* can be complete without a consideration of Diggory Venn's character. Critical reaction to Venn has been as diverse as that to any other character or aspect of the novel. To some he is a wholly noble character, while others take Hardy's phrase, a 'Mephistophelian visitant', about him quite literally. But there are those who wrongly see him as a purely allegorical figure: 'an emblematic expression or personification of the particular imaginative sense of bizarre incongruity which is the unifying principle of the entire book.'[28] Diggory's involvement in the action of the novel justifies his description as 'an emanation of the heath'. He is present in the story like a moral climate, just as the heath is an essential source of its ecology. He has no distracting personal or social identity, but becomes an almost anonymous medium for a certain kind of moral urgency: ' "I fancy I've seen that young man's face before," said Humphrey. "But where, or how, or what **his** name is, I don't know." ' (p. 59) He materialises on the heath at the most crucial moments to direct the course of events, makes 'providential counter-move[s]' (p. 293) and thus becomes the chief embodiment of the cultural-moral sensibility of the novel. The most memorable part he plays is winning Mrs Yeobright's guineas back from Wildeve. Both in its descriptive focus and its moral significance, the gambling episode is one of the major achievements of the novel. The farcical aspect of Venn, the aspect which makes people mistake him for the Devil, has no other meaning than its literal farcicality. Any man painted red will look a bit of a horror. He is not born red as he says himself. His belonging to a very definite rural tradition is made quite explicit:

Reddlemen of the old school are now but seldom seen. Since the introduction of railways Wessex farmers have managed to do without these Mephistophelian visitants, and the bright pigment so largely used by shepherds in preparing sheep for the fair is obtained by other routes. Even those who yet survive are losing the poetry of existence which characterized them... (p. 104)

The reddleman essentially is a product of that intimacy with a certain rhythm of life which is still active in *The Return of the Native*. He is not an answer to the exigencies of the plot, but an integral part of the true shape of the novel's image of life. No novel can yield its total meaning in any one image or statement. But there are certain kinds of sensitivity in a novel which betray its inmost rhythms of experience. Such a moment in *The Return of the Native* arises, I think, when Hardy merges his own consciousness with that of the dying Mrs Yeobright in trying to mark out the direction of her soul:

While she looked a heron arose on that side of the sky and flew on with his face towards the sun. He had come dripping wet from some pool in the valleys, and as he flew the edges and the lining of his wings, his thighs, and his breast were so caught by the bright sunbeams that he appeared as if formed of burnished silver. Up in the zenith where he was seemed a free and happy place, away from all contact with the earthly ball to which she was pinioned; and she wished that she could arise uncrushed from its surface and fly as he flew then.

But, being a mother, it was inevitable that she should soon cease to ruminate upon her own condition. Had the track of her next thought been marked by a streak in the air, like the path of a meteor, it would have shown a direction contrary to the heron's, and have descended to the eastward upon the roof of Clym's house. (p. 309)

In the undisguised clarity of that perception lies a clue to the true identity of Hardy's fictional imagination.

NOTES

1. Leonard W. Deen, 'Heroism and Pathos in *The Return of the Native*'.
2. Richard Benvenuto, '*The Return of the Native* as a Tragedy in Six Books'.
3. John Paterson, '*The Return of the Native* as Antichristian Document'.
4. David Eggenschwiler, 'Eustacia Vye, Queen of Night and Courtly Pretender'.
5. Ian Gregor, *The Great Web: The Form of Hardy's Major Fiction*, p. 88.
6. John Hagan, 'A Note on the Significance of Diggory Venn'.
7. Penelope Vigar, *The Novels of Thomas Hardy: Illusion and Reality*, p. 144.
8. Ibid., p. 145.
9. Gregor, *The Great Web*, p. 109.
10. Edmund Blunden, *Thomas Hardy*, p. 3.
11. Paterson, 'An Attempt at Grand Tragedy' in R. P. Draper, ed., *Hardy: The Tragic Novels*, p. 110.
12. Ibid., p. 111.
13. Ibid., p. 113.
14. Ibid., p. 111.
15. Ibid.
16. George Wing, *Hardy*, p. 55.
17. E. M. Forster, *Aspects of the Novel*, p. 89.
18. Paterson, 'An Attempt at Grand Tragedy', in R. P. Draper, ed., *Hardy: The Tragic Novels*, p. 109.
19. Walter Allen, *The English Novel* (London: Phoenix House, 1954), p. 238.
20. Merryn Williams, *Thomas Hardy and Rural England*, p. 144.
21. Wing, *Hardy*, p. 53.
22. Ian Gregor, 'What Kind of Fiction Did Hardy Write?'
23. Williams, *Thomas Hardy and Rural England*, p. 141.
24. Wing, *Hardy*, p. 56.
25. Paterson, *The Making of* The Return of the Native, p. 132.
26. F. G. Atkinson, ' "The Inevitable Movement Onward"—Some Aspects of *The Return of the Native*'.
27. Gregor, *The Great Web*, p. 108.
28. Hagan, 'A Note on the Significance of Diggory Venn'.

CHAPTER 4

The Mayor of Casterbridge
(1886)

'Character is fate' is true of *The Mayor of Casterbridge* in a less obvious sense than may at first appear. To say that the story of the rise and fall of Michael Henchard is a parable of how your own deeds come home to roost is to misrepresent the narrative angle of the novel. However, it has been argued that Hardy's *Mayor* is based on the central assumption of Christian literature that the gods are just and that, in the long run, one actually gets what one deserves. To see Hardy's novel as the working out of some inexorable moral absolute is to reduce it to a universalist formula, and thereby deflect attention from what is peculiar to itself. It means also to see Henchard as the irredeemable arch offender—a perspective hardly shared by the narrator. The whole movement of the novel in fact seems to be leading away from moralist assumptions. It is the story of a character not susceptible to conventional moral categories. It presents a character which has to be *discovered* and the novel unfolds itself as the process of that discovery. For one of his imaginative subtlety Hardy is an extremely straightforward novelist who does not leave central issues in his novels for resourceful critics to infer. It can be argued that this may not be sufficient guarantee for those unconscious forces which shape a work of art, but when acknowledged authorial intention and fictional processes cohere as effectively as they do in *The Mayor* it is futile to investigate the unconscious. The reading experience of this novel proves the instinctive rightness of Hardy's definition of his central characters in extended asides or, with greater economy, in rhetorical sub-titles such as that of *The Mayor*— 'A Story of a Man of Character'.

The simplest question with which one can begin an exam-

Page references to *The Mayor of Casterbridge* are to the New Wessex edition (1974).

ination of the novel is: what is Hardy's attitude towards his protagonist and how far does that attitude serve as a principle of viable fictional creation? Critics who judge Michael Hench-ard adversely usually point to the moral breach committed by him in selling his wife at a fair for five guineas. Henchard's later suffering, it is held, is a just retribution for a man who so wilfully violates the moral code. True that Henchard's sale of his wife is a callous and inhuman act; and the novel wants us to consider it as such. What needs equal consideration, how-ever, is the unhampered flow of moral feeling in this apparently disreputable character—his instinctive kindness, his craving for love, his primitive sense of justice, and his titanic capacity for endurance. This extraordinary sense of character is poised on a philosophical awareness that Man is more sinned against than sinning. Even as Hardy is describing the bestiality of Hench-ard's first act he betrays a profound tenderness and concern for mankind:

> The difference between the peacefulness of inferior nature and the wilful hostilities of mankind was very apparent at this place. In contrast with the harshness of the act just ended within the tent was the sight of several horses crossing their necks and rubbing each other lovingly as they waited in patience to be harnessed for the homeward journey.... In presence of this scene after the other there was a natural instinct to abjure man as the blot on the otherwise kindly universe; till it was remembered that all terrestrial conditions were intermittent, and that mankind might some night be innocently sleeping when these quiet objects were raging loud. (pp. 44–5)

Hardy's sympathies certainly do not qualify him to be a pro-secutor. *The Mayor of Casterbridge* cannot accommodate orthodox morality. Critics who have applied such a morality to the novel have been led to the absurd conclusion that Hardy's attitude towards his mayor is schizophrenic. What is suggested about 'the relationship of Henchard's character to his fate by the first part of the novel', they feel, 'is clearly inconsistent with the implications of its conclusion.'[1] The certainty and artistic deci-siveness with which Hardy treats his protagonist is made clear by the sub-title—'A Story of a Man of Character'. Unless one

treats the sub-title as ambiguous or ironic, it does not make
sense to argue, as some critics have done, that Hardy blows hot
and cold about Henchard. The later, more pointedly pro-Hen-
chard sections of the novel are explained by John Paterson as
an indulgence in 'humanistic apologetics'. He accuses Hardy of
double-think: 'Rebelling against the traditional frame he has
himself set up, rebelling against the moral dispensation that
Henchard himself has been great enough to accept as right and
just, Hardy will bitterly revile the mediocrities who have
supplanted his doomed and suffering protagonist.'[2] It seems
wrong to me to suggest that Hardy's attitude towards the
mayor undergoes any radical change towards the end. The
novel is throughout an imaginative exploration of Henchard's
unique character. The difficulty of that character consists in
its not being analysable by conventional standards of worth and
integrity. Henchard may be called, to adopt David Lodge's
phrase about Hardy, an 'in-spite-of' character. That is, in spite
of his obvious lapses of conduct he emerges as somehow superior
to everyone else in the novel. The force and inexplicable magnetism of Henchard's character have been recognised by all but
the most censorious of critics, despite their many differences of
approach and critical emphasis. R. L. Stevenson roundly
called Henchard 'a great fellow'.[3] More recently Henchard
has been called 'the most conscientious of bankrupts'[4] and 'by
far the most masculine and positive of Hardy's heroes'.[5] Irving
Howe's more informed appraisal points again to Henchard's
outstanding stature as a fictional character: 'He is that rarity in
modern fiction: an integrated characterization. . . . For a novelist to have created this image of character is a very great
achievement—it adds to the stock of archetypal possibilities
that inhabit our minds.'[6] There is the same recognition of
Henchard's epic status in the observation that: 'in Henchard's suffering passage towards self-awareness we can read
the suffering of an entire species in its struggles to master. . .a
destiny which demands the subjection of powerful instinctive
forces.'[7] Henchard's superiority has been widely recognised.
The cynicism with which he has been viewed by some critics
may be, as Donald Davidson has pointed out, the result of a
'Futurist bias'.[8] Davidson's eloquent plea for Henchardism
leads straight into the novel's centrality. He looks upon the

novel as inspired by 'Archaist' sympathies and as an exposé of the rival philosophy of 'Futurism'. Borrowing his terms of reference from Toynbee, Davidson sees the world of the novel as rooted in the necessary antithesis between Futurism and Archaism. In Futurist criticism, to continue with Davidson's terminology, the antithesis remains but Davidson's hero, and very probably Hardy's, becomes a villain. Farfrae is regarded as a descendant of Gabriel Oak,[9] a source of sweetness and light in the otherwise fallen world of the novel. To be left with cynical reservations about Henchard is, I think, to read the novel superficially, but to regard the Scotchman as anything but a foil is to refuse to read it altogether.

The Mayor of Casterbridge is a saga of the life and death of one man, who is conceived on so large a scale as to acquire legendary proportions. The greatness of the protagonist is not the greatness of the isolated, exceptional individual but the greatness and vitality of a whole culture. Henchard is not Faust. He is great only in his alignment with great natural forces, only to the extent that he is placed in the same dimension with a host of external symbols of a past civilisation of which he himself is in turn a potent symbol. His character commits him to a way of life which is deemed no longer necessary or desirable. In the visible social microcosm of the novel, Henchard is a total outsider, a grotesque anachronism. It is only on the outer fringes of this society that he finds any fulfilment or recognition. And if he still remains the unchallenged hero of the novel it is because these outer fringes of society come to acquire a peculiar importance in the total pattern of meaning in this novel. On these outer fringes is established a kind of archaist kingdom which spiritually reinstates Henchard.

Henchard's character expresses itself in memorable acts of archetypal piety. These acts usually occur when they are least expected. An early instance of this is his feeling of self-reproach after he has sold off his wife. The self-reproach in itself is an ordinary psychological phenomenon. What makes it an expression of character in Henchard's case is the manner in which it has been dramatically and psychically heightened by the man's ritualistic submission to his primitive sense of justice. To express his remorse Henchard 'required a fit place and imagery':

Dropping his head upon the clamped book which lay on the communion-table, he said aloud—'I, Michael Henchard, on this morning of the sixteenth of September, do take an oath before God here in this solemn place that I will avoid all strong liquors for the space of twenty-one years to come, being a year for every year that I have lived. And this I swear upon the book before me; and may I be strook dumb, blind, and helpless, if I break this my oath!' (p. 49)

Given Henchard's rebelliousness and the general latitudinarianism of the world around him such a gesture admits of a variety of implications. It could be ironic or absurd or simply counterfeit. But these words have an ingenuous, unconscious quality about them which leaves no room for interpretation. They are transparent and reveal Henchard's instinctive allegiance to ancestral forms of expiation. Hardy does not care for abstract, theological religion, but where the religious form is inherent in a cultural image, he accepts it without demur.

The action of the novel is so designed as to alienate Henchard progressively, to focus sharply on his otherness of being. He is startlingly different in appearance as well—'heavy frame, large features, and commanding voice'. (p. 64) His laughter has a discomforting ring: 'That laugh was not encouraging to strangers; and hence it may have been well that it was rarely heard. Many theories might have been built upon it. It fell in well with conjectures of a temperament which would have no pity for weakness, but would be ready to yield ungrudging admiration to greatness and strength.' (p. 64) In every detail, whether physical or psychic, Henchard has been differentiated from the social context in which he is placed. He sits abstracted like a visitant from another planet in the very assembly which has chosen him its civic head:

By this time toasts and speeches had given place to songs, the wheat subject being quite forgotten. Men were putting their heads together in twos and threes, telling good stories, with pantomimic laughter which reached convulsive grimace.... Only Henchard did not conform to these flexuous changes; he remained stately and vertical, silently thinking. (p. 70)

Henchard is all of a piece, integrated. He remains in full control of his will and does what he must, not what he ought to do. 'A man in a Hemingway novel, by comparison,' says Donald Davidson, 'is little more than a whining forked radish dressed up in a sports coat.'[10] Even men in 'contemporary' Casterbridge, with their 'pantomimic laughter' reaching 'convulsive grimace', do indeed suffer from the comparison. The novel invests a good deal of its resources in establishing Henchard's unique individuality through imagery, contrast, and narrational manipulation. Henchard is conceived as the only survivor of an ancient tribe, a primitive being with no more understanding of the niceties of social and commercial adjustment than of the new 'horse-drill' which replaces the 'venerable seed-lip' as an instrument of sowing. (p. 193)

The central mechanism employed by the novel to express this differential of character is a dialectic involving Henchard and Farfrae in a close personal and social relationship. Farfrae is not the villain of the piece, but an anti-hero. He negates Henchard with a philosophic thoroughness. To regard Farfrae as a norm character in the same way as Gabriel Oak or Giles Winterborne is a norm character is to turn the ideology of the novel upside down. Farfrae-oriented readings of the novel regard it as a treatise on the laws governing socio-economic progress. Hardy becomes a kind of Victorian Dale Carnegie with instant success formulas up his sleeve. The novel, however, is not a statement of what is conducive to social and economic betterment. True that *The Mayor of Casterbridge* touches upon a whole range of live social and economic questions in the period immediately preceding the repeal of the Corn Laws. But the perspective and the methods used by the novelist make it sufficiently clear that the chief interest of his novel is other than documentary or diagnostic. Hardy's personal attitude towards the contemporary socio-economic issues adds further support to the conclusion that he never treated material prosperity or social progress as an unmixed blessing. Any movement forward in history was for Hardy a cause of deep anxiety. His art consequently has a strong regressive instinct. Hardy expressed his personal reaction to the changing situation in Dorsetshire (Wessex) only twice— once in an article called 'The Dorsetshire Labourer', which I shall discuss in my conclusion and, on another occasion, in a letter he wrote to Rider Haggard. In the letter he agrees that 'their present life is almost without exception one of comfort, if the most ordinary thrift be observed. I could take you to the cottage of a shepherd not many miles from here that has brass-rods and carpeting to the staircase, and from the open door of which you hear a piano strumming within.'[11] But as he goes on his reflections become characteristically double-edged. What he recognises as progress and welcome material prosperity is also what he cannot help regretting as detrimental to the integrity of communal life:

> But changes at which we must all rejoice have brought other changes which are not so attractive. . . . For one thing, village tradition — a vast amount of unwritten folk-lore, local chronicle, local topography and nomenclature—is absolutely sinking, has nearly sunk, into eternal oblivion. I cannot recall a single instance of a labourer who still lives on the farm on which he was born, and I can only recall a few who have been five years on their present farm. Thus you see, there being no continuity of environment in their lives, there is no continuity of information, the names, stories, and relics of one place being speedily forgotten under the in-coming facts of the next. For example, if you ask one of the workfolk (they used always to be called 'workfolk' hereabout; 'labourers' is an imported word) the names of surrounding hills, streams, the character and circumstances of people buried in particular graves, at what spots parish personages lie interred; questions on local fairies, ghosts, herbs, &c. they can give no answer.[12]

Hardy's cultural instinct always seems to get the better of his disinterested reason. It is this operative cultural instinct which informs the philosophy of *The Mayor of Casterbridge*.

What has been said so far in this discussion falls in line with the view that this novel treats of the tragic conflict between the native countryman and the alien invader. At this point, however, certain important distinctions need to be made. Henchard is, unquestionably, the native countryman, but the native country is not as obviously there. Casterbridge is not the country to which Henchard naturally belongs. There are only isolated elements in Casterbridge society which vestigially constitute the native country but in its more dominant and popular forms of life Casterbridge is a commercial town. It is significant that Farfrae finds immediate acceptance and popularity in Casterbridge. When one thinks of the circumstances in which he enters upon the scene, the phrase 'alien invader' seems unduly harsh. At the Three Mariners, where he comes into contact with the natives for the first time, he is found by most to be wholly agreeable. There is only one doubting Thomas who questions the sentiment expressed in his song—'O hame, hame, hame to my ain countree!': ' "What did ye come away from yer own country for, young maister, if ye be so wownded about it?" inquired Christopher Coney, from the background ...'. But Christopher Coney is the odd man out whose opinions do not really matter: 'Christopher Coney was silenced, and as he could get no public sympathy, he mumbled his feelings to himself...'. (p. 83) The majority of people in Casterbridge take to Farfrae almost instinctively. To them he appears as 'the poet of a new school who takes his contemporaries by storm; who is not really new, but is the first to articulate what all his listeners have felt, though but dumbly till then.' (p. 84) He does not strike anyone as the scheming outsider. In fact, he is acclaimed by most as their natural leader. There is no suggestion of dissonance or alienness in his relationship with Casterbridge as such. There are only a few dissenters, voices in the background like Christopher Coney, to remind us that Farfrae is not in his 'ain countree'.

Henchard, on the other hand, is not as easily assimilated to 'contemporary' Casterbridge. He literally strays into the town in search of employment. Through extraordinary good luck and endeavour he rises to the eminence of mayoralty, but there is no indication anywhere that he has ever been a popular public figure who sways audiences. His mayoral profile is 'stately, vertical, silently thinking'. If there is anything in Casterbridge with which Henchard has an instinctive harmony, it is the ancient landscape and the Roman ruins. The Amphitheatre—'melancholy, impressive, lonely'—seems to be Henchard's nearest kin in the whole of Casterbridge. In times of crisis, he gravitates to the derelict, more remote points of the town or mounts the ramparts of the prehistoric fort Mai Dun to watch 'the progress of affairs'. The imagery used in portraying Henchard's character is without exception animistic or animalistic. He expresses his disappointment so strongly as to 'make itself felt like a damp atmosphere'. (p. 77) His affections are 'tigerish' (p. 120); his diplomacy is 'as wrong-headed as a buffalo's' (p. 324); finally, he stands 'like a dark ruin'. (p. 346) He has thus been alienated from the human society he inhabits through this naturalistic imagery. To lend further credence to the harmony between Henchard and the natural and primitive objects around him, the framing scenario has been charged with human expressiveness:

> To the east of Casterbridge lay moors and meadows through which much water flowed. The wanderer in this direction who should stand still for a few moments on a quiet night, might hear singular symphonies from these waters, as from a lampless orchestra, all playing in their sundry tones from near and far parts of the moor. At a hole in a rotten weir they executed a recitative; where a tributary brook fell over a stone breastwork they trilled cheerily; under an arch they performed a metallic cymballing; and at Durnover Hole they hissed. (p. 318)

The bridges where the failures of the town hang about have 'speaking countenances'. (p. 247) These objects become a kind of substitute for human understanding and fellowship. The actual human society in the novel cannot comprehend Henchard. The fact that he is the mayor of the town is entirely fortuitous, a satire of circumstance. In the very first appearance that he makes as the mayor he is seen as the butt of an enormous amount of hostile criticism. The humblest of men in Casterbridge rebel against Henchard's methods and do not have a moment's hesitation in voicing their protest:

> 'But what are you going to do to repay us for the past?' inquired the man who had before spoken, and who seemed to be a baker or miller. 'Will you replace the grown flour we've still got by sound grain?'
> Henchard's face had become still more stern at these

interruptions, and he drank from his tumbler of water as if to calm himself or gain time. Instead of vouchsafing a direct reply, he stiffly observed—

'If anybody will tell me how to turn grown wheat into wholesome wheat I'll take it back with pleasure. But it can't be done.'

Henchard was not to be drawn again. Having said this, he sat down. (p. 68)

It is not Farfrae who incites this rebellion against Henchard. It is simply the fact that in the given milieu Henchard is a total misfit. He stands in a 'refluent current'. He is not wanted. The world of Casterbridge belongs to Farfrae. When people want an opinion on any small matter of agriculture or business it is Farfrae they seek. Even Casterbridge children know by heart the language in which Henchard is condemned and Farfrae lionised:

'But please will Mr Farfrae come?' said the child.

'I am going that way .... Why Mr Farfrae?' said Henchard, with the fixed look of thought. 'Why do people always want Mr Farfrae?'

'I suppose because they like him so—that's what they say.'

'Oh—I see—that's what they say—hey? They like him because he's cleverer than Mr Henchard, and because he knows more; and in short, Mr Henchard can't hold a candle to him—hey?'

'Yes—that's just it, sir—some of it.'

'Oh, there's more? Of course there's more! What besides? Come, here's sixpence for a fairing.'

' "And he's better-tempered, and Henchard's a fool to him," they say. And when some of the women were a-walking home they said, "He's a diment—he's a chap o' wax—he's the best—he's the horse for my money," says they.' (pp. 129–30)

This is the voice of the people of Casterbridge speaking through the impartial medium of a child's memory.

It will be instructive at this point to look into the nature of Casterbridge itself. There is almost as much concern in the novel for Casterbridge as there is for the mayor. Casterbridge is not just a loose aggregate of the individuals it contains, but a powerful social organism with a predominant collective will and character. Casterbridge needs closer analysis than it has received in most critical discussions.

Ferdinand Toennies, the German sociologist, created two mutually antithetical sociological structures to bring out the fundamental differences between a traditional rural society and a modern urban complex. His pioneering book, *Gemeinschaft und Gesellschaft (Community and Association)*, published only a year after *The Mayor of Casterbridge*, is basically a response to the same processes of change and modernisation which are seen in Hardy's novels as destructive of an earlier, more primitive rural culture. Toennies defined *Gemeinschaft* as a society in which there was an instinctive, almost preternatural harmony between individuals whereas *Gesellschaft* is an artifice, a corporation brought into existence by the rational will of its members. He differentiated the two orders as follows: 'There exists a *Gemeinschaft* (community) of language, of folkways, or mores, or of beliefs; but, by way of contrast, *Gesellschaft* (society or company) exists in the realm of business, travel or sciences.'[13] *Gemeinschaft* is older than *Gesellschaft* 'as a name as well as a phenomenon'. The former is almost invariably manifest in rural societies whereas the latter is a corollary to urban development. 'Wherever the urban culture blossoms and bears fruits, *Gesellschaft* appears as its indispensable organ. The rural people knew little of it.'[14] There is no attempt in a *Gemeinschaft* to modify or upset the social hierarchy by disproportionate individualism or ambition: 'The social collective has the characteristics of *Gemeinschaft* in so far as the members think of such a grouping as a gift of nature or created by a supernatural will, as is expressed in the simplest and most naive manner in the Indian caste system.'[16] Toennies uses his antithetical categories to describe two radically different kinds of society as well as to characterise the different stages of development within one and the same society. Having made his fundamental distinctions, Toennies takes care to add that his two contrasting versions of society are difficult to find empirically in their pure, conceptual forms. What is actually verifiable is the approximation of any given society to the one or the other of his absolutes. But fictional societies, I think, should lend themselves better to Toennies's categories for they too, like the ideal types of the sociologist, are mental constructs reflecting certain social-moral attitudes.

To turn now to Casterbridge. There are elements in it that would justify its classification as a *Gemeinschaft*. It is old; it is sufficiently rural; and it has an appreciable sediment of old mores and customs and superstitions. However, these *Gemeinschaft* characteristics belong more to the history of Casterbridge than to its 'contemporary' situation. A sense of this history is kept alive in the novel through a rich evocation of ancient monuments and moors, but above all, through the cultural impulsion of the hero and through the subtle realignment of the reader's sympathies. Throughout the narrative one is being reminded of another Casterbridge, a mythical entity, of which the present town is but a shadow:

> through the long, straight, entrance passages thus unclosed could be seen, as through tunnels, the mossy gardens at the back, glowing with nasturtiums, fuchsias, scarlet geraniums, 'bloody warriors', snapdragons, and dahlias, this floral blaze being backed by crusted grey stone-work remaining from a yet remoter Casterbridge than the venerable one visible in the street. (p. 90)

But the Casterbridge 'visible in the street' has an altogether different character. It is a market-town where people from different neighbouring villages form a motley crowd. They constitute a kind of corporation for the smooth transaction of business. Otherwise they remain separate. Although Casterbridge 'announced Old Rome in every street, alley, and precinct' (p. 100) this is not to suggest continuity but only to see the past of Casterbridge as being totally incongruous with its present:

> Imaginative inhabitants, who would have felt an unpleasantness at the discovery of a comparatively modern skeleton in their gardens, were quite unmoved by these hoary shapes. They had lived so long ago, their time was so unlike the present, their hopes and motives were so widely removed

from ours, that between them and the living there seemed
to stretch a gulf too wide for even a spirit to pass.
(p. 100)

In a footnote to some of the features of Casterbridge described
in Chapter 9 Hardy says: 'The reader will scarcely need to be
reminded that time and progress have obliterated from the
town that suggested these descriptions many or most of the
old-fashioned features here enumerated.' (p. 91) What should
concern us, of course, is only what is evident in the novel. But
that footnote makes explicit the perspective in which Hardy
sees Casterbridge and his emotional reaction to the past and
the present of the town.

'Contemporary' Casterbridge, then, violates a most important condition of a *Gemeinschaft* in that it has no living links with
its past. It is a progressive, 'futuristic' society to, at least for
Hardy, a regrettable extent. In another respect, too, the living
society of the novel betrays a proneness to a *Gesellschaft* condition. It is a society devoid of any strong bonds among its
people. Many of them are maladjusted, cynical individuals
who dissipate themselves in scandal-mongering and anti-social
acts. They have no positive sentiments. When they hear a
patriotic song from Farfrae at the Three Mariners they express
their own deep-seated malaise as a kind of response to the
song:

> 'Danged if our country down here is worth singing about
> like that!' continued the glazier, as the Scotchman
> again melodized with a dying fall, 'My ain countree!'
> 'When you take away from among us the fools and the
> rogues, and the lammigers, and the wanton hussies,
> and the slatterns, and such like, there's cust few left to
> ornament a song with in Casterbridge, or the country
> round.'
> 'True,' said Buzzford, the dealer, looking at the grain of
> the table. 'Casterbridge is a old, hoary place o' wicked-
> ness by all account.' (p. 83)

Furthermore, Casterbridge contains slums which are un-
thinkable in a *Gemeinschaft*:

The lane and its surrounding thicket of thatched cottages, stretched out like a spit into the moist and misty lowland. Much that was sad, much that was low, some things that were baneful, could be seen in Mixen Lane. Vice ran freely in and out certain of the doors of the neighbourhood; recklessness dwelt under the roof with the crooked chimney; shame in some bow-windows; theft (in times of privation) in the thatched and mud-walled houses by the sallows. Even slaughter had not been altogether unknown here. In a block of cottages up an alley there might have been erected an altar to disease in years gone by. (p. 278)

Although Mixen Lane is only a 'mildewed leaf in the sturdy and flourishing Casterbridge' (p. 278) it does impinge upon the central experience of life in the town. The denizens of Mixen Lane are the people who form the body politic of Casterbridge. They include the people who organise the skimmity-ride and, as a more recent settler, the furmity-woman who persists like a malevolent fate in the unmaking of Michael Henchard. Notwithstanding the fairly neat stratification of society in three broad categories represented by the three inns in descending order—The King's Arms, the Three Mariners, and Peter's Finger—the distinction between the two lower strata—that is, between middle-class respectability and the iniquity of the poor—often disappears: 'The company at the Three Mariners were persons of quality in comparison with the company which gathered here; though it must be admitted that the lowest fringe of the Mariners' party touched the crest of Peter's at points.' (p. 280) There is a distinct subversive streak in these Casterbridge characters who hang about public places and sneer at authority. The man who explains the proceedings inside the municipal hall to Elizabeth-Jane speaks with obvious antipathy:

'Well, ye must be a stranger sure,' said the old man, without taking his eyes from the window. 'Why, 'tis a great public dinner of the gentle-people and such like leading volk—wi' the Mayor in the chair. As we plainer fellows bain't invited, they leave the winder-shutters open that we may get jist a sense o't out here.... Ah, lots of them when they begun life were no more than I be now!' (p. 63)

The words smack of a loss of faith in the ordered structure of society. They express the kind of thought which leads to a philosophy of anarchic violence.

The more closely one looks at Casterbridge as it stands in the 'now' of the novel, the more difficult it seems to describe it as a *Gemeinschaft*. Describing the most indispensable condition of a *Gemeinschaft* Toennies says: 'Reciprocal, binding sentiment as a peculiar will of a *Gemeinschaft* we shall call understanding *(Consensus)*. It represents the special social force and sympathy which keeps human beings together as members of a totality.'[16] In another phrase he describes this spirit as *Familiengeist* (family spirit). And this spirit has indeed departed from Casterbridge for good. A rival spirit is rising to overwhelm the town 'like a miasmatic fog'. (p. 290)

Laurence Lerner in his recent monograph on *The Mayor* sees the world of the Wessex novels only as a rich duality comprising the *Gemeinschaft* as well as the *Gesellschaft*. He does not find these novels, more particularly *The Mayor of Caster-bridge*, as at all involving a moral choice between the given alternatives: 'Literature is not simply an opportunity for moral choice, but an exploration of the nature of the alternatives, and Hardy's greatness lies not in his preference but in his full rendering of the life of *Gemeinschaft* warts and all.'[17] In my view this is reading too much impartiality or 'negative capability' in the novels. Hardy's story-telling is too straightforward, too traditional, to admit of such detachment. This, of course, is not to deny that his novels are a thorough 'exploration of the nature of the alternatives'. But when the alternatives involve Henchard and Farfrae, or Gabriel Oak and Francis Troy, or Casterbridge 'now' and 'then', the act of perception itself becomes a moral activity. He so perceives the alternatives as to make emotional indifference impossible. There is no clinical investigation of moral or psychological quality in Hardy. Behaviour or character for Hardy is conceivable only in terms of cultural images. Where individual character does not express itself in these images, it seems peculiarly impoverished and inferior. The battle between the alternatives is not a battle between abstract forces in the void. More often than not it is a struggle for pure human supremacy between two vivid personalities in a perspective made up largely of traditional moral and social attitudes. It is this perspective which makes Henchard's 'character', his moral worth axiomatic in *The Mayor*. The bluntness and utter lack of diplomacy which are so evident in Henchard's make-up also characterise the author's manner of demonstrating his character. The choice of the imagery itself in which Henchard is conceived is indicative of the kind of virtue or vitality that the author wants us to see in his character. This distinctive imagery is one significant feature of an artistic perception which is preceded and deeply motivated by a moral choice. Even Laurence Lerner concedes that Hardy's intention with regard to the mayor is expressed unequivocally in the sub-title, which ought to be treated as a simple key to the meaning of the book: 'But in the case of *The Mayor of Casterbridge* I believe the sub-title is a true guide, and corresponds to the experience of reading.'[18] Henchard's character is rooted in a natural, native sensibility which instinctively adheres to an older pattern of conduct. And the narrative never misses an opportunity for pointing out the difference between Henchard's characteristic responses and the general run of life and individual behaviour in the novel. Henchard has a strong sense of kinship which encompasses even his business relationships and acquaintances. When he first meets Farfrae he cannot but see him as resembling one of his own kin: 'Your forehead, Farfrae, is something like my poor brother's—now dead and gone; and the nose, too, isn't unlike his.' (p. 79) He instinctively trusts or distrusts people. He sees himself as 'bad at science ... bad at figures—a rule o' thumb sort of man'. (p. 79) Farfrae brings in science and a new business technology which throw Henchard's more personalised, rough-and-ready dealings overboard but which also throw them into greater relief:

The old crude *viva voce* system of Henchard, in which everything depended upon his memory, and bargains were made by the tongue alone, was swept away. Letters and ledgers took the place of 'I'll do't', and 'you shall hae't'; and, as in all such cases of advance, the rugged picturesqueness of the old method disappeared with its inconveniences. (p. 119)

It is worth noting that Hardy is not merely recording the

change from the one method to the other but is also implicitly evoking a response to the qualitative difference that the change brings about. He is using dramatic contrast as moral commentary. Henchard's behaviour in different spheres of life or in different situations evinces unvarying basic qualities. He is, through all the vicissitudes of his life, unmistakably himself. This is contrasted with Farfrae's automatic efficiency and his pleasant but shallow exterior. The unintegrated strands in his character can be recognised even by Lucetta: 'We common people are all one way or the other—warm or cold, passionate or frigid. You have both temperatures going on in you at the same time.' (p. 186) And Hardy confirms Lucetta's remark in an authorial comment: 'Whether its origin were national or personal, it was quite true what Lucetta had said, that the curious double strands in Farfrae's thread of life—the commercial and the romantic—were very distinct at times. Like the colours in a variegated cord those contrasts could be seen intertwisted, yet not mingling.' (p. 187) This is going out of the way for a novelist. It is gratuitous, even naive. But that kind of explicit judgement is the special signature of Hardy's fictional genius. Without being able to express a personal moral sentiment about his characters he does not seem to be able to do anything with them. Of course the personal sentiment is never without a basis in the perceived behaviour in the novel.

It is in character that Farfrae should offer seemingly better terms to his workers but remain indifferent to their more personal needs and problems. His hiring of Henchard as a daily labourer is an act of kindness. But it is a kindness done with a pair of tongs, a kind of mechanical kindness in which there is no scope for personal contact or feeling. He is kind when it suits him and knows no better principle than expediency. Moved by Henchard's plight he wants to set him up in a small business but never gets farther than contemplating it. It is not that Farfrae is evil. He will never lay himself open to that kind of a charge. Henchard's enmity, unlike Farfrae's, is ferocious. He hates Farfrae with a demonic intensity. The same impulse which once made him take a terrible oath in self-chastisement prompts him to command the choristers at the Three Mariners to sing the comminatory verses of Psalm Hundred-and-Ninth. Henchard's feelings are unreasonably vehement, but they also have a kind of instinctive sanity and goodness. His bark is worse than his bite. He threatens to destroy Lucetta's romance with Farfrae by divulging her past affairs with himself, but it is nothing more than a threat: 'Such wrecking of hearts appalled even him. His quality was such that he could have annihilated them both in the heat of action, but to accomplish the deed by oral poison was beyond the nerve of his enmity.' (p. 270) In the duel in the loft (Chapter 38) Henchard fights Farfrae with only one hand realising that he is the stronger of the two. In saying aloud to himself, 'I'm stronger than he' (p. 293) Henchard betrays an instinctive urge to fair-play and a total incapacity for unrestrained violence. From his appearance he might be described as an 'infuriated Prince of Darkness' (p. 296) but he is completely unmanned by a sudden upsurge of tenderness: ' "O Farfrae!—that's not true!" he said bitterly. "God is my witness that no man ever loved another as I did thee at one time....And now—though I came here to kill 'ee, I cannot hurt thee! Go and give me in charge—do what you will—I care nothing for what comes of me!" ' (p. 296) And Hardy hastens with his own comments lest one pass over this aspect of Henchard's character too quickly: 'So thoroughly subdued was he that he remained on the sacks in a crouching attitude, unusual for a man, and for such a man. Its womanliness sat tragically on the figure of so stern a piece of virility.' (p. 297) Henchard is indeed 'the most conscientious of bankrupts'. He will not keep a farthing which does not rightfully belong to him. In a deeply moving scene he turns over all his personal belongings to his creditors voluntarily. (Chapter 31) His creditors bow down to the gesture and recognise Henchard's overwhelming honesty. Their refusal to take his more personal belongings should have put an end to the matter. But Henchard will not rest until he has rid himself of what he thinks he has no right to. In making the offer he does not merely try to appear virtuous to appeal to the sentiments of his creditors, as becomes clear in what follows:

When they were gone Henchard regarded the watch they had returned to him. ' 'Tisn't mine by rights,' he said to himself. 'Why the devil didn't they take it?—I don't want

what don't belong to me!' Moved by a recollection he took
the watch to the maker's just opposite, sold it there and then
for what the tradesman offered, and went with the proceeds
to one among the smaller of his creditors, a cottager of
Durnover in straitened circumstances, to whom he handed
the money. (p. 244)

This is the kind of quick, unostentatious, compulsive morality
which distinguishes Henchard from his rival, Farfrae. Farfrae's
actions are unexceptionable, but they lack the spontaneity and
unworldliness of Henchard's moral feeling. The persistence of
Henchard's 'character' is the result of his being a product of an
altogether different culture. His loyalty to cultural paradigms
compels mythical parallels. Morality for Henchard is indistinguishable from his instinctive behaviour. He cannot be deliberately moral. His character is also distinguished by its powers
of memory and its sensitiveness to music. He has a peculiar
way of retaining past images and is 'transubstantiated' by
music. When he is about to kill Farfrae it is living memories of
his past friendship that suddenly rob his will: 'The scenes of
his first acquaintance with Farfrae rushed back upon him—
that time when the curious mixture of romance and thrift in
the young man's composition so commanded his heart that
Farfrae could play upon him as on an instrument.' (p. 297)
Farfrae, on the contrary, has a conveniently short memory and
lives undistractedly in the present: 'There are men whose
hearts insist upon a dogged fidelity to some image or cause
thrown by chance into their keeping, long after their judgement
has pronounced it no rarity—even the reverse, indeed; and
without them the band of the worthy is incomplete. But
Farfrae was not one of those.' (p. 323) Neither Farfrae nor
Casterbridge can comprehend Henchard fully. He is isolated
not by his sin, nor even by his bloated ego, but by the fact that
the fundamental assumptions and values of the world about
him are antagonistic to his defining personal traits—his rugged
manhood, his dogged fidelity to past images, his recklessness
and abandon, his unworldliness and honesty. The immediate
world around him is, in Burkean terms, the world of 'sophisters,
calculators, and economists'. Of course there are moral distinctions to be made even among these. But the best of sophisters

is a sophister still. As a last instance of the conflict between the two characters of Henchard and Farfrae, let us look at the rival entertainments they organise in Casterbridge: 'Charge admission at so much a head—just like a Scotchman!—who is going to pay anything a head?' (p. 133) That is what Henchard thinks of Farfrae's proposed show. But he is mistaken. The entire Casterbridge will go to Farfrae's camp even 'at so much a head'. Henchard gets up his rival entertainment on the outlying borders of Casterbridge, which is the traditional site for public entertainments:

> Close to the town was an elevated green spot surrounded by an ancient square earthwork—earthworks square, and not square, were as common as blackberries hereabout—a spot whereon the Casterbridge people usually held any kind of merry-making, meeting, or sheep-fair that required more space than the streets would afford. On one side it sloped to the river Froom, and from any point a view was obtained of the country round for miles. This pleasant upland was to be the scene of Henchard's exploit. (p. 133)

The physical distance of Henchard's camp from the central thoroughfares of the town is symbolic of the psychological distance between Farfrae-dominated Casterbridge and Henchard's ancient kingdom. It is not surprising that in spite of Henchard's greater hospitality (his entertainment is free) not a soul turns up at his show:

> 'But where are the folk?' said Henchard, after the lapse of half-an-hour, during which time only two men and a woman had stood up to dance. 'The shops are all shut. Why don't they come?'
> 'They are at Farfrae's affair in the West Walk,' answered a councilman who stood in the field with the Mayor.
> 'A few, I suppose. But where are the body o' 'em?'
> 'All out of doors are there.'
> 'Then the more fools they!' (pp. 134–5)

An anonymous remark heard in the streets of Casterbridge clinches the issue: " 'Mr Henchard's rejoicings couldn't say good morning to this," said one. "A man must be a headstrong stunpoll to think folk would go up to that bleak place to-day." ' (p. 136) No, folk would not go up to that bleak place today. That is the way in which Henchard is cut adrift from the mainstream of popular life in the novel.

But it will not be a gross exaggeration to say that the novel celebrates Henchard's isolation. I have said earlier that there are elements of life or sensibility in the novel which justify and acclaim Henchard. There are essences which put Henchard in perspective. There is a way in which the narrative telescopes Henchard and certain powerful cultural symbols of a remote past into an illuminating correspondence. Henchard is more and more alienated from the social context as the novel builds up a cumulative suggestion of his natural propensities. The dissonance between the hero and the 'contemporary' situation means, at one level, the total degradation and defeat of the discordant protagonist, but at another, and a more important, level it means a reassertion of the values represented through him. The various intermittent suggestions and comments and symbolic illuminations away from the material reality of the action are a prelude to that ultimate reassertion. We have seen how the narrative educates our response to Henchard, the man of character, with a purposeful consistency. It is in the fitness of things, therefore, that the end of the novel should recreate a mythical world which can fully express and exhaust the artistic consciousness which led to the creation of Michael Henchard—a man of character. As noted by Douglas Brown: 'The power of the story is a power to seem legendary, to suggest the scale of saga, and that power is most discernible where the movement of plot and character finds closest touch with the folklore behind—is animated by the deep convictions and acknowledgements that the folklore expresses.'[19]

The scene describing Henchard's return to an obscure corner of Egdon Heath creates a powerful myth to sustain Henchard's true identity. He leaves Casterbridge at last to be made one with the country which has always seemed present like an unforgettable dream without becoming existentially real. Now in Henchard's last heroic stride out of Casterbridge that country and its nameless inhabitants palpably gather round him. Waifs and strays from that country have been present throughout the story, but it is only in these concluding episodes that they become morally effective. It is only now that they can contribute to the image of life in the novel. In the earlier action in Casterbridge these elements have been somnolent, unable to exert themselves morally. Their presence in Casterbridge was comic or pathetic, just as Henchard's presence, too, at times bordered on the grotesque edges of comedy. Abel Whittle is an idiotic weakling in the town. Out of it, he comes into his own. He becomes a moral spokesman, a fit person to deliver the epilogue on Michael Henchard. The rustic plainness and concreteness of Abel's testimony have been unanimously regarded as one of the major triumphs of the novel. But the real source of that triumph has not been as readily recognised. It is not merely for the sake of quaintness or sentimentality that Hardy leaves the stage to Abel Whittle. Abel's testimony and the recreation of the world in which alone that testimony can have any meaning relates to the profoundest impulse of the novel. And this impulse is essentially conservative. It restores a frame of reference, a standard of feeling which will vindicate the suffering protagonist. Hardy envisions a world in which there is no redemption save through a community ethic of which both Abel and Henchard are exemplars. They both belong to the ancient country: 'whose surface never had been stirred to a finger's depth, save by the scratchings of rabbits, since brushed by the feet of the earliest tribes.' (p. 350) It is this country which Hardy inevitably counterpoises against a world vitiated as well by modern, *Gesellschaft* attitudes as by cosmic hostility. In the simple communities where time is still measured by 'the blue of the morning', there is an immediacy of feeling and a communal solicitude which will make the worst fate, Henchard's fate, powerless to negate the validity of individual life and character. Abel's words are a tragic reassertion that Henchard has not lived in vain:

'Yes, ma'm, he's gone! He was kind-like to mother when she wer here below, sending her the best ship-coal, and hardly any ashes from it all; and taties, and such-like that were very needful to her. I seed en go down street on the night of your worshipful's wedding to the lady at yer side, and I thought he looked low and faltering. And I followed en over Grey's Bridge, and he turned and zeed me, and said, "You go back!" But I followed, and he turned again, and said, "Do you hear, sir? Go back!" But I zeed that he was low, and I followed on still. Then 'a said, "Whittle, what do ye follow me for when I've told ye to go back all these times?" And I said, "Because, sir, I see things be bad with 'ee, and ye were kind-like to mother if ye were rough to me, and I would fain be kind-like to you." Then he walked on, and I followed; and he never complained at me no more. We walked on like that all night; and in the blue o' the morning, when 'twas hardly day, I looked ahead o' me, and I zeed that he wambled, and could hardly drag along. By that time we had got past here, but I had seen that his house was empty as I went by, and I got him to come back; and I took down the boards from the windows, and helped him inside. "What, Whittle," he said, "and can ye really be such a poor fond fool as to care for such a wretch as I!" Then I went on further, and some neighbourly woodmen lent me a bed, and a chair, and a few other traps, and we brought 'em here, and made him as comfortable as we could. But he didn't gain strength, for you see, ma'am, he couldn't eat—no, no appetite at all—and he got weaker; and to-day he died. One of the neighbours have gone to get a man to measure him.' (p. 352)

The speech is not simply an expression of individual sentiment. It evokes a whole cultural context, a standard of feeling and rectitude and ways of confronting life and death, which give to Henchard's career and character a kind of objective correlative. He is understandable only in relation to such a community. In the alien Casterbridge with its *Gesellschaft* men, he is clearly out of place. Henchard's return to this community before his death, and his apotheosis by Abel Whittle, is, I think, a measure of the novel's optimism about human possibilities and cultural continuity.

　　The Mayor of Casterbridge is the story of one man and the story of his culture. It of course involves other men and other cultures in order to create an occasion for revaluation. This is not to say that Hardy's moral judgement interferes with or weakens the dramatic objectivity of his tale. The other characters and forces in the story have been treated maturely and fairly but they depend for their significance centripetally on the way they respond to or influence Henchard's life. It is, on Hardy's own admission, the story of one man: 'The story is more particularly a study of one man's deeds and character than, perhaps, any other of those included in my Exhibition of Wessex life.' (Preface)

NOTES

1. Robert C. Schweik, 'Character and Fate in Hardy's *The Mayor of Casterbridge*'.
2. John Paterson, '*The Mayor of Casterbridge* as Tragedy'.
3. See Florence Emily Hardy, *The Life of Thomas Hardy, 1840–1928*, p. 179.
4. A. J. Guerard, *Thomas Hardy: The Novels and Stories*, p. 149.
5. Donald Davidson, *Still Rebels, Still Yankees and Other Essays* (Baton Rouge: Louisiana State University Press, 1957), p. 79.
6. Irving Howe, *Thomas Hardy*, p. 101.
7. F. R. Southerington, *Hardy's Vision of Man*, p. 104.
8. Davidson, *Still Rebels, Still Yankees*, p. 68.
9. This is the view held by Merryn Williams in *Thomas Hardy and Rural England*, p. 150. Reversing this judgement she concedes in her more recent book that: 'Such is the genius of Hardy's art that we begin to see unsuspected qualities of generosity and goodness in the Mayor, and something unpleasantly cold and scheming about his young rival.' *A Preface to Hardy*, p. 116.
10. Davidson, *Still Rebels, Still Yankees*, p. 79.
11. H. Rider Haggard, *Rural England*, 2 Vols., Vol. I (London: Longmans, 1902), p. 282.
12. Ibid., p. 283.
13. Ferdinand Toennies, *Community and Association* (*Gemeinschaft und Gesellschaft*), tr., Charles P. Loomis (London: Routledge & Kegan Paul, 1955), p. 38.
14. Ibid., p. 39.
15. Ibid., p. 24.
16 Ibid., p. 53.
17. Laurence Lerner, *Thomas Hardy's* The Mayor of Casterbridge—*Tragedy or Social History?*
18. Ibid., p. 11.
19. Douglas Brown, *Hardy: The Mayor of Casterbridge*, p. 39.

CHAPTER 5

The Woodlanders
(1887)

'If I had to name the finest English novel,' declared Arnold Bennett, 'I should undoubtedly choose *The Woodlanders*.'[1] This may seem hyperbolic but many discriminating readers have testified to the spell cast by this novel, to its irresistible charm and vividness. Hardy himself thought it to be his best story: 'On taking up *The Woodlanders* and reading it after many years I think I like it, *as a story*, the best of all. Perhaps that is owing to the locality and scenery of the action, a part I am very fond of. It seems a more quaint and fresh story than the *Native*, and the characters are very distinctly drawn.'[2] The locale of the novel is, indeed, superbly integrated with the human drama. The personality of place is seldom again as important a fictional ingredient in the Wessex novels as it is here. The *milieu naturel* is superbly achieved in *The Woodlanders*. Reading it against a background of 'bumpy, burnt-up' Indian landscape, E. M. Forster felt transported by its woodland atmosphere:

Trees, trees, undergrowth, English trees! How that book rustles with them! I read it looking out over my bumpy, burnt-up garden. Beyond the garden, on the farther side of the chaussee, rose Devi, a burnt up bump of a hill. . . . One day, as I raised my eyes to it, the trees I had been reading about transplanted themselves to its slopes and hung for a moment in a film of green. . . . The magic of Hardy had projected itself into this leafless spot.[3]

In some recent criticism of the novel there has been an objection to an entirely pastoral reading of nature in *The Woodlanders*. It has been argued that Hardy subjects the world of

Page references to *The Woodlanders* are to the New Wessex edition (1974).

nature to the same processes of decay and dementia as the urban world outside the woods. The point of the argument is that Hardy is not a simple pastoralist and that his view of reality is much more complex than a simple rural-urban antithesis can explain. David Lodge, in his recent introduction to the novel, cites the following passage as an example of Hardy's 'evolutionary pessimism':

> They went noiselessly over mats of starry moss, rustled through interspersed tracts of leaves, skirted trunks with spreading roots whose mossed rinds made them like hands wearing green gloves; elbowed old elms and ashes with great forks, in which stood pools of water that overflowed on rainy days and ran down their stems in green cascades. On older trees still than these huge lobes of fungi grew like lungs. Here, as everywhere, the Unfulfilled Intention, which makes life what it is, was as obvious as it could be among the depraved crowds of a city slum. The leaf was deformed, the curve was crippled, the taper was interrupted; the lichen ate the vigour of the stalk, and the ivy slowly strangled to death the promising sapling. (p. 83)

The passage certainly expresses Hardy's keen awareness of the cruelty in nature, but to regard it as a focal point of what the novel is trying to say as a whole is to grant it a structural significance it does not possess. In treating the passage as central to the novel's meaning David Lodge is perhaps over-reacting to Brown's opposing view that in passages like this 'Hardy stands aside from his invention in a new way, and provides a troubled, intrusive commentary, one that speaks for the despair from outside.'[4] Both Lodge and Brown err in offering systematic apologetics for what seems a moment in an unfolding vista. Hardy is too close and knowing an observer of nature to fail to see its darker side. Nor would he reduce nature to a trite literary symbol of peace and harmony associated with the pastoral. The passage in question, therefore, need not be explained away as an example of despair from outside just as it cannot bear a too schematic Darwinian reading. Lodge finds in the passage an echo of parts of *The Origin of Species*, and goes on to look for the Darwinian principle in the entire novel. However much Hardy's views may have been coloured by *The Origin of Species* and other expressions of the evolutionary philosophy of his times, his novels ultimately stand for the wholeness and integrity of human shapes in a world built for disintegration and decay. If he makes pointed references to the disorder and conflict in the state of nature, it is not to celebrate its finality but only to press home the urgency of his message of human and cultural shapes. Hardy's view of nature is far from Rousseauistic but his faith in the historical community is immense. He sees both nature and man entangled in a common mystery of suffering, but regards man as an improvement on nature because of his capacity for moral behaviour. The poem 'In a Wood' is an expression of just this sense of human capacity and responsibility. The poet comes to the world of nature in quest of peace and with conventional pastoral expectations:

> Heart-halt and spirit-lame,
>   City-opprest,
> Unto this wood I came
>   As to a nest;
> Dreaming that sylvan peace
> Offered the harrowed ease—
> Nature a soft release
>   From men's unrest.

But the woods offer him no escape, are in fact akin to the troubled world outside:

> But, having entered in,
>   Great growths and small
> Show them to men akin—
>   Combatants all!
> Sycamore shoulders oak,
> Bines the slim sapling yoke,
> Ivy-spun halters choke
>   Elms stout and tall.

The poem, however, goes on to assert human superiority and ends on a note of cautious but genuine optimism:

> Since, then, no grace I find
> Taught me of trees,
> Turn I back to my kind,
> Worthy as these.
> There at least smiles abound,
> There discourse trills around,
> There, now and then, are found
> Life-loyalties.[5]

The poem was written with the novel in mind as Hardy's note—'See "The Woodlanders" '—under the title of the poem makes clear. The novel, like the poem, emphasises the need for human community and human forms as a mainstay against the mindless mechanism of the universe. It does not present men as infallible or ideal but certainly sees them as capable of a superior moral order to that found in the state of nature. The archetypal Hardy hero is not the natural man, not the noble savage, but the communal man, the man capable of fellow-feeling and cultural inheritance. He can work, like Giles Winterborne, in accord with nature without being dominated by it. The communal ethic in *The Woodlanders* becomes a criticism both of the primary world of nature and of the modern civilisation represented by urbanites like Fitzpiers and Mrs Charmond. The plot of the novel is a metaphor of 'Unfulfilled Intention', but its action, which involves Hardy's deepest experiences, suggests a desperately human concern to find some answer to the chaos in nature. The communal ethic becomes for Hardy a metaphorical vehicle with which to confront despairing postulates about the human condition. The essential meaning of the Hardy novel resides in a sort of dialectical opposition between the mechanical plot and the moral action. *The Woodlanders* is the quintessential Hardy novel in that this fictional stance is nowhere more fully articulated than in this novel. It celebrates the triumph of human consciousness and memory over unthinking, speechless process and, furthermore, the triumph of the communal man over the rootless, self-seeking individual. Hardy's sentiment is not the easy, novelettish sentimentality of popular Victorian fiction but arises from the felt experience of his particular fictional world.

The central crisis of *The Woodlanders* issues from timber merchant Melbury's social pride and ambition. His decision to educate his daughter Grace beyond her station in the communal matrix brings about the central crisis through which Hardy pushes his vision of the enduring community. Melbury himself is treated with candour and even sympathy, where he deserves it, but the action of the novel is designed to confront him with the consequences of his overreaching ambition and snobbishness and finally to reconcile him to the community. He sends his daughter to school out of a desire to give her social advantages which he has been denied. He explains his reasons to the quizzical Hintock folk thus:

> 'I heard you wondering why I've kept my daughter so long at boarding-school,' said Mr Melbury, looking up from the letter.... 'Hey?' he asked with affected shrewdness. 'But you did, you know. Well now, though it is my own business more than anybody else's, I'll tell ye. When I was a boy, another boy—the pa'son's son—along with a lot of others, asked me "Who dragged Whom round the walls of What?" and I said, "Sam Barret, who dragged his wife in a wheeled chair round the tower when she went to be churched." They laughed at me so much that I went home and couldn't sleep for shame; and I cried that night till my pillow was wet; till I thought to myself—"They may laugh at me for my ignorance, but that was father's fault, and none o' my making, and I must bear it. But they shall never laugh at my children, if I have any; I'll starve first!" Thank God I've been able to keep her at school at the figure of near a hundred a year.... Mrs Charmond herself is not better informed than my girl Grace.' (pp. 59–60)

So far Melbury's motives are meant to evoke sympathy. Even the sceptical villagers to whom these words are addressed are rather disarmed by the innocent plea. 'There was something between high indifference and humble emotion in his delivery, which made it difficult for them to reply.' (p. 60) Education as a means to knowledge is an honourable pursuit. It is only when education is flaunted as a kind of wealth, a material possession leading to social enhancement, that it becomes suspect. Melbury whose initial motives in sending Grace to school are unexceptionable soon begins to treat education and his educated daughter as a means to escape his social situation. He even begins to hate the community, although this perhaps is due more to his ambitions about his daughter than to any other factor in his personality. Essentially a sound member of the community, Melbury becomes a victim of a 'humorous' obsession with social status. As a result, he fails to keep faith with Giles Winterborne to whom he is committed to wed his daughter in reparation of a wrong done to Giles's dead father. The mind trying to overthrow the accepted order and to rise above its allotted station in life is a commonplace literary motif. In *The Woodlanders*, however, it acquires a fresh urgency because of a central moral antithesis between community and the individual. Melbury's social pride leads to a disavowal of his earlier promises to Giles. The timber merchant is convinced that letting Grace marry Giles would mean wasting her education and his money behind that education:

> Here was the fact which could not be disguised: since seeing what an immense change her last twelve months of absence had produced in his daughter, after the heavy sum per annum that he had been spending for several years upon her education, he was reluctant to let her marry Giles Winterborne, indefinitely occupied as woodsman, cider-merchant, apple-farmer, and what not, even were she willing to marry him herself. (p. 111)

Suspecting that 'somewhere in the bottom of her heart there pulsed an old simple indigenous feeling favourable to Giles' (p. 112), he sets about to smother that feeling. Grace is no more than a pawn in a game of social climbing. She is 'the social hope of the family' (p. 117). He wants his daughter to bring him social rewards commensurate with the money spent on her education and upkeep. In a telling scene he asks her to study the counterfoil of his cheque-book with a view to making her aware of her price:

'I, too, cost a good deal, like the horses and waggons and corn!' she said, looking up sorrily.

'I didn't want you to look at those; I merely meant to give you an idea of my investment transactions. But if you do cost as much as they, never mind. You'll yield a better return.'

'Don't think of me like that!' she begged. 'A mere chattel.' (p. 119)

Melbury's yardstick has become grossly utilitarian and Gradgrindian. Guided solely by the prudential calculus and by class-consciousness he tries to force a breach between his daughter and her woodland lover, Giles. When, therefore, he finds the aristocratic Dr Fitzpiers inclined towards Grace he grasps at it as the opportunity of his life. His notions of gentility make him ridiculously deferential towards men like Fitzpiers. His foolish regard of Fitzpiers at their very first meeting and his readiness to accept Fitzpiers's proposal blindly are treated with gentle irony, the gesture being too much a result of foolishness and pathetic self-consciousness to arouse a deeper protest. But the narrator leaves one in no doubt that Melbury is making a fool of himself and inviting something other than felicity for his daughter. His interview with Fitzpiers brings out his obsequiousness very pointedly:

The timber-dealer was much surprised, and fairly agitated; his hand trembled as he laid by his walking-stick....

'... it would be deceit if I were to pretend to feel anything else than highly honoured by your wish; and it is a great credit to her to have drawn to her a man of such good professional station and venerable old family.' (p. 185)

The narrator ironically adds: 'That touching faith in members of long-established families as such, irrespective of their personal condition or character, which is still found among old-fashioned people in the rural districts, reached its full perfection in Melbury.' (p. 189) All that is left for Melbury now is to go through the bitter and humiliating experience of discovering the truth about Fitzpiers and trying unsuccessfully to undo his daughter's marriage with him. His credulity and simple-mindedness with regard to the divorce proceedings again border on the comic. Fully convinced that he has been duped by the lure of the civilised world, he would rather alienate his beloved daughter than have anything to do with that world again. It is he who is given the last cutting words on Fitzpiers after Grace has finally gone over to him:

> 'Well—he's her husband,' Melbury said to himself, 'and let her take him back to her bed if she will!....But let her bear in mind that the woman walks and laughs somewhere at this very moment whose neck he'll be coling next year as he does hers to-night; and as he did Felice Charmond's last year; and Suke Damson's the year afore!...It's a forlorn hope for her; and God knows how it will end!' (pp. 389–90)

Melbury's illusions about culture and education are thoroughly exploded and the action of the novel leaves him chastened and *en rapport* with the community sensibility in the end.

Grace is the more immediate victim of the identity crisis in which her father has participated vicariously, as it were. She is the native country girl spoiled by education and contact with external social currents. Her regrettable dissociation with the land is brought out vividly in the scene describing her drive home with Giles:

> However that might be, the fact at present was merely this, that where he was seeing John-apples and farm-buildings she was beholding a much contrasting scene: a broad lawn in the fashionable suburb of a fast city, the evergreen leaves shining in the evening sun, amid which bounding girls, gracefully clad in artistic arrangements of blue, brown, red, and white, were playing at games with laughter and chat in all the pride of life, the notes of piano and harp trembling in the air from the open windows adjoining. Moreover they were girls—and this was a fact which Grace Melbury's delicate femininity could not lose sight of—whose parents Giles would have addressed with a deferential Sir or Madam. Beside this visioned scene the homely farmsteads did not quite hold their own from her present twenty-year point of survey. (pp. 72–3)

On the ensuing conversation between the two, the trenchant authorial commentary is: 'cultivation had so far advanced in the soil of Miss Melbury's mind as to lead her to talk of anything save of that she knew well, and had the greatest interest in developing: herself. She had fallen from the good old Hintock ways.' (p. 74) Grace's unconscious snobbery and her restricting egotism are characteristics bred by education. She stands separated from the world of her childhood in her obvious responses and standard of judgement. Nevertheless, she has surprising moments of identification with the native world. After her acquaintance with Mrs Charmond, the alien *par excellence*, for instance, she confesses to Giles: 'And as for myself, I hate French books. And I love dear old Hintock, *and the people in it*, fifty times better than all the Continent! But the scheme; I think it an enchanting notion, don't you, Giles?' (p. 98) There are many similar instances which lend colour to Melbury's suspicion that there 'pulsed an old simple indigenous feeling' in Grace's heart. She is appalled by Fitzpiers's suggestion that their marriage take place at a registry instead of a church. The old cultural symbols are still active beneath her conscious estrangement from them. The dialogue about the form and place of the marriage reveals Grace's continuing reliance on inherited cultural images and her psychological inability to see them replaced:

'My inclination is not to be married at the horrid little church here, with all the yokels staring round at us, and a droning parson reading.'
'Where then can it be? At a church in town?'
'No. Not at a church at all. At a registry office. It is a quieter, snugger, and more convenient place in every way.'
'O,' said she with real distress. 'How can I be married except at church, and with all my dear friends round me!' (p. 195)

It is only after her desertion (in a moral sense) of Giles and her marriage with Fitzpiers, however, that her native susceptibilities acquire clarity and definition. A closer view of the glittering world of education and refinement reveals to her its internal vacuity and dullness. She can now look upon the world she has left behind, the world of Giles and of her own childhood, with something amounting to a sense of loss. The scene outside the window at the hotel in Sherton Abbas is a wistful recreation of the world irrevocably lost to her:

> In the yard between Grace and the orchards there progress-ed a scene natural to the locality at this time of the year. An apple-mill and press had been erected on the spot, to which some men were bringing fruit from divers points in mawn-baskets, while others were grinding them, and others wringing down the pomace, whose sweet juice gushed forth into tubs and pails. The superintendent of these proceedings, to whom the others spoke as master, was a young yeoman of prepossessing manner and aspect, whose form she recognized in a moment. He had hung his coat to a nail of the outhouse wall, and wore his shirt-sleeves rolled up beyond his elbows, to keep them unstained while he rammed the pomace into the bags of horsehair. Fragments of apple-rind had alighted upon the brim of his hat—probably from the bursting of a bag—while brown pips of the same fruit were sticking among the down upon his fine round arms, and in his beard.
>
> Grace watched the head man with interest. The slightest sigh escaped her. Perhaps she thought of the day—not so far distant—when that friend of her childhood had met her by her father's arrangement in this same town, warm with hope, though diffident, and trusting in a promise rather implied than given. Or she might have thought of days earlier yet—days of childhood....However, all that was over. She had felt superior to him then, and she felt superior to him now. (pp. 204–6)

What Grace sees out of her window evokes a whole culture and the detailed perception is the work of a regretful nostalgia which she tries in vain to conceal. The arch narratorial com-ment—'She had felt superior to him then, and she felt superior to him now'—is a piece of neat irony. After such seeing any feeling of superiority and distance can only be a clumsy defence mechanism. The bitter experience of marriage with a rank outsider brings a new keenness and piquancy to her reawakened

sense of communal identity. Her complete emotional identification with the tableau-like cultural scene outside her hotel
window is further clinched in the exchange she has about it
with her husband. To Fitzpiers's indecent and supercilious
remark—'. . . I do honestly confess to you that I feel as if I
belonged to a different species from the people who are working in that yard'—Grace unexpectedly retorts: 'And from me,
too, then. For my blood is no better than theirs.' (p. 209)
To this the author adds the following corroborative commentary: 'It was, indeed, a startling anomaly that this woman of
the tribe without should be standing there beside him as his
wife, if his sentiments were as he had said.' Some of the most
memorable and dramatically eloquent scenes in the novel
have their source in Grace's acute need for moral identification
in an anomalous social and marital situation. Hardy strategi-
cally endows her with a saddened perception of the relative
incorruptibility and purity of the woodlanders against the
schematic deceptions of the world she has married into. Sick
at the sight of her husband riding away to his 'new-found idol'
astride the very mare given her in pure love by Giles, she sees
the doubly wronged man emerging from the other side of the
wood and experiences a kind of epiphany in which Giles takes
on the restitutory role of a mythic racial hero. Grace's consciousness of betrayal, White Darling (a symbol perhaps of
purity and unselfishness) violated in the use she is being put to
by the promiscuous Fitzpiers, and Giles emerging in his wonted
guise from one corner of the wood—all these factors, dramatically and circumstantially irrefutable as they are, combine
into a deeper metaphorical meaning. The particular cultural
vision is Grace's and it restores to her, for a brief moment, her
natural sympathies. Appearing at a moment of acute loneliness
and betrayal, Giles becomes a point of articulation for her
ravaged sensibility:

He looked and smelt like Autumn's very brother, his face
being sunburnt to wheat-colour, his eyes blue as corn-flowers,
his sleeves and leggings dyed with fruit-stains, his hands
clammy with the sweet juice of apples, his hat sprinkled
with pips, and everywhere about him that atmosphere of
cider which at its first return each season has such an in-

describable fascination for those who have been born and bred among the orchards. Her heart rose from its late sadness like a released bough; her senses revelled in the sudden lapse back to Nature unadorned. The consciousness of having to be genteel because of her husband's profession, the veneer of artificiality which she had acquired at the fashionable schools, were thrown off, and she became the crude country girl of her latent early instincts. (pp. 235–6)

To see this account as a sentimental indulgence in pastoralism in an otherwise realistic novel would be to misinterpret it. There are obvious pastoral features in the description, but its central force is insufficiently explained by the pastoral formula. The poetic exuberance of feeling in the passage, its 'Keatsian sensuousness' is psychologically necessitated by the desperate nature of Grace's experience and helps to determine the quality of her nostalgia. The exchange that subsequently takes place between father and daughter shows her lamenting the ills brought her by education:

> 'I wish you had never, never thought of educating me. I wish I worked in the woods like Marty South! I hate genteel life, and I want to be no better than she!'
> 'Why?' said her amazed father.
> 'Because cultivation has only brought me inconveniences and troubles. I say again, I wish you had never sent me to those fashionable schools you set your mind on. It all arous out of that, father. If I had stayed at home I should have married—'
> She closed up her mouth suddenly and was silent; and he saw that she was not far from crying. (p. 251)

It is this cultural swing of her imagination which leads to the poignant idyll of her brief reunion with Giles, albeit a somewhat Platonic union, before the tragedy. In keeping with her emergent character she finally accepts Giles as her only true mate. 'There was one man on earth in whom she believed absolutely, and he was that man.' (p. 331) This is the voice of the omniscient narrator, not Grace's unreliable effusion. Grace and Giles have reached an instinctive understanding of each other through suffering and error, an understanding endorsed without irony or suspicion by the author: 'From long acquaintance they could read each other's heart-symptoms like books of large type.' (p. 334) Grace's self-reproach at keeping Giles out in the cold is unquestionably credible and expressive of her new understanding and honesty: ' "Giles, Giles!" she cried, with the full strength of her voice, and without any of the shamefacedness that had characterized her first cry. "O, come in—come in! Where are you? I have been wicked—I have thought too much of myself!" ' (p. 336) She acquires an unprecedented grandeur in her final haunting cry: '*Come to me, dearest! I don't mind what they say or what they think of us any more.*' (p. 337) The words memorably round out Grace's uninhibited acceptance of Giles and Giles's world. True to the communal ethic and standard of chivalry, Giles of course sacrifices his own life rather than bring any shame or embarrassment to the woman he loves. The fact that after Giles's death Grace lapses back into a numb acceptance of Fitzpiers has led many to look askance at her earlier emotional conduct in the novel. It has been suggested that she could never communicate effectively with Giles and that, therefore, the final reversal in the story is not as out of character as it might appear. In other words, Grace's essential character, warped by education and egotism, has all the while remained the same while she may be said to have had some 'spasmodic impulses'. Grace's reconciliation with Fitzpiers with a quiet conscience has been invoked as an instance of the 'open-endedness' of Hardy's mature fiction. However, such readings are based on a moral and artistic estimate of ambiguity not evident in *The Woodlanders*. There is no reason to believe that Grace's affirmation of the community and of the communal hero is insincere. The dramatic structure of that affirmation, its occasion, and verbal expression speak for its truth. Her last-minute capitulation to Fitzpiers, besides supplying the conventional happy ending, shows that she has contrary impulses or that she acts from desperation but it does not completely negate her earlier rapprochement with the community. A contemporary reviewer complained that 'the whole interest of the story is spoilt by our being expected to believe in that incredible event, the abiding repentance and amendment of a flippant profligate.'[6] That may not be true, for Hardy never intended Fitzpiers's professions of a change of heart to be taken seriously. His latter behaviour shows no radical departure from his former. He is all of a piece. Apropos of a request to dramatise *The Woodlanders* Hardy wrote to J. T. Grein:

> You have probably observed that the ending of the story— hinted rather than stated, is that the heroine is doomed to an unhappy life with an inconstant husband. I could not accentuate this strongly in the book, by reason of the conventions of the libraries, etc. Since the story was written, however, truth to character is not considered quite such a crime in literature as it was formerly; and it is therefore a question for you whether you will accent this ending, or prefer to obscure it.[7]

The mantrap incident which reconciles Grace to Fitzpiers by providing her evidence of his loyalty and love towards her is too clumsy and contrived, and Hardy knew it, to be mistaken for a real, impelling incident. Grace's choice in the end remains unconvincing and out of character and may be explained as a palliative to the Victorian conscience, 'truth to character' being such a 'crime' in contemporary judgement. The whole episode is too farcical to effect or reverse a deeper resonance. Grace's admission to Marty that no one deserved Giles better than she (Marty) has been cited as proof of Grace's alienation from Giles for all the ardour with which she returns to him and upholds his values.[8] Grace realises the natural compatibility between Giles and Marty and we have an inspired account of Grace's vision of this bond between them. Then the dialogue follows:

> 'He ought to have married *you*, Marty, and nobody else in the world!' said Grace with conviction, after thinking in the above strain.
> Marty shook her head. 'In all our outdoor days and years together, ma'am,' she replied, 'the one thing he never spoke of to me was love; nor I to him.'
> 'Yet you and he could speak in a tongue that nobody else knew—not even my father, though he came nearest

knowing—the tongue of the trees and fruits and flowers themselves.' (p. 358)

Grace's acknowledgement of Marty's equation with Giles does not suggest a loss of personal involvement. After Giles's death she can very well associate him and Marty without her own interests being at stake. Perhaps she also discovers in Marty an ideal of undemonstrative affection which she would fain possess herself. Marty is an ideal, a mythic counterpart of Giles Winterborne. This much Grace is brought to acknowledge. In giving expression to her sense of nearness between them she is not proposing a hypothetical marriage for their dead hero but giving evidence of her sensitivity to Giles's world, and Marty's, and of her awareness that she herself fell far short of the ideal. But this is not the same thing as a feeling of disengagement and separation.

Giles and Marty of course present an ideal of character and communal existence which becomes a central touchstone of human quality in the novel. They are poetic figures containing in themselves the genius of the ancient rural culture which the novel embodies. Although they never cease to be credible human beings, their metaphorical significance is beyond question. A contemporary review found Giles 'a little too consciously treated as the incarnation of a phase of village civilization, and not quite enough as an individual.'[9] Giles may often appear in his representative role as the cultural protagonist, but there is really no conflict between his dramatic and metaphorical functions. This is because of the cultural concept of character in the novel. Individuals here are not seen as moral entities, but as products of two antithetical social orders. The dramatic and metaphorical roles demanded of the dramatis personae in this novel are mutually supportive. Giles and Marty, inasmuch as they are norm characters, have to carry a special symbolic suggestiveness. They add a mythic dimension to the dramatic content. They are often placed in a pastoral perspective as in that superb evocation of their intimacy with nature:

to them the sights and sounds of night, winter, wind, storm, amid those dense boughs, which had to Grace a touch of the uncanny, and even of the supernatural, were simple occurrences whose origin, continuance, and laws they foreknew. They had planted together, and together they had felled; together they had, with the run of the years, mentally collected those remoter signs and symbols which seen in few were of runic obscurity, but all together made an alphabet. From the light lashings of the twigs upon their faces when brushing through them in the dark either could pronounce upon the species of the tree whence they stretched; from the quality of the wind's murmur through a bough either could in like manner name its sort afar off. They knew by a glance at a trunk if its heart were sound, or tainted with incipient decay; and by the state of its upper twigs the stratum that had been reached by its roots. The artifices of the seasons were seen by them from the conjuror's own point of view, and not from that of the spectator. (p. 358)

Giles Winterborne's mystic rapport with nature is emphasised on more than one occasion: 'He had a marvellous power of making trees grow. Although he would seem to shovel in the earth quite carelessly there was a sort of sympathy between himself and the fir, oak, or beech that he was operating on . . . '. (p. 93) His death, like the death of the pastoral hero, is mourned by all nature:

> The whole wood seemed to be a house of death, pervaded by loss to its uttermost length and breadth. Winterborne was gone, and the copses seemed to show the want of him; those young trees, so many of which he had planted, and of which he had spoken so truly when he said that he should fall before they fell, were at that very moment sending out their roots in the direction that he had given them with his subtle hand. (p. 353)

The sentiment here comes close, as David Lodge has remarked, to the 'sentiment of pastoral elegy'. But Giles finally emerges as more than a pastoral figure. He is remembered for his communal sympathy, rustic wisdom, loyalty and courage as much as for his 'intelligent intercourse with nature'. (p. 357) He is a loss to the community, to the real world of living men in Hintock. Creedle's elegy is not exactly a pastoral elegy:

> 'Well, I've knowed him from table-high; I knowed his
> father—used to bide about upon two sticks in the sun afore
> he died!—and now I've seen the end of the family, which
> we can ill afford to lose, wi' such a scanty lot of good folk
> in Hintock as we've got. And now Robert Creedle will be
> nailed up in parish boards 'a b'lieve; and nobody will glutch
> down a sigh for he!' (p. 353)

So Giles is not a mere orchardist, but an active, indispensable
member of a human community whose death leaves the
community poorer. He is ultimately judged, in Marty's deeply
moving elegy, a good man who *did* good things. It is the communal ethic which is active behind the closing memorial
tribute to Giles Winterborne:

> 'Now, my own, own love,' she whispered, 'you are mine,
> and only mine; for she has forgot 'ee at last, although for
> her you died! But I—whenever I get up I'll think of
> 'ee, and whenever I lie down I'll think of 'ee again.
> Whenever I plant the young larches I'll think that none
> can plant as you planted; and whenever I split a gad,
> and whenever I turn the cider wring, I'll say none could
> do it like you. If ever I forget your name let me forget home
> and heaven!:... But no, no, my love, I never can forget 'ee;
> for you was a good man, and did good things!' (p. 393)

Marty's lament is accompanied by a fitting determination to
carry on the work in the spirit she has imbibed from Giles's
example. Thus it is not a passive lament over a dead world
but a lament which stimulates moral action. We are assured
that Giles's memory will sustain those who, like Marty and
Creedle, have inherited the communal human adventure from
him. Marty's taking hold of Giles's tools together with her last
memorial tribute is a symbolic gesture expressing the novel's
profound belief in the continuing validity of the communal
bonds and forms of action in spite of its otherwise disturbing
vision of the human condition.

'Before the positive' says a recent work on literature and

culture, 'must come the negative, before the quest for a new ethic and a new culture we must be shown the anti-ethic, the anti-culture, the destruction of old, organic forms of work and life.'[10] The 'anti-ethic' of *The Woodlanders* is brilliantly fore-shadowed in the very first episode describing Barber Percomb's journey into Hintock to buy off Marty's hair to deck the faded and languorous Mrs Charmond. The loss of Marty's hair is followed by the felling of the tree which kills her father. The two incidents together form a symbolic context for the intro-duction of the central theme—the disruption of the simple and settled life of the traditional community at Hintock by external forces. The 'sophisticates' of the novel are regarded by some as stock characters of cheap sensational fiction. To one critic the portraits of Fitzpiers and Mrs Charmond appeared 'cut out with scissors from a vulgar fashion plate'.[11] Their insuffi-ciency and tawdriness, I think, is the very point of their exist-ence in the novel, not a fault in characterisation. They too are cultural symbols like the natives and, therefore, the differential characteristics of their culture, the 'anti-culture' of the novel, find their fullest expression through them. If they appear at times to be somewhat constrained, it is because they are metaphors of a milieu, not just individuals in their own right. Fitzpiers and Mrs Charmond are the philosophical opposites of the world of Giles and Marty.

Fitzpiers is a dilettante, a pseudo-scholar, a philanderer, and a snob. All these aspects of his personality are vividly dramatised. To the natives his practices and pre-occupations seem very suspicious and they even venture the opinion that he is in league with the Devil: 'It seems that our new neigh-bour, this young Doctor What's-his-name, is a strange, deep, perusing gentleman; and there's good reason for supposing that he has sold his soul to the wicked one.' (p. 60) He is 'like a tropical plant in a hedgerow' (p. 80) standing for 'a nucleus of advanced ideas and practices which had nothing in common with the life around'. (pp. 80–1) He lives an isolated life and prefers contemplation to action. But the natives can quite easily see through his pomposity and pretentiousness. The Arcadian innocent has innocence enough but he is no-body's fool. Giles can fling the truth in his face during an early conversation between them in which Fitzpiers tries to conceal his actual feelings about Grace, which Giles has already divined, in a maze of high-sounding words and allusions:

> 'You seem to be mightily in love with her, sir,' he said,
>   with a sensation of heart-sickness, and more than ever
>   resolved not to mention Grace by name.
> 'O no—I am not that, Winterborne; people living insulated,
>   as I do by the solitude of this place, get charged with
>   emotive fluid like a Leyden jar with electric, for want of
>   some conductor at hand to disperse it. Human love is a
>   subjective thing—the essence itself of man, as that great
>   thinker Spinoza says—*ipsa hominis essentia*—it is joy
>   accompanied by an idea which we project against any
>   suitable object in the line of our vision ... '
> 'Well, it is what we call being in love down in these parts,
>   whether or no,' said Winterborne. (pp. 146–7)

Fitzpiers's alienness from the country is emphasised throughout the narrative. The author explicitly lays down the conditions of fulfilled and authentic life in the village from which Fitzpiers must for ever remain debarred:

> They were present to the lives of Winterborne, Melbury, and
> Grace; but not to the doctor's. They are old association—
> an almost exhaustive biographical or historical acquaint-
> ance with every object, animate and inanimate, within the
> observer's horizon. He must know all about those invisible
> ones of the days gone by, whose feet have traversed the
> fields which look so grey from his windows; recall whose
> creaking plough has turned those sods from time to time;
> whose hands planted the trees that form a crest to the oppo-
> site hill; whose horses and hounds have torn through that
> underwood; what birds affect that particular brake....
> The spot may have beauty, grandeur, salubrity, convenience;
> but if it lack memories it will ultimately pall upon him who
> settles there without opportunity of intercourse with his
> kind. (p. 154)

His desire to settle in Hintock in pursuit of 'calm contentment'

(p. 170) has been well characterised as 'a whim so arbitrary as to be the mark of an aesthete'.[12] In actual fact, he hates, as he must, the woodland and its community. His boredom leads him to promiscuity and sensuality. Ostensibly given to professional studies he is often engrossed in literature of quite another kind: 'Though his aims were desultory Fitzpiers's mental constitution was not without its creditable side; a real inquirer he honestly was at times; even if the midnight rays of his lamp, visible so far through the trees of Hintock, lighted rank literatures of emotion and passion as often as, or oftener than, the books and *materiel* of science.' (p. 153) A 'subtlist in emotion' he goes through the novel making people, specially women, objects of his unrestrained passion. Grace discovers belatedly that she cannot cope with his 'double or treble-barrelled' heart. (p. 239) He is contemptuous of Melbury's position and social standing, but he has no aversion to sponging on him: 'Fitzpiers, like others of his character, while despising Melbury, and his station, did not at all disdain to spend Melbury's money.' (p. 234) But for all his armour of falsehood and cunning, Fitzpiers is known in the country for what he is. Melbury, who is first taken in by him, is also the one who passes the severest judgement on him later. Giles and Cawtree and all the rest of them have all along known the truth about Fitzpiers.

Mrs Charmond is a complement to the doctor. The two together constitute the anti-ethic of *The Woodlanders*. It is not for nothing that they turn out to have had a common past prior to their migration to Hintock. Like Fitzpiers, Mrs Charmond lives at the manor house in Hintock in self-imposed isolation with her curtains closed at daytime. The country palls on Mrs Charmond: 'Hintock has the curious effect of bottling up the emotions till one can no longer hold them; I am often obliged to fly away and discharge my sentiments somewhere, or I should die outright.' (p. 220) She is bored to death by her isolation and is always yawning on account of it. Fitzpiers, too, is always yawning. She has no sense of the past, is in fact afraid of past associations and in this, too, she presents a striking contrast to the community sensibility. This indifference about the past is 'a peculiarity that made her a piquant contrast to her neighbours'. (p. 91) She wants, as she tells

Grace at their very first meeting, to write a new *Sentimental Journey*, but needs someone at her elbow to put pen to paper on her behalf. As in the case of Fitzpiers, the villagers do not accept her any more than she accepts them. For them she only remains 'a strange woman come from nobody knows where'. (p. 123) They can confidently declare that 'she's the wrong sort of woman for Hintock—hardly knowing a beech from a woak.' (p. 275) When lost in the woods she is terrified and reduced to utter helplessness. Similarly when Melbury confronts her openly with the fact of her illicit relations with his son-in-law she is completely at a loss for a coherent answer. Her life is a structure of lies and deceptions and promiscuous sexuality: 'If one word could have expressed Felice Charmond it would have been Inconsequence. She was a woman of perversities, delighting in piquant contrasts.' (p. 224) Neither she nor Fitzpiers is able to affect the communal order of life substantially. They have only served to provide an antithesis, which is structurally necessary for establishing the positives of the novel. Mrs Charmond is a *deracine* who flits for a while on the Hintock landscape and soon flits out of it. Her miserable death on the continent fittingly brings her restless, rootless life to its close. The narrator adds with forgivable regional pride: 'Her body was not brought home. It seemed to accord well with the fitful fever of that impassioned woman's life that she should not have found an English grave.' (p. 361) Her successor is 'one who knew not Felice, one whose purpose seemed to be to blot out every vestige of her.' (p. 361) Against such pettiness and transitoriness are evoked the protective, shape-giving functions of memory and cultural continuity. Marty's spontaneous elegy is vibrant with this promise of continuity and remembrance. The values inherent in her words are final. The community stands at the end of the novel.

Some critics have emphasised the fact that in a novel so 'idyllic' as *The Woodlanders* Hardy should include such unseemly details as Suke Damson, the mantrap, and the presence of a primitive code of revenge. Such details, they argue, point to Hardy's disillusion with the country. There is no doubt that Hardy's image of rural society is free from the distortions of romance. So it is wrong in the first place to characterise *The Woodlanders* as an idyll. The unpleasant details of rustic culture do not detract from the validity of the deeper rhythms and sanctions of that culture. Suke Damson, after all, is not a native born, but a naturalised immigrant. And, in any case, her earthiness and vulgarity are not nearly as alarming as the malaise associated with the urbanites. The mantrap is indeed an evidence of a primitive code of revenge but it does not seriously disturb the normal tenor of life in Little Hintock. It is not something approved by the community as a whole, but only a surreptitious, guilty measure resorted to by the odd man like Tim under extreme provocation. However, there is no need to gloss over these details. They remain there, elements of the community which for Hardy becomes the repository of indispensable cultural and moral resources. It is a community of men 'with all the specks and flaws inseparable from concrete humanity', but still a community to which Giles Winterborne and Marty South can credibly belong.

NOTES

1. Quoted by Carl J. Weber in *Hardy of Wessex: His Life and Literary Career*, p. 159.
2. Florence Emily Hardy, *The Life of Thomas Hardy, 1840–1928* (London: Macmillan, 1962), p. 358.
3. E. M. Forster, 'Woodlanders on Devi'.
4. Douglas Brown, *Thomas Hardy*, p. 73.
5. The poem is included in *Wessex Poems* (1898).
6. Coventry Patmore in *St. James's Gazette* (2 April 1887).
7. Florence Emily Hardy, *The Life of Thomas Hardy*, p. 220.
8. David Lodge, Introduction to *The Woodlanders* (New Wessex edition, 1974) p. 17.
9. *Saturday Review* (2 April 1887).
10. David Meakin, *Man and Work: Literature and Culture in Industrial Society* (London: Methuen, 1976), p. 18.
11. William R. Rutland, *Thomas Hardy: A Study of His Writings and Their Background*, pp. 211–12.
12. Michael Millgate, *Thomas Hardy: His Career as a Novelist*, p. 252.

CHAPTER 6

Hardy's Shorter Fiction

Hardy wrote nearly fifty short stories the majority of which are available in *Wessex Tales* (1888), *A Group of Noble Dames* (1891), *Life's Little Ironies* (1894), and *A Changed Man and Other Tales* (1913). Most of these stories were written during the period 1874–1900 simultaneously with Hardy's major fiction. The care with which he revised and arranged many of these short stories suggests that he took as much interest in them as in his other writings. They should not be treated as hack-work any more than the novels which were written piecemeal under the same pressures from the 'Grundyist' and the subscriber. In both the novels and the stories Hardy was forced to pander to the demands of the magazines and consequently to inhibit or distort or bowdlerise his narratives. As well as being artistically satisfying to their creator these novels and stories also had to be commercially viable, saleable products. What is important is that he was as reluctant to perform these forced operations on the stories as on the novels. In the MSS of some of the stories in *A Group of Noble Dames* Hardy makes recurrent references to 'the tyranny of Mrs Grundy' and has blue-pencilled many lines which had to be deleted against his wish. There are other references as well to the difficulty and exasperation that Hardy experienced in getting his short stories accepted. An entry in *Life* reads: 'June 23. Called on Arthur Locker (editor) at the *Graphic* office in answer to his letter. He says he does not object to the stories (*A Group of Noble Dames*) but the Directors do. Here's a pretty job! Must smooth down these Directors somehow I suppose.'[1] And smooth them down he did, for not only were the stories published in 1891, but they seem to have paved the way for more. In a cancelled prefatory note to *A Changed Man and Other Tales* Hardy originally wrote: 'They would probably have never been collected by me at this

Page references to *Wessex Tales* and *Life's Little Ironies* are to the Greenwood edition (1966–67).

time of day if frequent reprints of some of them in America and elsewhere had not sent many readers inquiring for them in a volume.' With somewhat uncharacteristic aplomb Hardy inscribed copies of each of the four volumes of short stories to his literary friends. He presented copies of *Wessex Tales* to Browning on his birthday, and to Meredith. Similarly, he inscribed copies of *A Group of Noble Dames* in the very first week of its publication to Edward Clodd, Sir George Douglas, Theodore Watts, and Edmund Gosse; copies of *Life's Little Ironies* to Gosse, the Earl of Pembroke, and Sir Francis Jeune; and of *A Changed Man and Other Tales* to Edward Clodd and Edmund Gosse. This at least establishes the respectability of the short stories in Hardy's own reckoning.

An early reviewer of an anthology of Hardy's short stories observed: 'if he had produced nothing but the stories that have been assembled in this fat volume, what an abounding legacy of human histories he would have left behind him!'[2] Later critics, who have turned their attention to the stories at all, agree that in at least some of them one can find the real Hardy. Critics such as A. J. Guerard, George Wing, and Irving Howe, have called attention to the significance of the short stories, but their treatment of the stories is confined to a full discussion of only a very few of them and does not, on the whole, extend beyond a few suggestive remarks. Irving Howe and, more recently, Norman Page are the only two critics whose discussion of the stories is relatively serious and more detailed.

The stories are by and large stamped with all Hardy's habits of imagination. His individual style of perception is fully operative in them. The distinction between the real and the imagined, for instance, was always blurred for Hardy. He was thus able to transcend the limitations of conventional realism. The stories share this aesthetic psychology. He thought of the same story as the record of an actual event and as pure invention. In the Preface to the *Wessex Tales* he wrote:

I may add that the action of this story ['The Distracted Preacher'] is founded on certain smuggling exploits that occurred between 1825 and 1830, and were brought to a close in the latter year by the trial of the chief actors at the

Assizes before Baron Bolland for their desperate armed
resistance to the custom-house officers during the landing
of a cargo of spirits.

But by the time he comes to the end of the Preface he is assert-
ing that 'the stories are but dreams, and not records'. By their
compactness and thematic simplicity, the stories throw this
dream-reality dualism into greater relief. They vividly illustrate
the counterpoising, in Hardy, of the familiar with the exceptional, of the workaday and matter-of-fact with the magical
and the fantastic. The stories show Hardy's most compulsive
fictional impulses at work leading towards a ballad-like impersonality and artistic autonomy. The tragic quality of
Hardy's vision or his corrosively ironic understanding of life
is sufficiently evidenced by the stories, although it is true that
the more overtly philosophical concerns of the novels are in
abeyance. The stories are a more direct and unembarrassed
expression of an area of experience which never ceased to
attract Hardy. They bring us closer to the world he was born
into and to its problems and pre-occupations. They reveal a
world of tragic contingencies, a world rather out of joint, but
pitted against this vision of the world as a tragic arena is the
story of a 'coherent and self-explanatory' rural culture possessing in its tales and legends, and myths and traditions a complete
explanation of the phenomena. The stories are largely a
re-creation of the sources from which members of a rural
community derive their particular stance before experience.
Unlike most modern short stories they are not exploratory but
evocative. They do not take the reader forward into an unsuspected, unique eventuality, but refer him back to local
legend or tradition or actual history. The stories show Hardy
fully engaged with the unwritten history of an old agrarian
culture. In fact the possibility of being able to put his finger on
'something real in their history' was one positive inducement
for him to write such stories: ' A STORY–TELLER's interest in his
own stories is usually independent of any merits or demerits
they may show as specimens of narrative art; turning on something behind the scenes, something real in their history, which
may have no attraction for a reader even if known to him—a
consideration by no means likely.' (Preface to *Life's Little Ironies*).

It is this inwardness with his material in the stories which makes them inseparable from his total fictional achievement. It must be admitted, however, that the stories are not all uniformly successful. No one can quarrel with Wilfrid Gibson's frank admission that 'some of them are mere anecdotes; and others read too much like synopses of full-length novels: that here and there there are passages of perfunctory or careless writing.'³ Still, we are left with a sufficiently large number of short stories which merit serious consideration. Let us look at them. I have chosen for critical examination short stories which as well as being the products of Hardy's sociological imagination demonstrate the sheer verve and magnitude of his story-telling powers, which must be their final justification. 'We tale-tellers', Hardy wrote, 'are all Ancient Mariners.' These almost balladic stories of life in a primitive rural society speak eloquently of the Ancient Mariner in Thomas Hardy.

For a start let us look into a juvenile tale Hardy wrote for an American youth magazine in the summer of 1883, just before launching on *The Mayor of Casterbridge*. It was called 'Our Exploits at West Poley'. It was first salvaged from the American magazine by R. L. Purdy and published by him in 1952. Hardy's letter to the editors of *Youth's Companion*, the magazine which wanted the story, shows that his attitude to the story was far from flippant or perfunctory. He regarded it as a serious literary undertaking and gradually felt his way into the final product. In April 1883 he wrote to the American editors:

> I have roughly thought out a plot which at present seems promising. But I shall prefer not to commit myself to a title till later on in the year. The general scope, or sub-title, however, might be announced as 'A rural tale of adventure in the West of England'. You may depend upon my using my best efforts to please your numerous readers; and that the story shall have a healthy tone, suitable to intelligent youth of both sexes.⁴

While despatching the MS finally under the title 'Our Exploits at West Poley' Hardy further wrote: 'In constructing the story I have been careful to avoid making it a mere precept in narrative—a fatal defect, to my thinking, in tales for the young, or for the old. That it carries with it, nevertheless, a sufficiently apparent moral, will I think be admitted. The important features of plot and incident have received my best attention.'[5] The story seems to have hung fire for a long time, for in December 1886 Hardy is found writing to one of the editors of *Youth's Companion*:

> With regard to the short story I wrote for the Companion please do not pay any attention to the fact that I cannot avail myself of it here as long as you keep it unpublished. The proprietors of the Companion treated me very courteously in the matter, and I should much prefer that you hold it back as long as there is any chance of your having room for it to your publishing it elsewhere to oblige me. Possibly if you have no space for it at length you may some day think fit to produce it in a somewhat abridged form—it being a story of an imaginative kind suitable for a Christmas number, or such like. Our children here are younger for their age than yours; and possibly the story is too juvenile for your side of the sea. I fancy you may be mistaken in that; but of course I do not know as well as yourselves.[6]

Even in these purely business communications Hardy tries edgeways to offer his estimate of the story from a moral-artistic point of view. Without being professedly didactic the story has, he has told us, 'a sufficiently apparent moral'. If one regards it as mere tomfoolery for juvenile consumption, 'I fancy you may be mistaken in that'. Structurally, with regard to plot and incident it has received 'my best attention'.

'Our Exploits at West Poley' is a remarkable story in many ways. It records the youthful adventure of two boys, the narrator being one, in the Mendip Caves in West Poley, a village in Somersetshire. In innocent sport the two boys unwittingly divert the only water source it has from West Poley to the rival village, East Poley. The sudden disappearance of the stream from West Poley causes great distress in this village while East Poley is suddenly freed from years of waterlessness. The boys keep their secret to themselves and turn the stream one way or the other as they please. The situation is perfectly farcical till Steve, the more adventurous and, therefore, the

guiltier of the two, begins to realise the acute suffering that
results from the deprivation of water in either village. He finds
himself on the horns of a moral dilemma as he is not able to
decide whether one village has more right to the waters than
the other. Already, a deeper note of moral anxiety is struck in
the story than we expect from the comical procedure of surface
events. The two villages eventually clash over the issue and each
tries to turn the stream away from the other. Steve becomes
increasingly convinced that his own village of West Poley had
a natural right to the water and that had it not been for a freak
of his the East Poleyites would never have had access to it. In a
heroic act of conscience he, therefore, blasts the entire mass of
sand and stone forming the roof of the inner cave by gunpowder
thus obviating the possibility of further human interference with
the mouth of the stream. He nearly perishes in the explosion
himself. The story closes with this feat of restoring the water
to West Poley for good, heralding its boy-hero's entry into
adulthood and responsibility.

Although the story is told in the first person singular it never
loses its dramatic objectivity. The narrative is marked throughout by fair-mindedness and a consideration of relevance. Here
are the simple opening sentences which unobtrusively provide
a dramatic overture:

> On a certain fine evening of early autumn—I will not say
> how many years ago—I alighted from a green gig, before
> the door of a farmhouse at West Poley, a village in Somerset-
> shire. I had reached the age of thirteen, and though rather
> small for my age, I was robust and active....I had arrived
> on a visit to my aunt Draycot, a farmer's widow, who, with
> her son Stephen, or Steve, as he was invariably called by his
> friends, still managed the farm, which had been left on her
> hands by her deceased husband.[7]

The village is made sufficiently real and interesting. It has its
share of quaint and unexplainable individualities. The 'Man
who has Failed', as he calls himself, is a typical Hardyan mystic
who has a way of suddenly emerging from behind and making
his presence felt by offering gratuitous advice:

> 'Who is he?' I asked.

'Oh—he's nobody,' said Steve. 'He's a man who has been all over the world, and tried all sorts of lives, but he has never got rich, and now he has retired to this place for quietness. He calls himself the Man who has Failed.'[8]

But this seemingly comic character is not a figure of fun. He emerges as the voice of sanity and dispassionate goodwill in the village. In the words of Steve's mother: 'He is one who has failed, not from want of sense, but from want of energy; and people of that sort, when kindly, are better worth attending to than those successful ones, who have never seen the seamy side of things. I would advise you to listen to him.'[9] But there is no attempt on the part of the narrator to justify or indulge him. The narrative control is too rigid in this simple comic tale to allow of any disproportionate development of character. The miller, the baker, the dairyman, the blacksmith, the shoe-maker are all stock characters of rustic comedy. They help to form a lively and recognisable community but remain indistinct individuals. And it is against the background of their stolid and undifferentiated lives that the drama of adolescent adventurousness is delineated. Steve's freakish act stirs their dull and stagnant lives and draws them out of themselves, thus filling the canvas of the story with people caught in a flurry and getting up to act.

However, the real interest of the story centres on the impact of his childish prank on Steve's own moral sensibility. What first appears to be a harmless pastime soon turns out to have far-reaching moral consequences. In fact, the whole event becomes an object-lesson in moral education for Steve. 'I perceive', Steve is forced to confess, 'that it is next to impossible, in this world, to do good to one set of folks without doing harm to another.'[10] This is an awareness which leads to much anxiety and dismay in later Hardy. Here in 'West Poley' it is a passing thought which does not cause any tragic disorientation. Steve is left a prospering young farmer and philanthropist at peace with himself and his community. But this comic resolution of the story is leavened by a typical Hardyan awareness of the precariousness of human happiness and human success. The story leaves us with the sense of an unexpressed menace. 'As we left the cave, Steve, Job, Mrs Draycot and I walked behind the Man who had Failed. "Though this has worked well", he said to Steve, " it is by the merest chance in the world. " '11 Significantly, the epilogue is left to 'the Man who had Failed' and his last words bring into the story what Virginia Woolf, writing on Hardy's major novels, called the 'margin of the unexpressed'.

There is no planned symbolism in the story, but the author's understanding of events and their moral implication is so ripe as to give to his tale a quality of symbolic suggestiveness. Finding himself unable to solve the problem he has created Steve falls ill with anxiety. But the prospect of working unitedly with the village folk for the restoration of the stream works like medicine on his distraught mind. The recovery of the stream means for him a recovery of health, vitality, and freedom from a consciousness of guilt. It also means a renewal of the compact by which he shall live in the community. The story at the same time affords a quite different kind of interest approaching the burlesque and the recklessly farcical. The fateful encounter between the two rival villages, for instance, is seen from an entirely comic point of view regardless of the serious issue at stake The story thus preserves an atmosphere of rollicking comedy despite its perception of inescapable suffering and of the difficulty of moral choice. It is a story for children, but it does not exclude an adult perception of reality. And it has a tense structure of feeling which makes it genuine Hardy.

'The Three Strangers' is the first story in *Wessex Tales*. It was originally published in *Longman's Magazine* in March 1883 and concurrently in *Harper's Weekly* in America. Hardy wrote it at Wimbourne in the interval between *Two on a Tower* and *The Mayor of Casterbridge*.

It is a simple story of two contrasted aspects of life in Wessex. The dramatic juxtaposition of two antagonistic orders of being is achieved with remarkable speed and ingenuity. The story is memorable for its brilliant tableaux, for its bold opposition of light with shade. It lends itself easily to dramatisation and was in fact dramatised by Hardy as *The Three Wayfarers*, although he later called it 'a mere trifle'.

'The Three Strangers' lives as a gripping tale of the sudden invasion of the familiar and the snug by the alien and the unexpected, which is a recurrent motif in Hardy. Breaking into the homely conviviality of Shepherd Fennel's cottage come the three strangers from the world of crime and violence. Fennel Cottage is made particularly vulnerable because of its location: 'Higher Crowstairs, as the house was called, stood quite detached and undefended. The only reason for its precise situation seemed to be the crossing of two footpaths at right angles hard by, which may have crossed there and thus for a good five hundred years.' (*Wessex Tales*, pp. 3–4) Its crossroads location makes it 'undefended' and 'exposed to the elements on all sides'. It is at this halfway house that contraries meet. The absconding culprit and the hangman drink of the same mead and treat each other off Shepherd Fennel's skimmer-cake. The first stranger, who is a runaway convict, shows utter self-possession whereas the third stranger, who is the convict's innocent brother out looking for him, looks 'the picture of abject terror—his knees trembling, his hand shaking so violently that the door-latch by which he supported himself rattled audibly.' (p. 19) Fair is foul, foul is fair.

Higher Crowstairs takes on mythic qualities both in its pastoral setting and its human inhabitants. Its openness and hospitality constitute a grave risk. It is a typical country house not only in its external details but also in the unsuspecting openness of the people living in it. I do not think that Higher Crowstairs is a 'symbol' although it does provide a central focus. The polarities and incongruous occurrences witnessed at Higher Crowstairs do not symbolise anything beyond the rough geometry of rural experience. The story, on the whole, is free from any veiled meaning. Hardy emphasises the experience-sharing, 'conservative' susceptibilities of a rural people in noting that the incidents at Higher Crowstairs have taken on mythic perpetuity as they have been passed from one generation to the next:

> The grass has long been green on the graves of Shepherd Fennel and his frugal wife; the guests who made up the christening party have mainly followed their entertainers to the tomb; the baby in whose honour they all had met is a matron in the sere and yellow leaf. But the arrival of the three strangers at the shepherd's that night, and the details

connected therewith, is a story as well known as ever in the country about Higher Crowstairs. (pp. 28–9)

A continuing response to something that happened to a particular set of people at a point of time in the past is for Hardy a definition of culture. The village anecdote makes for a continuity of feeling. The story is also distinguished by the toughness and particularity of its natural details. Hardy's metaphorical style is in evidence in such masterly touches as this: ' . . . the tails of little birds trying to roost on some scraggy thorn were blown inside-out like umbrellas.' (p. 4) A fire of thorns 'crackle[s] like the "laughter of the fool" '. (p. 5) Thus the story brings together a whole living world through the vibrations of its emotively perceived details.

'A Tradition of Eighteen Hundred and Four' first appeared as 'A Legend of Eighteen Hundred and Four' in *Harper's Christmas* in December 1882. It was included in *Life's Little Ironies*, but Hardy transferred it to *Wessex Tales* in 1912. There is an interesting note in *Life* with regard to the actual truth of the incident recorded in this story:

A curious question arose in Hardy's mind at this date on whether a romancer was morally justified in going to extreme lengths of assurance—after the manner of Defoe—in respect of a tale he knew to be absolutely false. Thirty-seven years earlier, when much pressed to produce something of the nature of a fireside yarn, he had invented a picturesque account of a stealthy nocturnal visit to England by Napoleon in 1804, during the war, to spy out a good spot for invasion. Being struck with the extreme improbability of such a story, he added a circumstantial framework describing it as an old local tradition to blind the reader to the hoax. When it was published he was much surprised at people remarking to him: 'I see you have made use of that well-known tradition of Napoleon's landing.' He then supposed that, strange as it seemed, such a story must have been in existence without his knowledge, and that perhaps the event had happened. So the matter rested till the time at which we have arrived, when a friend who was interested made inquiries, and was assured by historians and annalists whom he consulted that such a visit would have been fatuous, and well nigh impossible. Moreover, that there had never existed any such improbable tradition. Hence arose Hardy's aforesaid case of conscience as to being too natural in the art he could practise so well. Had he not long discontinued the writing of romances he would, he said, have put at the beginning of each new one: 'Understand that however true this book may be in essence, in fact it is utterly untrue.'[12]

The story belongs to the class of fiction Hardy called 'Romances and Fantasies', where factual exactitude can be dispensed with easily. But, as it appears from the above note, Hardy's imagination was too perfectly attuned to the workings of the folk mind to 'fantasize' away from the innermost thought-patterns of that mind. So his fictitious chronicles produced a shock of recognition. Having ensured that, he needed not to bother much about factual corroboration. Truth 'in essence' was what he sought, refusing to be limited always by the more obvious truth of facts.

The story in question is narrated to the author by one of his characters, Solomon Selby. Attention is immediately drawn to the local institution of the inveterate teller of tales. This story-mongering lends a depth and expressiveness to the collective consciousness of the people and unites individuals within a common experience. The tradition has a mystique which makes incredulity sacrilegious, an act of betrayal. Part of the success of 'A Tradition of Eighteen Hundred and Four' lies in its full-bodied evocation of the milieu which creates such narratives. The personality of the internal narrator is emphasised: 'Withdrawing the stem of his pipe from the dental notch in which it habitually rested, he leaned back in the recess behind him and smiled into the fire. The smile was neither mirthful nor sad, not precisely humorous nor altogether thoughtful. We who knew him recognized it in a moment: it was his narrative smile.' (*Wessex Tales*, p. 33) The queer incident he narrates of Napoleon's trial landings on the shore above the cove is known only to him: ' . . . and certainly to no maker of newspapers or printer of books, or my account o't would not have had so many heads shaken over it as it has by gentry who only believe what they see in printed lines.' (p. 36) The story, then, is a deliberate assault on the cynical, print-happy 'gentry'. The shepherd-narrator of the story is an artist with a commanding style: 'Thanks to the incredulity of the age his tale has been seldom repeated. But if anything short of the direct testimony of his own eyes could persuade an auditor that Bonaparte had examined these shores...it would have been Solomon Selby's manner of narrating the adventure which befell him on the down.' (pp. 40-1) The listeners who have gathered round Solomon Selby's 'yawning chimney-corner' form an important part of the total conception of the story. In their collaborative response to the story they—tellers and listeners—evince a unifying cultural sensibility.

'The Melancholy Hussar of the German Legion' first appeared as 'The Melancholy Hussar' in *Bristol Times and Mirror* in January 1890. It was reprinted in *Three Notable Stories* (Spencer Blackett, London, June 1890) together with 'Love and Peril' by Marquis of Lorne and 'To Be or Not to Be' by Mrs Alexander. It was included in *Life's Little Ironies* but later transferred to *Wessex Tales* in the Uniform edition in 1927. The story was probably written in 1887. A note made by Hardy in 1876 contains the seed of the story: 'July 27. James Bushrod of Broadmayne saw the two German soldiers [of the York Hussars] shot [for desertion] on Bincombe Down in 1801. It was in the path across the Down, or near it. James Selby of the same village thinks there is a mark.'[13] Here is another story, then, which has its origins in the village anecdote, a determinant not only of theme but of the entire *modus operandi* in the tales of Thomas Hardy. Phyllis Grove, the young heroine of this story leads the life of a semi-recluse with her father in a village in the downs five miles from Budmouth. The weariness of her life is expressed through a brilliant evocation of the supine and changeless atmosphere around her:

> When a noise like the brushing skirt of a visitor was heard on the doorstep, it proved to be a scudding leaf; when a carriage seemed to be nearing the door, it was her father grinding his sickle on the stone in the garden for his favourite relaxation of trimming the box-tree borders to the plots. A sound like luggage thrown down from the coach was a gun far away at sea; and what looked like a tall man by the gate

at dusk was a yew bush cut into a quaint and attenuated shape. (*Wessex Tales*, p. 46)

This is a memorable rendering of the young girl's bored existence in terms of ordinary sensory experiences and disappointed expectations. Suddenly the quiet of her environment is invaded by the York Hussars in their 'brilliant uniform, their splendid horses, and above all, their foreign air and mustachios'. The entire region is caught up in the excitement of their exotic presence: 'At this point of time a golden radiance flashed in upon the lives of the people here.' (p. 49) Phyllis falls in love with one of these German Hussars, Matthäus Tina, whose heart is as sad as his appearance is flashing. Although engaged to marry a man called Humphrey Gould, who is away at Bath and maintains the engagement by erratic correspondence, Phyllis agrees to her lover's plan to elope to Germany. While waiting for Matthäus on the highway on the fateful evening of their flight, she sees a passenger alight from a stage-coach who turns out to be her fiancé, Humphrey Gould. From his conversation with his companion regarding a present he has brought for her she understands that he is still loyal to her. 'Bracing herself to an exceptional fortitude', therefore she tells Matthäus off at the last moment. There is no going back for Matthäus and his friend Christopher, however, who have decamped from the Regiment and must press on for their very lives. Phyllis returns home to discover that Humphrey Gould is already married while the two runaway German Hussars land in Jersey mistaking it for the French coast. They are delivered up to the authorities for trial and subsequently sentenced to military execution. From her garden perch Phyllis sees the soldiers being shot into their coffins. Their bodies are buried at the back of the church. Even after their graves are overgrown with nettles and barely recognisable, the older villagers can still recollect the spot where they lie. Hard by is Phyllis's grave. Thus the story has come down from generation to generation. There is no denying that the story is highly melodramatic. The fact that Hardy had a penchant for the bizarre and the sensational must be faced. His achievement consists in the suppleness and ease with which he can create an irrefutable story of human endurance and suffering on a legendary scale. The legendary nature of the characters makes them singularly fitted for more than an ordinary share of the tragic predicament. The rich concentration on the human material, the thick texture of life and human motivation in the story, promotes a sense of nearness and identity. Through such controlling devices Hardy is able to construct a powerful tale of ironic mischance and human waste. The subtlety of his narrative makes the mythically distant seem dangerously near and urgent. Given his fundamental bias that suffering is central to human existence, the story of Phyllis Grove and her hapless lover becomes artistically necessary. But the tragic vision is not imposed upon the story; it is inherent in the chosen material. In reading the story one does not feel the presence of a personalised manoeuvring consciousness. The story acquires the impersonality of a fable.

'The Withered Arm', one of Hardy's finest tales, again belongs to the local lore. At the time of writing there are still among his friends people who have seen it happen (see Preface to *Wessex Tales*). This story invokes local tradition as a criterion of truth. Within this central focus the otherwise improbable and grotesque features of the story—its neurotic dreams and weird circumstances—seem to melt into a valid form of self-definition for the characters and issues at stake. The story centres on Rhoda Brook, a hard-worked, egocentric, coarse milkmaid possessing all the qualifications of the village witch. That she is in fact looked upon by some as possessing evil powers adds a strain of morbidity to her natural self-consciousness. She is deserted by her lover, Farmer Lodge, and, thus despised and isolated, lives self-absorbedly with their illegitimate son. The news that Farmer Lodge is bringing a new bride home adds fuel to her smouldering sexual jealousy. She develops a jealous obsession with the appearance of the new bride because she is reputed to be fair of looks. She sends her son to verify the bride's appearance and to find out for sure if she is taller than herself. Rhoda Brook contemplates the form of her rival so intently that she turns into an incubus. In the dream the spectre 'thrust forward its left hand mockingly, so as to make the wedding-ring it wore glitter in Rhoda's eyes'. (*Wessex Tales*, p. 77) Nearly choked to death by the incubus she seizes it by the left arm and hurls it down to the floor. At exactly the same hour of the night Gertrude, the bride, is awakened by a twinge in her left arm and thereafter the arm begins to shrivel. When they actually meet, Rhoda discerns a faint shadow of her own finger prints on the wrinkled and discoloured spot on Gertrude's arm: ' "O, can it be," she said to herself, when her visitor had departed, "that I exercise a malignant power over people against my own will?" ' (p. 81) As time passes the finger print on the afflicted arm becomes even more prominent. It is Conjuror Trendle— the 'white wizard' of Egdon Heath—who shows Gertrude an image of the enemy who has brought this curse upon her. Soon after her visit to Conjuror Trendle with Gertrude, Rhoda and her son disappear from the neighbourhood. Six years later Gertrude is seen riding to Casterbridge to bring her arm into contact with the neck of a man who has been hanged—this being the only cure according to the conjuror. The conjuror has promised that the touch will 'turn the blood' and change her entire constitution. So, indeed, it does. The corpse she puts her arm to is the corpse of Rhoda's son who is hanged for having been present at a rick-burning. The outraged Rhoda snatches Gertrude away from her son's corpse exclaiming: 'This is the meaning of what Satan showed me in the vision! You are like her at last!' (pp. 106–7) Gertrude dies of shock, but Rhoda, after a temporary absence, returns to her parish and resumes her familiar way of life.

The central motif of the story is sexual jealousy in all its symptoms—obsession, vindictiveness, violence. To illustrate this primal drive the story creates a condition in which it becomes so compulsive and implacable as to acquire a demonic power. 'My art', wrote Hardy, 'is to intensify the expression of things, as is done by Crivelli, Bellini, etc., so that the heart and inner meaning is made vividly visible.'[14] In order to get at 'the heart and inner meaning' he had to go sometimes beyond the limits of ordinary rationality and bring the occult and the irrational into the workings of primary human impulses. And he could do so without sacrificing plausibility. Hardy's ability to domesticate the occult is fully illustrated by 'The Withered Arm'. The rural context of his stories gives Hardy a license to freely use customs, beliefs, and totems which would be otherwise considered highly improbable. However, he does not use

them for documentary purposes, but as instruments of exploration and analysis of the basic emotions involved in his stories.
In 'The Withered Arm' the central theme is corrosive jealousy
leading to psychosis. The story uses superstition as a natural
response to the absurdities and contradictions of human experience. It premises that: 'Apprehension is a great element
in imagination. It is a semi-madness, which sees enemies, etc.,
in inanimate objects.'[15] This truth is inherent in the material
of the story. To understand the metaphoric significance of the
story it is necessary that we first take everything literally.
Rhoda Brook is a real woman; her nightmare is a real nightmare. It is because of their reality that these occurrences
acquire a metaphoric suggestiveness. The story is not a piece of
horror fiction. It has at the centre of its concern a more fundamental crisis, which finds in the peasant characters and
superstitions a kind of 'objective correlative'.

It is Rhoda Brook who survives all the violence of her life
and emotion. When the story opens she is seen 'buried in the
flank of that motionless beast' (p. 69) she is milking. At the
end of her turbulent career in the story she returns to her
'monotonous milking at the dairy'. (p. 108) Thus a sense of
the indestructible security of a non-imaginative, functional
life is part of the total consciousness of the story. Imagination
is seen in its proper context as an agent of power and peril.
Imagination has as much power for evil as it has for good, as
much for hate as for love. It helps Rhoda Brook to express her
internal, non-social self with artistic completeness. But there is
no attempt to equate her entire personality with her charged
imagination. She often acts as one possessed, but she is equally
convincingly a lorn milkmaid, a part of the landscape in which
she appears, so completely identified with the natural world
around her that when she speaks 'the voice seemed to proceed
from the belly of the cow called Cherry . . .'. (p. 69)

'The Distracted Preacher' was written at Upper Tooting in
the interval between *The Return of the Native* and *The Trumpet
Major*. It was published in *The New Quarterly Magazine* in
April 1879 and also in *Harper's Weekly* in five instalments
(19 April–17 May 1879). This too is a story based on actual
events to which Hardy draws attention in the Preface to
Wessex Tales. Here again historical circumstance has been

transmuted into an imaginative structure of experience. The notable thing about the story, however, is not its factual veracity but its moral and imaginative response to the given facts.

The story opens with a matter-of-fact description of the arrival in Nether-Moynton of the new Methodist preacher, Mr Stockdale. The preacher falls in love with his landlady—a skittish young widow called Mrs Newberry. One night she offers to get the priest some liquor to cure his cold and asks him to escort her to the cellar. The minister is appalled to find himself in the church with tubs of contraband liquor rolling in front of him. Lizzy is deliciously nonchalant:

> 'Smuggling is carried on here by some of the people,' she said in a gentle, apologetic voice. 'It has been their practice for generations, and they think it no harm. Now, will you roll out one of the tubs?'
> 'What to do with it?' said the minister.
> 'To draw a little from it to cure your cold,' she answered. 'It is so 'nation strong that it drives away that sort of thing in a jiffy.' (*Wessex Tales*, p. 224)

Stockdale is yet innocent of the full scale of Lizzy's involvement in the trade. It is a little later that her sudden disappearance from home, her irregular hours of sleep, and her possession of men's clothes arouse his suspicion. He follows her one night to see her fire a bough of furze as a danger signal to an incoming cargo. Next, she confesses to Stockdale that she and her cousin Owlett were active smugglers and that they had the support of the local men. The minister tries to win her back to 'correctness of conduct', but to no avail:

> 'Then you will go, Lizzy?' he said as he stood on the step beside her; who now again appeared as a little man with a face altogether unsuited to his clothes.
> 'I must,' she said, repressed by his stern manner.
> 'Then I shall go too,' said he.
> 'And I am sure you will enjoy it!' she exclaimed in more buoyant tones. 'Everybody does who tries it.'
> 'God forbid that I should!' he said. 'But I must look after you.' (p. 253)

The smugglers are all strong, enterprising men who can easily
outwit the Preventive-men and so carry on with impunity.
Once while returning with the contraband they have seized
from Owlett's orchard the Preventive-men are waylaid by the
disguised smugglers and tied to the trees. They are later released by Stockdale. Soon after this incident the minister delivers
his last sermon in Nether-Moynton and leaves for another
place. The smugglers are eventually brought to book. Owlett is
badly wounded in the affray and migrates to America. Stockdale returns and marries Lizzy. But this was an ending forced
on Hardy by the conventions of the magazines, as he explains
in the following postscript:

> Note–The ending of this story with the marriage of Lizzy
> and the minister was almost *de rigueur* in an English
> magazine at the time of writing. But at this late date,
> thirty years after, it may not be amiss to give the ending
> that would have been preferred by the writer to the
> convention used above. Moreover it corresponds more
> closely with the true incidents of which the tale is a
> vague and flickering shadow. Lizzy did not, in fact,
> marry the minister, but—much to her credit in the
> author's opinion—stuck to Jim the smuggler, and
> emigrated with him after their marriage, an expatrial
> step rather forced upon him by his adventurous
> antecedents. They both died in Wisconsin between
> 1850 and 1860.

Clearly, the homiletic conclusion that in after years Lizzy
Newberry wrote an excellent tract called *Render Unto Caesar: or,
The Repentant Villagers* is a hoax for the Victorian conscience.

Lizzy's involvement in smuggling is free from any self-
questioning or qualms of conscience. She has a profound
instinctive trust in what she is doing: 'No, I must go on as
I have begun. I was born to it. It is in my blood, and I can't
be cured.' (p. 282) Her motives lie not in considerations
of gain but in the deeper compulsion in her blood. She loves
the hazards, the hairbreadth escapes, the deep secrecy, and
the sheer physical strenuousness of a smuggling career. It
brings to her a sense of freedom and fulfilment: 'It stirs up

one's dull life at this time o' the year, and gives excitement, which I have got so used to now that I should hardly know how to do 'ithout it. At nights when the wind blows, instead of being dull and stupid, and not noticing whether it do blow or not, your mind is afield.' (pp. 281-2) This is a plea which makes nonsense of the preacher's moral objections. He is reduced to contemplating: 'If I had only stuck to father's little grocery business, instead of going in for the ministry, she would have suited me beautifully!' (p. 251) Lizzy has a purity of instinct which most forms of civilised life—grocery business or priesthood—deny. She can survive only as an outlaw. To ask her to adhere to a prescribed 'correctness of conduct' is to violate her authentic self. She is opposed to the precepts of civilisation. But for all her outlawry and intransigence Lizzy is not an individualist in the anarchic, subversive sense of the word. She is part of a community consisting of people like herself bound together by common needs and hazards. Within this society Lizzy is good and kind and even fastidiously altruistic. It is to abstractions that she is opposed. She loves the priest but is indifferent to his dogmas. She knows that the officers of the law are her mortal enemies, but she can think of doing them no harm as individuals. When Stockdale expresses his fear that they might be murdered by her gang, she is shocked: ' "Murdered!" said Lizzy impatiently. "We don't do murder here." ' (p. 278) She will not deny a living man his right, but she feels in no way obliged to the State. Church and State are abstractions beyond her range of moral consciousness: 'My conscience is clear. I know my mother, but the King I have never seen. His dues are nothing to me. But it is a great deal to me that my mother and I should live.' (p. 281) Lizzy's character has a 'quickness', an untutored sense of justice and fair-play and moral discrimination which cannot be codified. She would be an 'aristocrat' in Lawrence's terminology. It is important that her values are not arrived at individually but are commonly shared by a whole community of people, a community which, in Frank O'Connor's phrase, may be described as 'submerged'. Frank O'Connor uses the phrase 'submerged population group'[16] to describe communities on the frontiers of civilisation which have not been adequately treated in the novel which, according to him, adheres to 'the classical concept of civilized society'.[17] The short story, on the other hand, provides a domain for these émigrés and exiles. Whatever the value of O'Connor's general argument, his terms seem appropriate for the kind of society which creates Lizzy Newberry. It is a community of criminals who, however, are meant to offer a criticism of the evasions and insensitivities of less culpable men in the eyes of the law. Lizzy is the most moral character in the story, subversive of the law but redeemed by her extraordinary compassion and truthfulness. She sets a standard for a whole community of fugitives.

The two stories from *Life's Little Ironies* that I want to consider here are 'An Imaginative Woman' and 'The Son's Veto'. The first was transferred from *Wessex Tales* to *Life's Little Ironies* in 1912 'as being more nearly in its place, turning as it does upon a trick of Nature, so to speak.' It is the story of a middle-aged, married woman with three children whose infatuation with a young poet, though entirely unrealised, leaves strange imprints on her life. Mrs Ella Marchmill is an 'impressionable, palpitating creature' who can barely put up with her tradesman husband. So she keeps 'letting off her delicate and ethereal emotions in imaginative occupations, day-dreams, and night-sighs, which perhaps would not much have disturbed William if he had known of them.' (*Life's Little Ironies*, p. 4) When the Marchmills take up their new lodgings at Thirteen, New Parade, Ella discovers that one of the rooms they are using is under the tenancy of a young poet, Robert Trewe, who has gone away temporarily. Mrs Marchmill promptly falls in love with the absent poet. She makes several attempts to meet him but the nearest she comes to it is being visited by a painter friend of the poet's—a dreadful bore who has affinities with her husband. Then suddenly she receives news that the poet has committed suicide. She runs away to the cemetery to embrace his corpse. Time passes and she is now to have her fourth child. As the time draws near she develops a strange premonition of her death. Then she calls her husband and asks his forgiveness for her past conduct. Soon she is dead after being delivered of her fourth child. Had the story ended there it would have been an unbearably sentimental and trite story of transgression and remorse. As it is, it assumes a strange obliquity and depth. Two years after Ella's death her husband lights upon a lock of hair and a photograph of the deceased poet among his wife's possessions:

> Marchmill looked long and musingly at the hair and portrait, for something struck him. Fetching the little boy who had been the death of his mother, now a noisy toddler, he took him on his knee, held the lock of hair against the child's head, and set up the photograph on the table behind, so that he could closely compare the features each countenance presented. By a known but inexplicable trick of nature there were undoubtedly strong traces of resemblance to the man Ella had never seen; the dreamy and peculiar expression of the poet's face sat, as the transmitted idea, upon the child's, and the hair was of the same hue. (pp. 30–1)

'I'm damned if I didn't think so!' murmured Marchmill. But it is meant to be a profound mystery. In its blending of the ordinary and the fantastic 'An Imaginative Woman' is a typical Hardy story. And this combination is not merely a literary genre-mixing. It expresses Hardy's oft-repeated belief that the unexpected or the fantastic is co-present with the normal. 'A "sensation-novel"', Hardy wrote, 'is possible in which the sensationalism is not casualty, but evolution; not physical but psychical.'[18] 'An Imaginative Woman' is an experiment in psychical sensationalism.

'The Son's Veto' originally appeared in the Christmas number of *The Illustrated London News* in 1891, and was later included in *Life's Little Ironies*. It is a poignant story of social antagonism between a mother and her son.

Sophy is a parlour-maid in the service of Mr Twycott, the local vicar in a village in Wessex. The vicar falls in love with Sophy after the death of his wife. Sophy has a lover already but she is too overawed by the vicar's august proposal to turn it down: 'Sophy did not exactly love him, but she had a respect for him which almost amounted to veneration. Even if she had wished to get away from him she hardly dared refuse a personage so reverend and august in her eyes, and she assented forthwith to be his wife.' (*Life's Little Ironies*, p. 40) Marriage with a servant girl is a 'social suicide' which obliges the vicar

to move out of the small world of his Wessex living into the
anonymity of London. The vicar dies after a while leaving
Sophy with a son who is attending the Public school. Sophy is
left alone in the dreariness of her suburban home. When the
boy comes home for vacation he finds his mother's lack of
refinement exasperating. The tendency in the boy to reproach
his mother for her uncouthness of speech and demeanour
gradually hardens into downright derision. Sophy finds solace
only in thoughts of her lost rural world where she had a place
of her own. She sits at the window gazing upon the vegetable
carts that come daily into the city from the direction of her
village. On one of these carts one day she spots Sam Hobson,
the man she might have married, and calls after him. They go
for a ride and find much comfort in each other's company:
'They spoke of their native village in dear old North Wessex,
the spots in which they had played together as children. She
tried to feel that she was a dignified personage now, that she
must not be too confidential with Sam. But she could not keep
it up, and the tears hanging in her eyes were indicated in her
voice.' (p. 45) Sam proposes to Sophy and she is greatly
revived by the prospect of a return to her native village. But
Randolph, her son, is incensed at the idea: 'I am ashamed of
you! It will ruin me! A miserable boor! a churl! a clown!
It will degrade me in the eyes of all the gentlemen of England!'
(p. 50) She lives in the hope that he might withdraw his
objections once he was ordained and independent: 'But he
did not. His education had by this time sufficiently ousted his
humanity to keep him quite firm; though his mother might
have led an idyllic life with her faithful fruiterer and green-
grocer, and nobody have been anything the worse in the
world.' (pp. 51–2) In fact, he finally makes her swear in front
of a little cross and altar that she would never wed Sam Hobson
without his consent. Sophy spends the rest of her days pining
and murmuring to herself, 'Why mayn't I say to Sam that I'll
marry him? Why mayn't I?' (p. 52) The story closes with a
scene in which Sam Hobson is seen standing in a suit of
black in front of his half-shuttered fruiterer's shop. A funeral
procession is seen approaching from the railway station.
He stands tearfully, hat in hand, as the vehicles move past
him. And from the mourning coach a young smooth-shaven

priest looks 'black as a cloud at the shopkeeper standing there'.

Fate, chance, coincidence—the notorious imponderables of Hardy's fiction—have nothing to do here. It is a story of man's callousness to man. More specifically, it is a story of the cruelty of social ambition. It is indeed a vindication of the values expressed through Sophy. The author's loyalties are un-ambiguous. He makes no pretence of detachment. He sees the advancing civilisation of the city as trivial and dehumanising. At the cricket-match at Lord's Sophy sees the contents of this civilisation:

> They promenaded under the lurid July sun, this pair, so wide apart, yet so near, and Sophy saw the large proportion of boys like her own, in their broad white collars and dwarf hats, and all around the rows of great coaches under which was jumbled the *debris* of luxurious luncheons; bones, pie-crusts, champagne-bottles, glasses, plates, napkins, and the family silver; while on the coaches sat the proud fathers and mothers; but never a poor mother like her. If Randolph had not appertained to these, had not centred all his interests in them, had not cared exclusively for the class they belonged to, how happy would things have been! (p. 49)

Randolph is a cad spoiled by his notions of gentility. Quite explicitly, his education has 'ousted his humanity'. He is no Prince Hamlet opposed to the idea of his mother's re-marriage on compulsive moral and psychological grounds. His reasons are mundane and impish. He looks upon everything from the point of view of social decorum: 'Somehow, her boy, with his aristocratic school-knowledge, his grammars, and his aversions, was losing those wide infantine sympathies, extending as far as to the sun and moon themselves, with which he, like other children, had been born, and which his mother, a child of nature herself, had loved in him.' (pp. 42–3)

His mother, on the contrary, belongs to a culture which fosters a philosophical sense of community even with the inanimate objects of nature which make up one's environment. In her anguish and privation she looks upon the vegetable carriers for a sense of familiarity and home:

walls of baskets enclosing masses of beans and peas, pyramids of snow-white turnips.... Wrapped in a cloak, it was soothing to watch and sympathize with them when depression and nervousness hindered sleep, and to see how the fresh green-stuff brightened to life as it came opposite the lamp, and how the sweating animals steamed and shone with their miles of travel. (p. 44)

Education and culture are counterpoised in pitiless antagonism. They are irreconcilable. When they meet as in the relationship of mother and son, the result is a tragic clash of identities: '... I almost fancy when I am miserable sometimes that he is not really mine, but one I hold in trust for my late husband. He seems to belong so little to me personally, so entirely to his dead father. He is so much educated and I so little that I do not feel dignified enough to be his mother.' (p. 48) That is an eloquent testimony to the tragic rift. Perhaps it is the story's challenging moral and cultural standpoint which made it Hardy's favourite. He is said to have told Rebekah Owen that he thought it to be his best short story.[19]

Taken together the stories constitute a significant body of fictional output informed by Hardy's characteristic moral and artistic predilections. In their balladic simplicity, their moral consciousness, and their experiential data, they stand close to the heart of Hardy's fiction.

NOTES

1. See Florence Emily Hardy, *The Life of Thomas Hardy: 1840–1928*, p. 227.
2. Wilfrid Gibson, 'Hardy's Short Stories'.
3. Ibid.
4. R. L. Purdy, Introduction to *Our Exploits at West Poley* (London: Oxford University Press, 1952; reprinted, The Folcroft Press Inc., 1970), pp. vi–viii.
5. Ibid., p. viii.
6. Ibid., pp. ix–x.
7. Ibid., p. 1.
8. Ibid., pp. 2–3.
9. Ibid., pp. 97–8.
10. Ibid., p. 39.
11. Ibid., p. 97.

12. Florence Emily Hardy, *The Life of Thomas Hardy*, pp. 391–2.
13. Ibid., p. 116.
14. Ibid., p. 204.
15. Ibid.
16. Frank O'Connor, *The Lonely Voice: A Study of the Short Story* (1962; London: Macmillan, 1965), p. 18.
17. Ibid., p. 21.
18. Florence Emily Hardy, *The Life of Thomas Hardy*, p. 204.
19. See F. B. Pinion, *A Hardy Companion: A Guide to the Works of Thomas Hardy and Their Background*, p. 91.

CHAPTER 7

Tess of the d'Urbervilles (1891)

Tess of the d'Urbervilles has continued to be the subject of much critical controversy and speculation in spite of the 'commandingly simple outline of the book'.[1] Different elements of the novel have been wrenched apart to do duty for vastly differing moral, philosophical, and aesthetic assumptions to which the novel as a whole is not susceptible. The result has been a bewildering variety of *Tess*, each version trying to encapsulate the narrative invention into a quasi-rational theory deduced from abstracted features of the story. The novel has been read as an indictment of Christianity, as simple social polemics—a frontal attack on the Victorian establishment—or, more recently, it has been seen as having for its *telos* the inner drama of individual consciousness. The novel is very obviously an *exposé* of religious and social obscurantism as it is also, equally vividly, a demonstration of the loneliness and uniqueness of each individual soul in a harsh and unresponding world, but to identify the entire perceived world we have here with either of these critical formulas seems somehow to obscure and deny that world. Parts of the novel, seen by themselves, do seem to promise a philosophical and ideational orientation, but as the action progresses the central imaginative concern becomes progressively aphilosophical so much so that by the end of the novel the more philosophical bits of the story call for a redefinition. Joyce Cary's remark about the totality of the literary experience seems relevant:

the form of a book, page by page, is not the book, the work of art. All these separate pages and chapters, like the

Page references to *Tess of the d'Urbervilles* are to the New Wessex edition (1974).

movements of a symphony, do not have a complete significance until the whole work is known. They are, so to speak, partly in suspension, until at the end of the last movement, the last chapter, they suddenly fall into their place. This is only to say again that the separate forms do not possess their whole content until the work is complete. That's why I call the book a total symbol. It is both richer than its parts and actually different from them.[2]

Tess is, I think, a 'total symbol' subsuming, but not identical with, the different 'parts' which have come under critical scrutiny and have been subsequently praised or blamed. It is not a structure of rationalisation designed to support a dogma, but the story of a woman whose struggle for self-fulfilment follows a universal or archetypal tragic pattern individualised by the cultural imagination of the novelist. The cultural conditioning both redeems and intensifies the experience of tragic suffering for Tess. It redeems her suffering inasmuch as it keeps intact and active her memorable identity to the very last. But this 'rootedness' also makes the suffering more difficult to bear, both for her and for the reader who vicariously participates in that suffering, and makes the final reduction much more tragic. The peculiar resonance and form of this tale of the village maiden is the work of an ineluctable cultural memory. It is this memory which makes the novel what it is.

The adverse contemporary reaction to *Tess* stung Hardy into contemplating the end of his fictional career: 'How strange that one may write a book without knowing what one puts into it—or rather, the reader reads into it. Well, if this sort of thing continues no more novel-writing for me. A man must be a fool to deliberately stand up to be shot at.'[3] *Tess*, perhaps his most successful experiment in fiction, proved by a Hardyesque irony, as it were, to be the beginning of the end of his career as a novelist. In the 1892 Preface to the novel Hardy offers a succinct summary of the creative principle in *Tess*: 'Nevertheless, though the novel was intended to be neither didactic nor aggressive, but in the scenic parts to be representative simply, and in the contemplative to be oftener charged with impressions than with conviction, there have been objec-

tors both to the matter and to the rendering.' He quotes from
Schiller's letters to Goethe to explain his own aesthetic of the
novel: 'As soon as I observe that anyone, when judging of
poetical representations, considers anything more important
than the inner Necessity and Truth, I have done with him.' As
far as he was concerned *Tess* was simply a story as it occurred
to him, 'an impression, not an argument'. There were some at
least even among the contemporary critics who took the novel
on its own terms. *The Bookman*, for instance, wrote: 'We think
Mr Hardy will be much misunderstood if, in this great
tragedy, he is taken as dealing primarily with moral problems.'[4]
William Watson came to a similar conclusion about the moral
of the story: 'He himself proposes no remedy, suggests no
escape—his business not being to deal in nostrums of social
therapeutics. He is content to make his readers pause, and
consider, and pity.'[5] More recently, *Tess* has been interpreted
rigorously in thematic and metaphorical terms. The thematic
critic insists that the subject of *Tess of the d'Urbervilles* is 'the
destruction of the English peasantry'.[6] At the other end of the
spectrum we have some brilliant analyses of the pattern of
imagery and symbol in the novel as constituting its essential
core of meaning, its reality. Dorothy Van Ghent and Tony
Tanner, to mention just two outstanding critics of the novel,
have treated the novel as a tissue of symbolic or imagistic
constituents forming a pattern 'deeper than lines of rational
cause and effect'.[7] But, unlike so many other symbol-hunting
critics, they do not regard symbolism in *Tess* as mere literary
expediency but see it arising out of the cultural compulsions
behind the tale. As Dorothy Van Ghent puts it: 'It is Hardy's
incorruptible feeling for the actual that allows his symbolism
its amazingly blunt privileges and that at the same time subdues it to and absorbs it into the concrete circumstance of
experience, real as touch.'[8] Many of these recent critics, however, share with their predecessors a certain uneasiness about
the philosophical voice in or over the narrative. A voice which
was described as 'argumentative, theological, dogmatic,
philosophical or what you will, but which is not intrinsic to the
picture'[9] has repeatedly come under fire even in the most
sympathetic criticism of the novel. Bits of 'philosophical adhe-
sive tape' have been contrasted with 'the deeply animated

vision of experience'[10] in the narrative. The spontaneity of theme and metaphor, it has been argued, is rudely interrupted by 'raids of philosophic speculation'.[11] David Lodge has argued that Hardy, after his own Tess, 'spoke two languages' but 'to regard the second Hardy as a regrettable excrescence super-imposed upon the first, "true" Hardy would be mistaken.'[12] The final impact of this duality of voice, however, still remains in David Lodge's analysis surprisingly similar to the response of the earlier critics: 'Alternately dazzled by his sublimity and exasperated by his bathos, false notes, confusions, and contradic-tions, we are, while reading him, tantalized by a sense of great-ness not quite achieved.'[13] I think some work still needs to be done on the philosophical rhetoric of the novel, on its precise relationship with the dramatic material of the story. It is necessary to remember that Hardy is working in a convention which thrives on the irrelevant detail, which allows a suspension of narrative movement for moral and philosophical contem-plation. Hardy specifically described *Tess*, as we have seen, as consisting of two distinct movements—'the scenic' and 'the contemplative'. Post-Jamesian criteria of *nouvelle critique* have led to a too exclusive belief in 'dramatic economy' and 'rel-evance'. This has resulted in a literary discrimination which has rightly been described as attempting to turn 'the large, loose baggy monster' into an 'original Jamesian streamlined beast' to the unwarranted exclusion of a great deal which was not meant to be excised from the narrative.

The philosophical consciousness in *Tess* is expressed through two different narrative modes. It is sometimes attributed to the characters and is expressed as a given, ingrained tendency, but oftener than not it takes the form of authorial interjection and commentary. Those who find the philosophy gratuitous and ill-placed try, through exegetical manipulation, to exorcise the author out of his tale. They see the philosophical idiom as totally external to the grain of the story and localised only in occasional instances of artistic failure. It appears to me, how-ever, that the tendency to philosophise, to indulge in question-ing and protest, to declare loyalties, and make uninhibited comments on the procedure of events in the novel is of the very genius of the story. It is in *Tess* so pervasive and normal a strain that to imagine the novel without it would be to imagine a very different novel indeed. An early instance of the philosophical voice in the novel is the following passage:

> All these young souls were passengers in the Durbeyfield ship— entirely dependent on the judgment of the two Durbeyfield adults for their pleasures, their necessities, their health, even their existence. If the heads of the Durbeyfield household chose to sail into difficulty, disaster, starvation, disease, degradation, death, thither were these half-dozen little captives under hatches compelled to sail with them—six helpless creatures, who had never been asked if they wished for life on any terms, much less if they wished for it on such hard conditions as were involved in being of the shiftless house of Durbeyfield. Some people would like to know whence the poet whose philosophy is in these days deemed as profound and trustworthy as his song is breezy and pure, gets his authority for speaking of 'Nature's holy plan'. (p. 51)

Commenting on this passage Dorothy Van Ghent writes: 'Whenever, in this book, Hardy finds either a butt or a sanction in a poet, one can expect the inevitable intrusion of a form of discourse that infers proofs and opinions and competition in "truth" that belongs to an intellectual battlefield alien from the novel's imaginative concretions.'[14]

'Intellectual' is precisely what the comment in question is not. In fact it is decidedly anti-intellectual. It is emotive, unrestrained, even vaguely sentimental. It has none of the objectivity and rationality that belong to the manner of a competitor in 'truth'. It is an emotional response to the sordidness and poverty of the Durbeyfield household. It may leave a certain kind of reader cold but it is a necessary and inescapable consequence of the temperament that goes into the story. Part of the reason why the passage offends our sensibilities may be its heretical dismissal of Wordsworth. But what seems to be a satire is, in the actual context of feeling created by the situation, only a layman's curse. It has all the abruptness and impetuosity of an instinctive rejection on the spur of the moment. Not all Hardy's learning and his formidable range of allusions can blur the cultural clarity of his response. It is as a Dorsetshire peasant that he challenges Wordsworth, not as an agnostic philosopher nor as a judge of poetry. That such questionings and expostulations are an essential habit of the mind that invents the story is proved by the rhythmic regularity of such outbursts. The chapter describing Tess's evil encounter with Alec ends with the following authorial commentary:

> In the ill-judged execution of the well-judged plan of things the call seldom produces the comer, the man to love rarely coincides with the hour for loving. Nature does not often say 'See!' to her poor creature at a time when seeing can lead to happy doing; or reply 'Here!' to a body's cry of 'Where?' till the hide-and-seek has become an irksome, outworn game. We may wonder whether at the acme and summit of the human progress these anachronisms will be corrected by a finer intuition, a closer interaction of the social machinery than that which now jolts us round and along; but such completeness is not to be prophesied, or even conceived as possible. Enough that in the present case, as in millions, it was not the two halves of a perfect whole that confronted each other at the perfect moment; a missing counterpart wandered independently about the earth waiting in crass obtuseness till the late time came. Out of which maladroit delay sprang anxieties, disappointments, shocks, catastrophes, and passing-strange destinies. (p. 72)

This is a piece of meditation which does not add to the story structurally. But in a novel of this kind perhaps the concept of structure itself is somewhat limiting and inadequate. It is to the 'action' of the novel, as opposed to its 'story', that the commentary makes a contribution; and the 'action' of the novel owes as much to the sledge-hammer directness with which the emergent experience of the story is shaped and controlled as to the dramatic notation. The two processes are parts of the single vision which continually opposes the depersonalising conditions of life to the active demands of personality and culture. That is why nothing in Hardy is mere dramatic property. Even his most objective scenes and turns of narration are played upon by his conscious moral commitment to the human characters and issues of his story. The great symbolic scenes of the novel just stop short of erupting into a furious tirade. Some of these great moments of the story are, as David Lodge has rightly remarked, as much the work of the second Hardy as of the first. The philosophical voice is not a far cry from the eloquent symbolism of *Tess*. It becomes axiomatic in the given world of the novel. But authorial presence here is by no means confined to detachable passages. It is built into the syntactic and symbolic tissues of the narrative. Hardy hovers over his story like a ghost.

Tess seems to me to be motivated by a powerful nostalgia and this sense of the absolute validity of the past is at the heart of the emotional impact the novel makes. Nostalgia in *Tess* does not end in romantic pastoralism, but evokes levels of moral experience beyond the reach of romanticised fiction. Critics looking for a thematic core in the novel have alleged that it is confused and full of contradictions rather than complexity. But they have, nevertheless, acknowledged its emotional integrity, its 'over-arching unity of feeling'. Some have argued that the novel is an uneasy co-existence of different perspectives and ways of responding to experience. It is true that Hardy can, indeed often does, use a variety of contrasting perspectives to bring out the full ambience of a scene or incident. He can masterfully turn the kaleidoscope, but his central values are too assured to warrant a suspicion of moral multiplicity in his fictional arrangement. Ambiguity has its limits in Hardy's novels. *Tess*, in any case, is conspicuous for its unswerving singleness of perspective. The novel achieves its unity through its vindication of Tess both as an individual and as a metaphor of a certain quality of consciousness. It seems highly improbable that a novel with such clear commitment can indulge in an inconsequential plurality of perspective. Hardy's vision is dogmatically selectivist and it has no pretensions to philosophical cosmopolitanism. This is evident in the blunt finality of the cultural and moral framework of the story. Even the tell-tale chapter heads—'The Maiden', 'Maiden No More', etc.—suggest the traditionalism of the basic terms of reference in the novel. It is, indeed, true that Hardy's involvement with Tess becomes an obsessive narrative attitude. He treats Tess's sensibility as a moral touchstone and makes her an absolute woman. But in thus treating Tess he is not championing individual consciousness against social and cultural barriers—nor even dallying with the kind of total subjectivism that Lawrence saw existing but, much to his dismay, eventually frustrated and withheld in the Wessex novels. Tess's personality issues from cultural compulsions. Her profoundest responses in the novel are so evocative of cultural archetypes that she sometimes acquires the impersonality of the immemorial ballad heroine. There is no opposition between her intense self-awareness and her representative role as the 'cultural' woman wronged. Bernard J. Paris, in his probing study of the novel, argues that Hardy's identification with Tess leads to a rejection of every norm and perspective except 'the phenomenological' which means sacrificing all communal sanctions to the passionate intransigence of individual will and imagination:

> Hardy is committed in *Tess* to the point of view of the individual.... What is missing in the novel is communal perspective which sees the individual in terms other than his own and which provides shared values toward the realization of which a whole society can move. This is why Hardy lacks the moral toughness, the recognition of human evil, and the insistence on goodness that Guerard admires in a writer like Conrad; it is also why *Tess* fails as a novel of social protest.[15]

I think there is some basic confusion here. First, if *Tess* is committed to 'the point of view of the individual' and negates socially realisable goals it should make a novel of social protest *par excellence*, rather than otherwise. Then the comparison with Conrad is uncalled-for and it deflects attention from the questions asked about *Tess*. In any case, the charge that *Tess* excludes 'a communal perspective' seems to me patently absurd. Tess's own individual vision is largely made up of communal perspectives. Hardy's rhetorical question—'Moreover, alone in a desert island would she have been wretched at what had happened to her?' (p. 127)—inversely stresses the inevitability, for Tess, of a non-desert, a world with cultural agreements and expectations impinging upon individual psyche. Her 'conventional aspect' (p. 127) is both her strength and her weakness. The rapport between Tess's consciousness and her community is evidenced in the remarkable ease and spontaneity with which her private experience is all too often signalised through common cultural forms and symbols of experience. These public metaphors provide a modality for the articulation of life in the novel. They are also operative in the moral imagination of the story. The glaring, almost melodramatically externalised distinction that exists in *Tess* between good and evil is owing to the novel's imaginative alliance with the fluent moral idiom of an established culture. That is why there is little moral anxiety or uncertainty in this story. Hardy's philosophical despair is dramatically useful not because it opposes but because it coincides with the inherent moods and meanings of the culture he portrays. *Tess* claims uniqueness as a work of art in the sheer scope of its visualisation and externality rather than in any moral difficulty or subtlety. So much that is meaningful in the novel is right on the surface, easily accessible. If, in spite of its cultural clarity, certain elements in the novel appear to us morally indeterminate it is because we bring to bear upon these elements our typically modern aversion to the finality of recognition. We ought to remember that Tess herself evinces no moral hesitancy or confusion. She can separate her rights and desirables from her wrongs and nullities with remarkable volitional and emotional economy—a fact which makes all our assumptions about moral and social discontinuity in the novel seem fanciful and academic. Tess is a child of unconscious propensity actuated in the great psychological moments of her life by 'ancestral passion'. Let us look at the cultural pattern that the novel traces through the action of her vivid personality.

Tess is shocked into self-awareness and adulthood by the degrading sexual experience she undergoes at Trantridge. Before this 'Tess Durbeyfield . . . was a mere vessel of emotion untinctured by experience.' (p. 42) She is so much a part of her surroundings that she is hardly distinguishable from the natural life around her. The village of Marlott in which she was born and reared acquires an ethnic personality, so that in leaving it she leaves more than a place:

The Vale of Blackmoor was to her the world, and its

inhabitants the races thereof. From the gates and stiles of Marlott she had looked down its length in the wondering days of infancy, and what had been mystery to her then was not much less than mystery to her now. She had seen daily from her chamber-window towers, villages, faint white mansions; above all the town of Shaston standing majestically on its height; its windows shining like lamps in the evening sun. She had hardly ever visited the place, only a small tract even of the Vale and its environs being known to her by close inspection. Much less had she been far outside the valley. *Every contour of the surrounding hills was as personal to her as that of her relatives' faces*; but for what lay beyond her judgment was dependent on the teaching of the village school, where she had held a leading place at the time of her leaving, a year or two before this date. (italics mine) (p. 65)

Significantly, she decides to go to Trantridge to claim kinship with the Stoke d'Urbervilles not out of any physical or psychological requirement of her own but from a sense of responsibility towards her family. She is able to subordinate the needs of her own ego to the more fundamental needs of her family. Such self-abnegation may or may not be morally desirable in absolute terms, but it is a cultural value which Tess accepts without hesitation: 'And to please her parent the girl put herself quite in Joan's hands, saying serenely—"Do what you like with me, mother." ' (p. 78) At Trantridge, of course, Tess finds herself in a situation for which she is not prepared. The incident at The Chase leaves her petrified and, while it lasts, in a state of amnesia, which is conveyed in startling physical detail:

The obscurity was now so great that he could see absolutely nothing but a pale nebulousness at his feet, which represented the white muslin figure he had left upon the dead leaves. Everything else was blackness alike. d'Urberville stooped; and heard a gentle regular breathing. He knelt and bent lower, till her breath warmed his face, and in a moment his cheek was in contact with hers. She was sleeping soundly, and upon her eyelashes there lingered tears. (p. 107)

But after this accidental capitulation she totally recovers her earlier integrity of vision. Rather than try to adapt herself to her changed situation she betrays, in her instinctive response to the facts of her experience, an annoying fidelity to conventional, cultural categories. This is suggested in Hardy's own occasional bafflement and irritation at her incurable conventionality, in spite of his deeper understanding of why it must be so:

> At times her whimsical fancy would intensify natural processes around her till they seemed a part of her own story. Rather they became a part of it; for the world is only a psychological phenomenon, and what they seemed they were. The midnight airs and gusts, moaning against the tightly-wrapped buds and bark of the winter twigs, were formulae of bitter reproach. A wet day was the expression of irremediable grief at her weakness in the mind of some vague ethical being whom she could not class definitely as the God of her childhood, and could not comprehend as any other.
>
> But this encompassment of her own characterization, based on shreds of convention, peopled by phantoms and voices antipathetic to her, was a sorry and mistaken creation of Tess's fancy—a cloud of moral hobgoblins by which she was terrified without reason. (p. 120)

I think this remark serves to stress the cultural orientation of Tess's personality rather than discredit cultural and societal pressures within her. It has been read as an expression of Hardy's disenchantment with culture. It is true that Hardy is dismayed by the pain-giving aspects of social values, but he does not forget for long that a total transcendence of culture is not humanly possible, or even desirable. The world of the novel takes its dramatic concreteness and plausibility from its evocation of cultural and communal values, and not from its occasional holiday away from them. When Tess translates the innocent natural world around her into her own 'story' she is only renewing her earlier habit of communication with nature fostered by her pastoral culture. In saving that 'the world is only a psychological phenomenon, and what they seemed they were' Hardy is not referring, as the context of the statement makes amply clear, to the operations of the separated individual

psyche, but to the 'encompassment' of the individual psyche
within a predictable pattern of behaviour, which is a function
of culture. Tess's sense of sexual guilt and violation is a consequence of cultural determinism. It cannot be wished away. It
is simply there as an essential response. The stark simplicity
and recognisability of the dramatic property Hardy uses to
objectify Tess's reaction to her sexual experience provide a
further clue to the cultural origins of her conscience. On her
journey home from Trantridge she is accosted, as it were, by
her own conscience embattled with its pot of red paint and an
array of biblical injunctions:

> As she walked, however, some footsteps approached behind
> her, the footsteps of a man; and owing to the briskness of his
> advance he was close at her heels and had said 'Good morn-
> ing' before she had been long aware of his propinquity. He
> appeared to be an artisan of some sort, and carried a tin
> pot of red paint in his hand....
> 'It is early to be astir this Sabbath morn!' he said cheer-
> fully.
> 'Yes,' said Tess.
> 'When most people are at rest from their week's work.'
>   She also assented to this.
> 'Though I do more real work to-day than all the week
> besides.'
> 'Do you?'
> 'All the week I work for the glory of man, and on Sunday for
> the glory of God. That's more real than the other—hey? I
> have a little to do here at this stile.' The man turned as
> he spoke to an opening at the roadside leading into a
> pasture. 'If you'll wait a moment,' he added, 'I shall not
> be long.'
>   As he had her basket she could not well do otherwise;
> and she waited, observing him. He set down her basket and
> the tin pot, and stirring the paint with the brush that was in
> it began painting large square letters on the middle board of
> the three composing the stile, placing a comma after each
> word, as if to give pause while that word was driven well
> home to the reader's heart—

THY, DAMNATION, SLUMBERETH, NOT
2 Pet. II 3

Against the peaceful landscape, the pale, decaying tints of the copses, the blue air of the horizon, and the lichened stile-boards, these staring vermilion words shone forth. They seemed to shout themselves out and make the atmosphere ring. Some people might have cried 'Alas, poor Theology!' at the hideous defacement—the last grotesque phase of a creed which had served mankind well in its time. But the words entered Tess with accusatory horror. It was as if this man had known her recent history; yet he was a total stranger. (pp. 114–15)

As a piece of realistic fictional invention the episode is superb. But it acquires its special significance by providing a cultural rationale for Tess's sense of guilt and self-accusation. Hardy makes it very clear that it is not the theological content of the 'staring vermilion words' so much as their cultural force which overwhelms Tess. This episode also exemplifies Hardy's reliance on culturally sensitive material for communication of meaning. And he adopts these forms wholly seriously. There is no suggestion of irony or intellectual superiority in the above episode. Hardy treats the man with the pot of red paint realistically and he is emotionally involved in the way in which the whole episode impinges on Tess's sensibility. The result is the emergent authenticity of his character-study of Tess and the inherence of cultural compulsions in the working of the story.

Another superb instance of Tess's cultural sensitivity is her christening of her dying child. Here again the focus is on the cultural concept of mother-child relationship. In Tess's anxiety for the soul of her baby Hardy is renewing and revalidating one of the primary cultural myths—the infinite solicitude of the mother for her child regardless of the circumstances of the child's conception and birth. Tess's maternal anxiety further stresses her allegiance to cultural roles. But her determination to save her child from damnation by baptising him before he is dead also underscores the survival of religious imagery into culture. Hardy calls the secularised ritual 'an act of approximation' (p. 131) which it truly is, for its validity for Tess lies in its form and imagery rather than in its theological implications. She has done away with the church and the clergy but retained the basic emotional understanding of the ritual because it has come to her naturally in the ordinary process of growing up within a certain culture. The baptism scene grows out of a cultural-religious stereotype. So powerful is its hold on Tess's imagination that she has nightmarish visions of her child being tortured in hell because he has died unbaptised. The baptismal proceedings into which Tess is prompted by her vivid imagination are described in a vignette memorable for its demonstration of the transfiguring, hypnotic effect of religio-cultural rituals, especially on children:

> Then their sister, with much augmented confidence in the efficacy of this sacrament, poured forth from the bottom of her heart the thanksgiving that follows, uttering it boldly and triumphantly in the stopt-diapason note which her voice acquired when her heart was in her speech, and which will never be forgotten by those who knew her. The ecstasy of faith almost apotheosized her; it set upon her face a glowing irradiation.... The children gazed up at her with more and more reverence, and no longer had a will for questioning. She did not look like Sissy to them now, but as a being large, towering, and awful—a divine personage with whom they had nothing in common. (p. 131)

By the time Tess reaches Talbothays her personality has been firmly and irreversibly defined in terms of its cultural susceptibility. The Talbothays idyll provides an extended context for the celebration of her personality. Talbothays is a kind of paradise not because it offers immunity to suffering but because it restores to Tess's life its natural context. It offers an external social microcosm which becomes an 'objective correlative' of Tess's personality. It makes Tess more credible. Talbothays breeds a sensibility which is continuous with the past. Dairyman Crick presides over the life of the dairy as a patriarchal figure in a close-knit, culturally coherent society. His stories reveal his consciousness of the earlier beliefs and practices which continue to be meaningful and relevant for him. Particularly revealing is Angel Clare's reaction to his story of the bull's response to the ' 'Tivity Hymn':

'It's a curious story; it carries us back to mediaeval times, when faith was a living thing!' [says Angel Clare]

The remark, singular for a dairy-yard, was murmured by the voice behind the dun cow; but as nobody understood the reference no notice was taken, except that the narrator seemed to think it might imply scepticism as to his tale.

'Well, 'tis quite true, sir, whether or no. I knowed the man well.'

'Oh yes; I have no doubt of it,' said the person behind the dun cow. (p. 148)

Angel's remark implies a dissonance between the terms of Crick's story and the needs of modern imagination. This is so because Angel Clare, if anybody, is a victim of historic schizophrenia. But we shall return to him later. The fact that his remark is not even intelligible to his listeners emphasises the gulf that exists between him and Talbothays. It may be noted, incidentally, that his appeal for Tess is not simply a matter of instant sexual magnetism. Nor does her passion for Angel cancel the ingrained drives of her personality. A major force in her involvement with this man is her unceasing quest for emotional integrity, a quest which is tragically frustrated, but which, nevertheless, remains a ruling drive in her personality. She is meeting Angel for the second time at Talbothays. He is not a total stranger but one with whom she has an earlier emotional acquaintance, one whom she has seen in a dreamlike episode of her innocent youth. That vision of him is active in her second encounter:

But the details of his aspect were temporarily thrust aside by the discovery that he was one whom she had seen before. Such vicissitudes had Tess passed through since that time that for a moment she could not remember where she had met him; and then it flashed upon her that he was the pedestrian who had joined in the club-dance at Marlott— the passing stranger who had come she knew not whence, had danced with others but not with her, had slightingly left her, and gone on his way with his friends. (p. 149)

The congenial atmosphere of the dairy aids Tess's struggle

towards wholeness and spiritual survival. The world begins to come together for a brief while in the love, companionship, and continuity of physical and spiritual environment that she finds at Talbothays. This is not to say that it allows Tess total self-fulfilment and serenity. The tragic vision of the novel demands that she be always struggling, always on the rack. Suffering is an inescapable condition of her life. And she suffers as much and as well at Talbothays as anywhere else. The Talbothays interlude, in fact, is in many ways a symbolic summary of the central quality of her experience of life. On the positive side, it offers her meaningful work, conviviality, love, and a sense of belonging. In short, it offers her a harmonious existence:

> Either the change in the quality of the air from heavy to light, or the sense of being amid new scenes where there were no invidious eyes upon her, sent up her spirits wonderfully. Her hopes mingled with the sunshine in an ideal photosphere which surrounded her as she bounded along against the soft south wind. She heard a pleasant voice in every breeze, and in every bird's note seemed to lurk a joy. (p. 140)

Her sense of harmony with the natural and human world of Talbothays touches beatific sublimity:

> The outskirt of the garden in which Tess found herself had been left uncultivated for some years, and was now damp and rank with juicy grass which sent up mists of pollen at a touch; and with tall blooming weeds emitting offensive smells—weeds whose red and yellow and purple hues formed a polychrome as dazzling as that of cultivated flowers. She went stealthily as a cat through this profusion of growth, gathering cuckoo-spittle on her skirts, cracking snails that were underfoot, staining her hands with thistle-milk and slug-slime, and rubbing off upon her naked arms sticky blights which, though snow-white on the apple-tree trunks, made madder stains on her skin; thus she drew quite near to Clare, still unobserved of him.
>
> Tess was conscious of neither time nor space. The exaltation which she had described as being producible at will by gazing at a star, came now without any determination of

hers; she undulated upon the thin notes of the second-hand harp, and their harmonies passed like breezes through her, bringing tears into her eyes. The floating pollen seemed to be his notes made visible, and the dampness of the garden the weeping of the garden's sensibility. Though near nightfall, the rank-smelling, weed-flowers glowed as if they would not close for intentness, and the waves of colour mixed with the waves of sound. (pp. 161–2)

The first part of this quotation has been the subject of much critical controversy. Dorothy Van Ghent sees the weeds as symbolic of the degeneracy of Angel Clare. She sees Tess as a victim in keeping with her metaphorical reading of the weeds. David Lodge challenges her reading and persuasively argues that it is only by taking liberties with the grammar of the passage, as Dorothy Van Ghent has done, that one can see Tess as an innocent victim in it. He says: 'The participles *gathering*, *cracking*, *staining*, and *rubbing off*, of which the grammatical subject is Tess, as well as imitating her physical movement, stress the active nature of her relationship with the natural world.'[16] I think the weed passage has been read much too metaphorically and out of context. Read together, the two passages I have quoted suggest a somewhat different concern. No one can deny that Hardy is emphasising 'the active nature of her relationship with the natural world', but the natural world need not be read in strictly Darwinian terms. I think the natural phenomenon here does not have any overweening metaphysical connotation. What mobilises the natural world and gives it meaning is the human sensibility. So powerful is Tess's sense of harmony with her world at this particular moment that she makes even the least romantic aspects of nature fulfil some need of her excited imagination—'The floating pollen seemed to be his notes made visible, and the dampness of the garden the weeping of the garden's sensibility.' But this is only one aspect of her experience at Talbothays.

The inevitability of suffering for Tess comes through in the sudden forebodings and fears aroused in her in spite of all the apparent blessedness of life in these primeval haunts. Dairyman Crick's story of the widow, for instance, suddenly fills Tess's mind with gloom and sad presentiments. Even her final

decision to marry Angel Clare is attended by a nagging fear
that his having passed her by at the Marlott dance might be an
ill omen for them:

> 'Ah, then I *have* seen you before this summer—'
> 'Yes; at that dance on the green; but you would not dance
> with me. O, I hope that is of no ill-omen for us now!'
> (p. 232)

Her sense of happiness is alloyed with her acute consciousness
of the fragility of love and of the stigma of her past. Dairyman
Crick's stories parody her predicament, but his stories also
reveal that the culture of their origin can absorb and transcend
youthful mishaps and indiscretions. In any case, Tess achieves
a wholeness and integrity of being at Talbothays which will
now be subjected to pressures yet unknown.

Her marriage with Angel Clare, marking the end of the
Talbothays idyll, is only a prelude to her great, grotesque career
of suffering and victimisation. Angel's rejection of Tess on the
night of their honeymoon initiates for her the process of de-
personalisation and separation from meaning. She is suddenly
left in a world without identity, a world where personality
and emotion are anomalous. Material objects, no less than
familiar human beings, betray a total loss of sympathy and
habitude:

> But the complexion even of external things seemed to suffer
> transmutation as her announcement progressed. The fire
> in the grate looked impish—demoniacally funny, as if it did
> not care in the least about her strait. The fender grinned idly,
> as if it too did not care. The light from the waterbottle was
> merely engaged in a chromatic problem. All material
> objects around announced their irresponsibility with terrible
> iteration. (p. 270)

This severence makes Tess's life increasingly automatic, devoid
of will and imagination:

> and there was something of the habitude of the wild animal
> in the unreflecting instinct with which she rambled on—

disconnecting herself by littles from her eventful past at every step, obliterating her identity, giving no thought to accidents or contingencies which might make a quick discovery of her whereabouts by others of importance to her own happiness, if not to theirs. (p. 321)

But despite the dehumanisation and shock that she undergoes, her moral and cultural imagination is never totally paralysed. She has springs of compassion and moral sympathy which no adversity can anathematise. An outstanding assertion of her moral identity comes in the deep compassion which the sight of the wounded pheasants arouses in her on her way to Flint-comb-Ash:

> With the impulse of a soul who could feel for kindred sufferers as much as for herself, Tess's first thought was to put the still living birds out of their torture, and to this end with her own hands she broke the necks of as many as she could find, leaving them to lie where she had found them till the game-keepers should come—as they probably would come—to look for them a second time.
>
> 'Poor darlings—to suppose myself the most miserable being on earth in the sight o' such misery as yours!' she exclaimed, her tears running down as she killed the birds tenderly. 'And not a twinge of bodily pain about me! I be not mangled, and I be not bleeding, and I have two hands to feed and clothe me.' (p. 324)

This assertion of her superior moral imagination becomes all the more remarkable because, in the circumstances, she herself is little more than a hunted animal. In fact she discovers the pheasants because in flight from the evil attentions of the Trantridge passer-by she runs into the deep undergrowth where the birds lie dying. Her mode of self-defence is no different from theirs: 'She scraped together the dead leaves till she had formed them into a large heap, making a sort of nest in the middle. Into this Tess crept.' (p. 322) Physically reduced to a sub-human level of vulnerability and resourcelessness, she can yet evince her powerful human identity and potentiality.

It is at Flintcomb-Ash that the forces opposed to Tess's sensibility and culture are most vividly dramatised. The mechanical, meaningless toil, the inclement weather, the brooding ennui, and hostile human presences all combine to create an 'anti-utopia' in which Tess's soul is cast to starve and perish. It is a vision of hell:

> it was a complexion without features, as if a face, from chin to brow, should be only an expanse of skin. The sky wore, in another colour, the same likeness; a white vacuity of countenance with the lineaments gone. So these two upper and nether visages confronted each other all day long, the white face looking down on the brown face, and the brown face looking up at the white face, without anything standing between them but the two girls crawling over the surface of the former like flies. (p. 331)

Even the rain falls differently in this place. Rather than fall it races along 'horizontally upon the yelling wind, sticking into them like glass splinters till they were wet through.' (p. 332) Detail by detail Hardy establishes the horrific dreariness of Flintcomb-Ash. Even the birds that land here in winter seem to be the very messengers of doom:

> strange birds from behind the North Pole began to arrive silently on the upland of Flintcomb-Ash; gaunt spectral creatures with tragical eyes—eyes which had witnessed scenes of cataclysmal horror in inaccessible polar regions of a magnitude such as no human being had ever conceived, in curdling temperatures that no man could endure; which had beheld the crash of icebergs and the slide of snow-hills by the shooting light of the Aurora....(p. 334)

But the most telling symbols of dehumanisation and oppression in Flintcomb-Ash are the threshing-machine described as the 'red tyrant' (the colour, apart from its usual associations, has a particular significance in Tess's life)[17] and the itinerant engine-man whom Hardy presents with a fascinated disgust:

> By the engine stood a dark motionless being, a sooty and grimy embodiment of tallness, in a sort of trance, with a heap of coals by his side: it was the engineman. The isolation

of his manner and colour lent him the appearance of a creature from Tophet, who had strayed into the pellucid smokelessness of this region of yellow grain and pale soil, with which he had nothing in common, to amaze and to discompose its aborigines.

What he looked he felt. He was in the agricultural world, but not of it. He served fire and smoke; these denizens of the fields served vegetable, weather, frost, and sun. He travelled with his engine from farm to farm, from county to county....He spoke in a strange northern accent; his thoughts being turned inwards upon himself, his eye on his iron charge, hardly perceiving the scenes around him, and caring for them not at all: holding only strictly necessary intercourse with the natives, as if some ancient doom compelled him to wander here against his will in the service of his Plutonic master. (pp. 372–3)

All these features of life at Flintcomb-Ash combine to dissolve the world which has produced Tess. She seems to have been separated from her essential self and become a female automaton toiling through the sheer force of exhaustion: 'Then the threshing-machine started afresh; and amid the renewed rustle of the straw Tess resumed her position by the buzzing drum as one in a dream, untying sheaf after sheaf in endless succession.' (p. 379) But even amidst all this reduction and atrophy she keeps struggling for survival and moral identity. Just when it seems to have lost all its resistance and élan, her dormant personality rises up, in a memorable feat of self-definition, against the predatory forces of lust and mechanisation contending for her body and soul. The dramatic moment comes when Alec approaches her on the upland farm to renew his offer of love and protection. It is a great scene, visualised with an aptness and concentration of dramatic detail which make it irrefutable. All we are given is an assemblage of physical details descriptive of a physical action, but the final impression conveyed by this terse and realistic account is that of a deeper spiritual rhythm, of a distinct psychological movement shaped by cultural and historical factors. The very abruptness of the action suggests an unconscious cultural motivation:

'You have been the cause of my backsliding,' he continued,

stretching his arm towards her waist; 'you should be willing to share it, and leave that mule you call husband for ever.'

One of her leather gloves, which she had taken off to eat her skimmer-cake, lay in her lap, and without the slightest warning she passionately swung the glove by the gauntlet directly in his face. It was heavy and thick as a warrior's, and it struck him flat on the mouth. Fancy might have regarded the act as the recrudescence of a trick in which her armed progenitors were not unpractised. Alec fiercely started up from his reclining position. A scarlet oozing appeared where her blow had alighted, and in a moment the blood began dropping from his mouth upon the straw. (pp. 378–9)

Her final submission to Alec d'Urberville is motivated by the same force which first brought her under his sway. It is because of her sensitivity to the needs of her family that she agrees to live as Alec's mistress. The circumstantial pressure that brings Tess to such humiliating and self-denying compromise arouses profound despair in her creator:

If she could only believe what the children were singing; if she were only sure how different all would now be; how confidently she would leave them to Providence and their future kingdom! But, in default of that, it behoved her to do something; to be their Providence; for to Tess, as to not a few millions of others, there was ghastly satire in the poet's lines—

> Not in utter nakedness
> But trailing clouds of glory do we come.

To her and her like, birth itself was an ordeal of degrading personal compulsion, whose gratuitousness nothing in the result seemed to justify, and at best could only palliate. (p. 406)

Critics have objected to Hardy's generalisation from Tess's predicament. But the generalisation is not as gratuitous as it appears to be. It is against a background of general uprooting and cultural dislocation that Hardy places the particular destiny of Tess and her family:

These annual migrations from farm to farm were on the increase here. When Tess's mother was a child the majority of the field-folk about Marlott had remained all their lives on one farm, which had been the home also of their fathers and grandfathers; but latterly the desire for yearly removal had risen to a high pitch....

However, all the mutations so increasingly discernible in village life did not originate entirely in the agricultural unrest. A depopulation was also going on.... These families, who had formed the backbone of the village life in the past, who were the depositaries of the village traditions, had to seek refuge in the large centres; the process, humorously designated by statisticians as 'the tendency of the rural population towards the large towns', being really the tendency of water to flow uphill when forced by machinery. (pp. 400-1)

In the context in which Tess's family is rendered homeless, making it inevitable for her to subdue her nobler instincts to a brutal necessity, the emotionalism and excessive despair of Hardy's remarks do have a moral justification. His sensibility is deeply involved in the tradition which is being so rapidly destroyed. What gives him a novelistic attitude is not a sense of historical inevitability, and understanding of change, but a profound nostalgia for the vanishing past. His imagination is the opposite of the historical: 'History is concerned with mutation, and Hardy, a Poet first and last, was concerned with the immutable.'[18] For Hardy, as for Tess, the ancestral village and home are correlates of the human personality: 'Part of her body and life it ever seemed to be; the slope of its dormers, the finish of its gables, the broken courses of brick which topped the chimney, all had something in common with her personal character. A stupefaction had come into these features, to her regard; it meant the illness of her mother.' (p. 394) To be forced out of this habitat is to be intrinsically violated. The novel expresses strong resistance to the incongruous city surroundings in which Tess finds herself after her forced migration from her native village. The city of Sandbourne seems:

like a fairy place suddenly created by the stroke of a wand, and allowed to get a little dusty. An out-lying eastern tract of the enormous Egdon Waste was close at hand, yet on the very verge of that tawny piece of antiquity such a glittering novelty as this pleasure city had chosen to spring up. Within the space of a mile from its outskirts every irregularity of the soil was prehistoric, every channel an undisturbed British track-way; not a sod having been turned there since the days of the Caesars. Yet the exotic had grown here, suddenly as the prophet's gourd; and had drawn hither Tess. (p. 426)

The novelist's deep resentment at Tess's degradation and detribalisation demands nothing less than a knife-wielding gesture. The end of *Tess* is characterised by a profound cultural optimism. For all the circumstantial opposition and hostility to her character and culture, Tess never fails to produce herself at the psychological moment. She perishes in the end but not without having passed the image on. Her stabbing of Alec is dangerously close to the melodramatic. But it is only the most natural climax of the movement of her personality. In her desperate struggle for identity she has already drawn blood from Alec's face. And she is aware of her propensities: 'I feared long ago, when I struck him on the mouth with my glove, that I might do it someday for the trap he set for me in my simple youth . . . '. (p. 436) She kills Alec with an almost moral earnestness. If we do not feel shocked by the murder, it is because the murder seems to be the natural response, considering the circumstantial provocation, of a whole culture rather than the culpable act of one aberrant criminal. It is perhaps right to say that the murder is the only means of cultural redemption left to her: 'But her stabbing of Alec is her heroic return through the "door" into the folk fold, the fold of nature and instinct, the anonymous community.'[19] The murder firmly establishes Tess's cultural identity. After it there is no mistaking her. It is a magical strategy through which she is made to transcend the psychological limitation accruing from her role as a credible character in a realistic novel and achieve the authority of a poetical symbol or a mythological figure. We accept this enlargement of her personality because it accords with the principle of cultural mythicisation implicit in the whole novel. To many critics the later manifestations of Tess have appeared somewhat blurred and not sufficiently individuated. Meredith complained that the late Tess was 'a smudge in vapour'. A more recent critic finds Tess of the closing section, 'a mere cliche, a sentimentalized angelic figure like Dickens's Agnes Wickfield'.[20] There is no denying that Tess is poetically distanced towards the end of the novel. But this fading of her individuated behaviour into a larger cultural configuration means only a capping imaginative recognition of the forces that made her defiant particularity possible. Her individuality, as we have seen, is not the result of the anchorless ego of existentialist fiction but of cultural and hereditary determinism. The mythologisation and symbolic extension of her personality, therefore, are in keeping with the central assumption of the novel that culture to a great extent determines individual consciousness. Tess's last acts, while being adequately motivated in terms of psychological realism, achieve the grander illumination of the larger, mythical attitudes and impulses of a particular culture. It is significant that her last thoughts centre on questions of familial and cultural futurity and continuity. In committing Angel Clare to her sister she is handing on to them a mandate for pursuing the cultural identity to which she herself has been a martyr. In seeing Liza-Lu as a 'spiritualised image' of Tess Hardy balances his disturbing vision of cultural impasse with a tragic but affirmative vision of cultural continuity and persistence through defeat and disruption. Tess dies but not till she has fully acted out her cultural latency and made her compulsions the starting point of life where the novel ends. She dies with a vision.

There has been some critical attempt recently at a denigration of Tess and a moral elevation of the two disasters in her life—Alec d'Urberville and Angel Clare. Robert Heilman, for instance, has argued that Alec is 'a plausible complex figure' rather than the simple villain of melodrama. Angel similarly becomes 'a divided man incapable of peace-producing singleness'. He goes on to call him 'a potential Othello'. Defending his view of Angel Clare he adds: 'much of the talk about the conventional in Angel seems like editorializing that springs from historical annoyance rather than insight into character.'[21] The world of the book, in this view, becomes a modern democracy of conflicting egos and personalities where moral distinctions are not obtainable. Heilman is mistaken, I think, in

assuming that what he calls 'historical annoyance' is an attri-
bute of critical illiteracy. In claiming the status of authentic
and adequate human beings for the two commonly but rightly
denounced characters of the novel he is displaying as much
'historical annoyance' or perhaps historical reaction as those
he accuses of insufficient insight into character. There is a
basis for 'historical annoyance' in the novel itself. Hardy is not
striving for ambiguity and open-endedness. The action of *Tess*,
its emotional and moral impact upon the reader, depends
on the operation of clear-cut moral categories and attitudes.
Alec d'Urberville is quite emphatically a sensualist and an
unscrupulous philanderer and his whole life is governed by
bogus and inauthentic attitudes. He is seen as the product of a
money-grabbing, materialistic chicken-culture, at one remove
from the traditional pieties celebrated in the normative purity
of Tess. His typicality serves Hardy's purposes well because he
is interested in Alec only negatively, only inasmuch as he can be
Tess's counterpoint. All the details that go into his making—
his loud clothes, his stock phrases, his artificially stimulated
proselytising zeal—make him a stereotype antagonist of the
culture celebrated in the novel. No charity and ingenuity of
critical imagination can alter those basic facts about him. He
is meant to be despised unless of course we import irrelevant
associations into the book. Angel Clare is likewise opposed to
the ideal of an adequate life. He too belongs to the world
outside. Alec and Angel are anomalies against which Hardy
tries to order and sustain his authentic vision of a culture.
They belong to the negative side of his creative vision, dramatically necessary but morally repugnant. This is another way of
saying that the flow of meaning in the novel is governed solely
by the cultural authority of Tess's actions and responses. The
world of the novel clearly and indivisibly belongs to Tess who
is quite simply, in Tomlinson's phrase, 'a country girl'.[22]

NOTES

1. T. B. Tomlinson, *The English Middle Class Novel* (London: Macmillan, 1976),
   p. 140.
2. Joyce Cary, *Art and Reality* (Cambridge: University Press, 1958), p. 103.
3. See Florence Emily Hardy, *The Life of Thomas Hardy, 1840–1928*, p. 246.

4. See Laurence Lerner and John Holmstorm, eds., *Thomas Hardy and His Readers: A Selection of Contemporary Reviews* (London: Bodley Head, 1968), p. 74.

5. See R. G. Cox, ed., *Thomas Hardy: The Critical Heritage*, p. 202.

6. Arnold Kettle, *An Introduction to the English Novel*, second edition, Vol. II (London: Hutchinson, 1967), p. 45.

7. Tony Tanner, 'Colour and Movement in Hardy's *Tess of the d'Urbervilles*'.

8. Dorothy Van Ghent, *The English Novel: Form and Function* (1953; New York: Harper & Row, 1961), p. 201.

9. William R. Rutland, *Thomas Hardy: A Study of His Writings and Their Background*, p. 234.

10. Van Ghent, *The English Novel*, p. 196.

11. Ian Gregor and Brian Nicholas, *The Moral and the Story* (London: Faber & Faber, 1962), p. 144.

12. David Lodge, *Language of Fiction* (London: Routledge & Kegan Paul; New York: Columbia University Press, 1966), p. 168.

13. Ibid., p. 188.

14. Van Ghent, *The English Novel*, p. 196.

15. Bernard J. Paris, '"A Confusion of Many Standards": Conflicting Value Systems in *Tess of the d'Urbervilles*'.

16. Lodge, *Language of Fiction*, p. 182.

17. See Tanner, 'Colour and Movement in Hardy's *Tess*'.

18. R. J. White, *Thomas Hardy and History*, p. 11.

19. Van Ghent, *The English Novel*, p. 209.

20. J. T. Laird, *The Shaping of* Tess of the d'Urbervilles, p. 101.

21. Robert B. Heilman, '*Gulliver* and Hardy's *Tess*: Houyhnhnms, Yahoos, and Ambiguities'.

22. Tomlinson, *The English Middle Class Novel*, p. 141.

CHAPTER 8

Jude the Obscure
(1895)

Jude is rooted in the central sociological typology
of Hardy's Wessex fiction. It is a vision of the chaotic absurdity
of human life outside the shaping matrices of history and
culture and thus a powerful vindication of the norms embodied
in his comprehensive fictional metaphor 'Wessex'. The many
departures that this novel makes from 'Wessex' are made
obliquely to recall and continually exploit that magic metaphor as a central criterion of quality. That is why I consider
Jude a logical completion of Hardy's sociological fiction. It is
obviously a novel embodying very different social structures
from those of the earlier novels, but this in itself is no proof that
the novelist welcomes the change or is even reconciled to it.
On the contrary, it seems to me that *Jude* is an expression of
Hardy's dismay and bewilderment at the final disruption of
the rural community. It is an exploration of the chaos that
follows from excessive individualism and rationality. It is
indeed the story of a difficult and tragic journey beyond culture,
but the narrative point of view still evokes a moral sensibility
continuous with the past. Hence the difficulty and the tragedy,
which would be inconceivable without this apparatus of feeling
and memory and a whole standard of reference built into the
novel. Hardy's last novel is an antithesis, as he himself pointed
out, which rather than undermine the thesis, is its necessary
structural complement.

Edmund Gosse, friend of Hardy and one of the earliest
critics of *Jude*, was the first to treat the harsh topography and
sociology of this novel not as a cancellation of the Wessex milieu
but as indicative of its opposition by new economic and social
values.[1] Hardy revealed some of his most intimate feelings

Page references to *Jude the Obscure* are to the New Wessex edition (1974).

about the novel to Gosse in response to his review. In a letter
dated 10 November 1895 Hardy wrote to him:

> Your review [of *Jude the Obscure*] is the most discriminating
> that has yet appeared. It required an artist to see that the
> plot is almost geometrically constructed—I ought not to say
> *constructed*, for, beyond a certain point, the characters
> necessitated it, and I simply let it come. As for the story
> itself, it is really sent out to those into whose souls the iron
> has entered, and has entered deeply at some time of their
> lives. But one cannot choose one's readers.[2]

There is no gainsaying the fact that *Jude* is 'woven from the
materials of historical change, the transformation and uprooting of traditional English life.'[3] But what needs emphasising
is that the changed atmosphere in this novel does not mean a
loss of faith in the cultural assumptions inherent in the preceding fiction. Hardy always saw traditional rural society in a
dialectical opposition to the new urban and industrial milieu.
Here in *Jude the Obscure* rural society is almost non-existent,
but its disappearance does not imply a breach in the novelist's
sensibility. *Jude* is a tragic vision of deracination and of the
loss of traditional values and mores. But in contemplating the
change Hardy does not evince a change of heart, a spiritual
acclimatisation. *Jude* is the final proof of the integrity and
'resolving sincerity' of Hardy's cultural imagination. The
belief that it is a 'modernist' novel seems to be a critical
fiction based on an identification of the novel's total meaning
with the spectacle of mental and physical chaos that it exhibits,
but does not regard as an inevitable consequence of its vision
of the world. Wherever there is any disorientation or moral
impasse in Hardy's world it is imputed confidently to a perversion or denial of the communal verities and rhythms of life,
whatever that perversion or denial may be due to. The dwindl-
ing away of the visible forms of the communal order primes
the cultural memory to a new pitch of imaginative action. It
seems to me that *Jude* is a final demonstration of the undeviat-
ing principle, for Hardy, that his humans 'wilt out of their
natural habitat and communal order'.[4]
Most modern interpreters of the novel, however, regard it

as given exclusively to twentieth-century predilections. Very few critics have noted the fact that in depicting chaos Hardy is not proposing that order is an illusion or that it means an inferior level of moral existence. Ian Gregor is right in thinking that *Jude* involves problems which it is beyond Hardy's fictional means to treat imaginatively, but he is perhaps mistaken in attributing to Hardy an increasing cynicism about his imagined world:

> From *Under the Greenwood Tree* to *Jude*, his pursuit of 'the series of seemings' led him to an increasing scepticism about the validity of his imagined world, the world in which his fictional imagination had taken root. The more he sought the truth, the more Wessex faded before his eyes. . . . As his 'seemings' became ever more inclusive, the fictional world in which he could believe became smaller and smaller, so that by the time he came to write *Jude*, his whole truth was contained in the relationship between a man and a woman. Implied in that relationship was a whole social dimension, but imaginatively Hardy had no access to it, and when Jude dies in a rented lodging, Hardy's fictional world is stripped bare.[5]

It would be more true to say that Hardy is dramatising cynicism rather than being cynical himself. The novelistic sensibility in *Jude* is at bottom continuous with that in the more obviously affirmative novels. Hardy is 'unable', as Frederick MacDowell has remarked, 'to efface his temperament'[6] from *Jude the Obscure*. Jean R. Brooks's differentiation of Jude from the anti-heroes of modernist fiction also provides a clue to the controlling conservatism of the novel: 'Jude Fawley differs from most anti-heroes, to his credit, in knowing what he wants to escape from and where he wants to go to, in holding fast to his ideal Christminster, and in refusing to demean his integrity in order to survive.'[7] The values that Hardy brings to his experience of 'wounding isolation' are the values of Wessex, not of the modern metropolis. By bringing his characters into contact with modern ideas and new forms of life he is only exposing the inadequacy of those ideas and forms for a humanly satisfying existence. It is in thus treating the anti-Wessex elements in *Jude* that Hardy evinces an irreversible faith in a cultural-moral centrality and achieves in his last, seemingly modern, novel an acute indictment of modern society.

The description of Marygreen, with which the novel opens, provides the focal point for an examination of the moral perspective in *Jude*. Marygreen is completely denatured as a result of its invasion by an alien ethos. But Hardy's description of the desiccated and denaturalised village involves a regret for the change and a nostalgic evocation of its cultural past. By looking at the village in the dual perspective of past and present Hardy is initiating the reader, at the very outset of his story, into a mood of compliance with his implied preference for the past. His vision of Marygreen is not much different from his vision of central Casterbridge in *The Mayor* or of Flintcomb-Ash in *Tess*. In all these instances he presents change antithetically to set off his more positive vision of an irreplaceable cultural past, and not naturalistically as a fact to be faced. To turn to Marygreen:

> It was as old-fashioned as it was small.... Old as it was, however, the well-shaft was probably the only relic of the local history that remained absolutely unchanged. Many of the thatched and dormered dwelling-houses had been pulled down of late years, and many trees felled on the green. Above all, the original church, hump-backed, wood-turreted, and quaintly hipped, had been taken down, and either cracked up into heaps of road-metal in the lane, or utilized as pig-sty walls, garden seats, guard-stones to fences, and rockeries in the flower-beds of the neighbourhood. In place of it a tall new building of modern Gothic design, unfamiliar to English eyes, had been erected on a new piece of ground by a certain obliterator of historic records who had run down from London and back in a day. The site whereon so long had stood the ancient temple to the Christian divinities was not even recorded on the green and level grass-plot that had immemorially been the churchyard, the obliterated graves being commemorated by eighteenpenny cast-iron crosses warranted to last five years. (pp. 30–1)

In depicting the change Hardy is not, as Arnold Kettle has

pointed out, giving way to easy nostalgia but is trying to capture 'the actual processes of historical change in their complex ramifications upon the countryside and its people'.[8] A further point is that Hardy is not merely describing the material impact of the change, but is concerned with its moral and cultural consequences. Kettle has rightly observed that Hardy is not against metal based roads and, one might add, he is not particularly for the church as an abstract institution either, but when it comes to the depradation of the old familiar church in order to create a new metal based road his cultural imagination gets the better of his more rational judgement. The breaking up of the church becomes more than the utilisation of inert matter for purposes of reconstruction. It is seen as an expulsion of all traditional cultural images by an aggressive utilitarianism. And this the novelist deeply regrets. As a result, in the very process of dramatically defining the change Hardy sets in motion a certain moral and emotional dimension within which the change is felt and evaluated. Implicit in the very objects in terms of which he tells his story of cultural transformation are certain ineradicable social and moral attitudes and a controlled but poignant nostalgia. To be told that obliterated graves are renewed by 'eighteenpenny cast-iron crosses warranted to last five years' is to be given more than the terms of the change; it is to be made to see through the change with the cultural-moral vision of the novelist.

Marygreen is a metaphor of the clash of two antagonistic cultures. The past or passing cultural qualities and mores of the village take on a renewed validity and imaginative urgency as they are drawn through the meshes of their present condition. Even the landscape is contemplated through a memory of its earlier cultural personality:

> The fresh harrow-lines seemed to stretch like the channellings in a piece of new corduroy, lending a meanly utilitarian air to the expanse...and depriving it of all history beyond that of the few recent months, though to every clod and stone there really attached associations enough and to spare— echoes of songs from ancient harvest-days, of spoken words, and of sturdy deeds. (pp. 33–4)

The novelist's consciousness of the past provides him with a standard by which to judge the present. It is the awareness of earlier expanses which makes the present landscape appear 'meanly utilitarian'. The same awareness of past values is implied in the satirisation of the people of modern Marygreen. Farmer Troutham is the new economic man in whose scheme of things compassion either towards man or beast is the greatest anomaly. He punishes Jude for having fed the birds off his crop and owning up to his act of kindness:

> This truthful explanation seemed to exasperate the farmer even more than if Jude had stoutly denied saying anything at all; and he still smacked the whirling urchin, the clacks of the instrument continuing to resound all across the field and as far as the ears of distant workers...and echoing from the brand-new church tower just behind the mist, towards the building of which structure the farmer had largely subscribed, to testify his love for God and man. (p. 35)

The farmer's apathy and paltriness are given an ironic clinch by Jude's imaginative animism: 'He [Jude] could scarcely bear to see trees cut down or lopped, from a fancy that it hurt them; and late pruning, when the sap was up and the tree bled profusely, had been a positive grief to him in his infancy.' (p. 36) Another character brought in to define the *Gesellschaft* condition into which the village is rapidly falling is Physician Vilbert. He is a confidence trickster who passes among the ignorant for a physician. But his vileness is not confined to the sham medicines he sells as rare potions. He is an important factor in precipitating Jude's decision to leave the village for good. In letting Jude discover the quack, Hardy creates an occasion for an undisguised denunciation of the man: 'He was an unsophisticated boy, but the gift of sudden insight which is sometimes vouchsafed to children showed him all at once what shoddy humanity the quack was made of.' (pp. 48-9) Hardy's vision of Marygreen as a *Gesellschaft* society reaches a climax in the creation of Arabella, who is spiritually akin to the farmer and the quack. Her entire conduct is governed by sensuality and down-to-earth utilitarianism. This 'substantial female animal' (p. 59) does not even possess a spontaneous animality but remains a curious example of calculated coquetry. Her charm and sexual seductiveness are not natural endowments but a matter of 'supernumerary hair-coils' and 'optional dimples'. (p. 310) She is in the village but not of it. Her deceit and artfulness are not a reflection on the country but a measure of her alienation from, and antipathy to, the values associated with rural innocence in Hardy. It is made explicit in her dialogue with Jude following the latter's shocked discovery of her detachable hair-piece:

'What—it wasn't your own?' he said, with a sudden distaste for her.
'O no—it never is nowadays with the better class.'
'Nonsense! Perhaps not in towns. But in the country it is supposed to be different. Besides, you've enough of your own, surely?'
'Yes, enough as country notions go. But in towns the men expect more, and when I was barmaid at Aldbrickham—'
(p. 79)

She tricks Jude into marriage by feigning pregnancy. Having married him she wants to exploit his 'earning power' (p. 79) rather than find any other kind of marital fulfilment. The pig symbolism used for Arabella successfully brings out her essential sickness. Her actions are designed to shock the moral-cultural premises of the novel mediated through the lonely consciousness of the author and his protagonist. Her sale of Jude's photograph establishes her solidarity with the new utilitarian ethos and marks the cultural void that separates her from her husband: 'The utter death of every tender sentiment in his wife, as brought home to him by this mute and undesigned evidence of her sale of his portrait and gift, was the conclusive little stroke required to demolish all sentiment in him.' (p. 93) Her philosophy of marriage is irredeemably Benthamite: 'Life with a man is more business-like after it, and money matters work better.' (p. 288) She forces Jude into remarriage by so manipulating his presence in her house as to make him appear compromised. He marries her because he is still sensitive to such abandoned concepts as 'honour' and 'integrity': 'If I am bound in honour to marry her—as I suppose I am—though how I came to be here with her I know no more than a dead man—marry her I will, so help me God! I have never behaved dishonourably to a woman or to any living thing'. (p. 401) In her desertion of Jude on his death-bed Arabella stands ultimately exiled from the possibility of redemption in the novel.

Imposing a non-moral perspective on the novel, to suit their own naturalistic assumptions about life and literature, some critics have tried to find ambivalence in Hardy's treatment of Arabella. D. H. Lawrence blamed Hardy for attributing 'pig-sticking, false hair crudities' to Arabella because 'he must have his personal revenge on her for her coarseness, which offends him, because he is something of an Angel Clare.'[9] Whatever Lawrence's own views he at least has no illusions about Hardy's attitude towards her. Arabella offends a vital sense in Hardy. That Lawrence does not approve of that sense or regards Hardy's stigmatisation of Arabella as a result of his squeamishness is another matter. An altogether different view of her character, which has gained currency lately, makes such astounding claims as these: 'Despite the constricting implications of his symbolism, he would not have wished readers and critics to translate completely into abstractions the multiform impressions of reality and the complications of motive he was trying to record in Arabella.'[10] This is mere wishful thinking, entirely unsupported by the evidence of the text, for the point of Arabella's existence in the novel, as of so much else, is that it provides a dramatic counterpoint to the normative cultural order. That is why, much to the disappointment of those who go to the novel looking for polychromatic characters, the case against Arabella is 'exaggerated...almost to the point of parody'.[11]

Jude's disenchantment with Marygreen (anti-Wessex) leads him to an obsession with Christminster and Sue Bridehead. Hardy treats both his obsessions sympathetically, but without identifying his authorial consciousness with Jude's adventures; which is yet another proof of cultural monism in the novel. The simple truth emerging from all this is that there is no substitute for Wessex as a moral and cultural symbol. Disruption of this central symbol accounts for the apocalyptic vision of anomie and frustration in *Jude the Obscure*. Hardy records all the poignancy and pathos of Jude's yearning for Christminster only to prove that he is a victim of misplaced romanticism and Christminster a cultural illusion. Christminster is presented in the dual perspective of Jude's beatific vision and a cancelling, critical irony that sometimes borders on open satire. Viewed in itself the satirical treatment of Christminster seems cheaply vengeful, but understood in terms of cultural resistance the satire loses much of its offensive gratuitousness.

For Jude's starved imagination Christminster is 'the heavenly Jerusalem' (p. 40) whispering from its magical towers an angelic message of intellectual and spiritual fulfilment: 'Suddenly there came along this wind something towards him—a message from the place—from some soul residing there, it seemed. Surely it was the sound of bells, the voice of the city, faint and musical, calling to him, "We are happy here!"' (p. 43) Jude's mystical rapport with his imagined city of light is ironically juxtaposed with a carter's view of Christminster:

'O, they never look at anything that folks like we can understand,' the carter continued, by way of passing the time. 'On'y foreign tongues used in the days of the Tower of Babel, when no two families spoke alike. They read that sort of thing as fast as a night-hawk will whir. 'Tis all learning there—nothing but learning, except religion. And that's learning too, for I never could understand it. Yes, 'tis a serious-minded place. Not but there's wenches in the streets o' nights....You know, I suppose, that they raise pa'sons there like radishes in a bed? And though it do take—how many years, Bob?—five years to turn a lirruping hobble-dehoy chap into a solemn preaching man with no corrupt passions, they'll do it, if it can be done, and polish un off like the workmen they be, and turn un out wi' a long face, and a long black coat and waistcoat, and a religious collar and hat, same as they used to wear in the Scriptures, so that his own mother wouldn't know un sometimes....There, 'tis their business, like anybody else's.' (pp. 43–4)

In the first flush of his adolescent infatuation Jude, of course, ignores the carter's account and proceeds unheeding on his pilgrimage; which brings incremental irony into the narrative in a way which makes the carter's seem a voice of authorised judgement. Hardy emphasises the mistakenness of Jude's image of the city. His blindness about Christminster is stated in as many words:

> After many turnings he came up to the first ancient mediaeval pile that he had encountered. It was a college, as he could see by the gateway. He entered it, walked round, and penetrated to dark corners which no lamplight reached. Close to this college was another; and a little further on another; and then he began to be encircled as it were with the breath and sentiment of the venerable city. When he passed objects out of harmony with its general expression he allowed his eyes to slip over them as if he did not see them. (p. 98)

The narrative stresses the ironic disjunction between the reality of Christminster and Jude's idealised image of it. His imaginative audition of Arnold's celebrated apostrophe—'Beautiful city! so venerable, so lovely, so unravaged by the fierce intellectual life of our century, so serene!'—is ironically imputed to his ignorance of Arnold's later characterisation of Christminster (Oxford) as 'the home of lost causes'. (p. 100) To sustain the ironic perspective Jude is given momentary insights into the illusory nature of his image of Christminster: 'For a moment there fell on Jude a true illumination; that here in the stone yard was a centre of effort as worthy as that dignified by the name of scholarly study within the noblest of the colleges. But he lost it under stress of his old idea.' (p. 104) His communal and proletarian instincts assert themselves in reaction to his superimposed ideals of intellectual excellence and a university career. He realises that deep down, in some essential compulsions and needs of his personality, he belongs with those working men in Christminster who have not the least idea of the university and are exempt from its illusions: 'He began to see that the town life was a book of humanity infinitely more palpitating, varied, and compendious than the gown life. These struggling men and women before him were the reality of Christminster, though they knew little of Christ or Minster. That was one of the humours of things.' (p. 137) The irony is that such awareness does not cure him entirely of his academic ambition. In Jude's continuing infatuation with the university the novelist finds scope for its satiric exposure. In inverse proportion to Jude's fascination with it Hardy's view of the university grows harsher and more damaging:

> At some distance opposite, the outer walls of Sarcophagus College—silent, black and windowless—threw their four centuries of gloom, bigotry, and decay into the little room. . . . The outlines of Rubric College also were discernible beyond the other, and the tower of a third further off still. She thought of the strange operation of a simple-minded man's ruling passion, that it should have led Jude, who loved her and the children so tenderly, to place them here in this depressing purlieu, because he was still haunted by his dream. Even now he did not distinctly hear the freezing negative that those scholared walls had echoed to his desire. (p. 352)

The obvious theme of the novel is the University's rejection of Jude. Hardy had for long contemplated the story of a youth miserably unsuccessful in his efforts to enter the University. But in the novel we have this is only half the story. In tension with the initial conception of the University's rejection of Jude is Jude's and Hardy's rejection of the University as a moral and cultural symbol. It is this rejection which unifies *Jude the Obscure* with the cultural sensibility of the earlier novels. Given the cultural determinism that I find central to Hardy's fiction, the University can only be the subject of ironic exploration and rejection. Jude stands biblically defiant against the impenetrable masonry of Christminster. On the gates of Biblioll, whose Master has sent him a chilling reply to his application, he writes with a lump of chalk: ' "*I have understanding as well as you; I am not inferior to you: yes, who knoweth not such things as these?*"—Job xii. 3.' (p. 138) This is not mere lachrymose despair in the face of ill-treatment and undeserved indifference but a falling back upon reserves of moral and spiritual resourcefulness. Jude's challenging inscription invokes ethical and human standards which make the University seem hopelessly inadequate as a cultural agent. The sustained criticism and exposure of Christminster in the novel implies the availability of cultural and moral standpoints which are generally believed to be compromised in *Jude the Obscure*. Most critical accounts of the novel proceed from the assumption that it is a negative footnote to Hardy's Wessex fiction. We have seen how in its treatment of the University the novel evokes the typical Hardyan values. The narrative structure, too, has the same features of ironic juxtaposition, unequivocal moral commentary, and a guiding authorial voice which characterised the earlier fictions. The changed scenario with its discrete individualities in *Jude the Obscure* is of course a far cry from Wessex, but it is seen and estimated from a point of view sufficiently alive to Wessex as a moral referent.

Jude's relationship with Sue repeats the pattern of his relationship with Christminster. He falls in love with Sue's photograph just as he once got 'romantically attached' (p. 43) to Christminster 'miraged' (p. 41) in mist. In his blind love for Sue he sees, in fact, a continuation and consummation of his visionary experience of the great University. On receiving Sue's photograph from his aunt, 'Jude, a ridiculously affectionate fellow...put the photograph on the mantelpiece, kissed it—he did not know why—and felt more at home. She seemed to look down and preside over his tea. It was cheering—the one thing uniting him to the emotions of the living city.' (pp. 104–5) She is for him 'an ideal character, about whose form he began to weave curious and fantastic day-dreams.' (p. 108) He sees in her 'almost a divinity'. (p. 165) The ironic reverse of Jude's image of Sue is Aunt Drusilla's profile of her:

'A pert little thing, that's what she was too often, with her tight-strained nerves. Many's the time I've smacked her for her impertinence. Why, one day when she was walking into the pond with her shoes and stockings off, and her petticoats pulled above her knees, afore I could cry out for shame, she said: "Move on, aunty! This is no sight for modest eyes!" ' (p. 130)

At this stage in the narrative, of course, Aunt Drusilla's account of Sue's aberrant behaviour seems little more than the expression of an old woman's prejudices against adventurous girlhood. But, as it turns out, the old woman's words acquire a lasting resonance in the development of Sue's character in the novel.

In her conscious personality Sue is a product of new conditions—'the slight, pale "bachelor" girl—the intellectualised, emancipated bundle of nerves that modern conditions were producing'. (1912 Preface to *Jude the Obscure*) Her representative role as the New Woman consists not just in her sexual independence and fickleness, but in her doctrinal justification of a nomadic and preferably asexual state of being. She looks upon all the symbols of a communal order as anachronistic, wanting to live her emancipated life in 'railway stations, bridges, theatres, music-halls, hotels—everything that has no connection with conduct'. (p. 325) She reproaches Jude for taking 'so much tradition on trust'. (p. 173) For her 'the social moulds civilization fits us into have no more relation to our actual shapes than the conventional shapes of the constellations have to the real star-patterns.' (p. 226) She chafes at the social constraints upon individual freedom: 'When people of a later age look back upon the barbarous customs and superstitions of the times that we have the unhappiness to live in, what *will* they say!' (p. 236) She is, in Jude's words, 'quite Voltairean'. (p. 172) Her law-givers are not Moses and St. Paul, but Lempriere, Catullus, Martial, Juvenal, Lucian, Beaumont and Fletcher. She is, in her own words, 'a sort of negation' (p. 167) of everything that goes under the name of civilisation. She wants to live in a world without memories, without associations and obligations of common human existence. To live in a house with any history or habitational tradition is a mortification to her: 'Such houses are very well to visit, but not to live in—I feel crushed into the earth by the weight of so many previous lives there spent.' (p. 223) Her intellectualism saps her femininity and breeds in her a 'curious unconsciousness of gender'. (p. 169) She cannot conceive of men sexually: 'I have no fear of men, as such, nor of their books. I have mixed with them .. almost as one of their own sex.' (p. 167) With her first man— the Christminster undergraduate—she 'used to go about together—on walking tours, reading tours, and things of that sort—like two men almost.' (p. 223) She is 'so uncarnate as to

seem at times impossible as a human wife to any average man.'
(p. 207) Jude calls her 'a phantasmal, bodiless creature' in
comparison with whose etherealness most ordinary men are
'poor unfortunate wretches of grosser substance'. (p. 279) The
intellectualist, instinct-denying aspects of her personality are
vividly dramatised in a series of situations. Her career in the
novel is prefaced by her fatal jilting of a sensitive Christminster
undergraduate. She is opposed to marriage because, in her
view, it means total self-abnegation for the woman: 'I am
called Mrs Richard Phillotson, living a calm wedded life with
my counterpart of that name. But I am not really Mrs Richard
Phillotson, but a woman tossed about, all alone, with aberrant
passions, and unaccountable antipathies.' (p. 226) But
she has married Phillotson in full knowledge of what marriage
means. It is only after the marriage that she begins to kick
over the traces. The pattern of Sue's behaviour in the novel
is a study in schizophrenia. She is a 'maddening compound
of sympathy and averseness'. (p. 272) Jude characterises her
wrongly when he says: 'You are, upon the whole, a sort of fay, or
sprite—not a woman!' (p. 373) He is not so wide of the mark
when, in a moment of forthrightness, he calls her 'a flirt'.
(p. 225) Sue's coquetry is distinguished by a strong sadistic
strain: 'she would go on inflicting such pains again and again,
and grieving for the sufferer again and again, in all her colossal
inconsistency.' (p. 194) Having encouraged Jude to make
advances to her she tells him abruptly, 'You mustn't love me.
You are to like me—that's all!' The next morning Jude gets
a letter from her saying, '*If you want to love me, Jude, you may*:
I don't mind at all; and I'll never say again that you mustn't!'
(p. 176) This prompts Jude to comment—'you are often not
so nice in your real presence as you are in your letters!' (p. 185)
But her letters are not consistently 'nice' either. When she next
writes to Jude it is to announce her decision to marry Phillotson.
What is more, out of a strange sadistic compulsion she asks
Jude to give her away in marriage. On the morning of her
marriage to Phillotson, she rehearses the ceremony with Jude
with unaccountable relish:

He passively acquiesced in her wish to go in, and they
entered by the western door....Sue still held Jude's arm,

almost as if she loved him. Cruelly sweet, indeed, she had been to him that morning.... They strolled undemonstratively up the nave towards the altar railing, which they stood against in silence, turning then and walking down the nave again, her hand still on his arm, precisely like a couple just married. The too suggestive incident, entirely of her making, nearly broke down Jude.

'I like to do things like this,' she said in the delicate voice of an epicure in emotions, which left no doubt that she spoke the truth. (p. 192)

After the wilful marriage she returns to Jude to confide her afflictions to him: 'What tortures me so much is the necessity of being responsive to this man whenever he wishes, good as he is morally!—the dreadful contract to feel in a particular way in a matter whose essence is its voluntariness!' (p. 233) Having thus aroused fresh feelings in Jude she decides on her return journey from the visit to retract again and gloats over the prospect of keeping Jude in suspense: 'I won't write to him any more, or at least for a long time, to impress him with my dignity! And I hope it will hurt him very much.... He'll suffer then with suspense—won't he, that's all!—and I am very glad of it!' (p. 239) Her horror of Phillotson compels him, kind-hearted and unselfish as he is, to let her live independently. But no sooner is she free to live with Jude than she turns, predictably, cool towards him. It is now out of consideration for Phillotson that she refuses to live with Jude:

'I *may* feel as well as you that I have a perfect right to live with you as you thought—from this moment. I *may* hold the opinion that, in a proper state of society, the father of a woman's child will be as much a private matter of hers as the cut of her under-linen, on whom nobody will have any right to question her. But partly, perhaps, because it is by his generosity that I am now free, I would rather not be other than a little rigid....But don't press me and criticize me, Jude! Assume that I haven't the courage of my opinions.' (p. 260)

Jude is by this time beginning to understand the predicament he is in: 'That episode in her past history of which she had told him—of the poor Christminster graduate whom she had handled thus, returned to Jude's mind; and he saw himself as a possible second in such a torturing destiny.' (p. 261) She keeps Jude at bay until, driven by a stronger emotion than she had reckoned with, she finally gives in to him. It is jealousy which breaks down her defences and reduces her to tempting Jude with a pretence of sexuality: 'She ran across and flung her arms round his neck. "I am not a cold-natured, sexless creature, am I, for keeping you at such a distance? I am sure you don't think so! Wait and see! I do belong to you, don't I? I give in!" ' (p. 286) This is the first chink in her armour. It shows how even in her decision to lead an unconventional life she is actuated by utterly conventional motives. Her involuntary conventionality is an ironic commentary on the rationalist position she has tried, but failed, to live up to. As Robert Heilman has perceptively remarked: 'At the heart of the drama of Sue is the always simmering revolt of the modes of life which she rejects, the devious self-assertion of the rejected values.'[12] After the gruesome death of the children she develops a morbid guilt-consciousness. The emotional strain under which she has tried to live an unconventional life is symbolically concentrated in her shocked and self-flagellating reaction to the murder of her children by Arabella's son. The only terms in which she can understand the incident are the non-rational, dogmatic terms of traditional religion. 'Arabella's child killing mine', she thinks, 'was a judgment—the right slaying the wrong.' (p. 370) The psychology of religious dread, which now dominates Sue, is explained by Hardy thus:

Vague and quaint imaginings had haunted Sue in the days when her intellect scintillated like a star, that the world resembled a stanza or melody composed in a dream; it was wonderfully excellent to the half-aroused intelligence, but hopelessly absurd at the full waking; that the First Cause worked automatically like a somnambulist, and not reflectively like a sage....But affliction makes opposing forces loom anthropomorphous; and those ideas were now exchanged for a sense of Jude and herself fleeing from a persecutor. (p. 362)

In reaction to her own rationality Sue now becomes fanatically religious and looks upon all her earlier attempts at a morally and culturally independent selfhood as a sinful error. Her career in the novel might well be described as the triumph of the traditional imagination. It illustrates the inescapability of community and culture. There is a quotation from *Amiel's Journal* in Hardy's notebook which seems to accord with the indirect emphasis he puts on the cultural sources of behaviour in the character of Sue. It says: ' No one can think but through the general thought, refined by centuries of culture & experience, absolute individualism is nonsense.'[13] Here in his last novel, then, Hardy is as true to the dictates of his cultural imagination as he was in the early fiction. If he presents Sue, without admonishment or interference, as a rational, independent mind seeking to fulfil itself in entirely individualistic terms, it is only to demonstrate that, in his fictional world, such a quest can only result in the imbalance and morbidity that characterise Sue's later behaviour in the novel. In saying that she has grown 'superstitious as a savage' (p. 362) she provides an eloquent testimony to her ultimate capitulation to forms and conditions of life which she has tried in vain to deny. In the light of this final revelation, it seems erroneous to argue that in the character of Sue Hardy sought a form for his own disenchantment with convention.

The cultural consciousness, which we have seen to be still active in *Jude the Obscure*, finds direct representation through the presence of such characters as Mrs Edlin, the kindly Marygreen widow. Mrs Edlin offers a rectifying sensibility. In her continuing solicitude for Jude and her moral participation in the action, especially towards the end, she stands for just those bases of communal life whose validity the novel finally asserts. She is not, as is often thought, a concession to passing nostalgia or a crude cultural anachronism. She is an important figure in the meaning and moral discovery of the novel. When she reprimands Sue for her mechanical religiosity or refers back to the very different experience of marriage in her youth, she touches on the central problematics of the novel. In her self-assurance and sanity and natural affection the novel proposes a standard of rectitude and moral feeling which it is impossible, after the ironic exposure of the principles opposed to it, to regard as irrelevant. Her nostalgia is necessitated by the action of the novel: 'I don't know what the times be coming to! Matrimony have growed to be that serious in these days that one really do feel afeard to move in it at all. In my time we took it more careless; and I don't know that we was any the worse for it!' (p. 387) It is this cultural memory which provides a moral and human standard of evaluation in a world without absolutes.

Little Father Time is a somewhat strained symbol of the modern conditions that Hardy dramatises in *Jude the Obscure*. He does not symbolise metaphysical absurdity, but only the ascendancy of an urban, *Gesellschaft* society. He is specifically made an outcome of cultural crisis and dislocation: 'The doctor says there are such boys springing up amongst us—boys of a sort unknown in the last generation—the outcome of new views of life. They seem to see all its terrors before they are old enough to have staying power to resist them. He says it is the beginning of the coming universal wish not to live.' (p. 356) He summarises all the aberrations and absurdities of adult behaviour in the novel. He is 'their nodal point, their focus, their expression in a single term.' (p. 356) His suicide and murder of his younger brothers is not a piece of grotesquerie, but is adequately motivated in his background and his representative role as the new child. The killing, '*Done because we are too menny*', is a dramatic, perhaps melodramatic demonstration of the cruelty and senseless violence inherent in the new order of society. The point of the murderous conduct seems to be that without communal bonds man would inevitably come under the withering effects of alienation, which the French sociologist Durkheim found to be the main cause of suicide in modern cities.[14] Hardy's intuitive grasp of the social causes behind Father Time's suicide and multiple murder is prophetic of Durkheim's *Suicide*. There is evidence in Hardy's personal journal that he was aware of the social causes of suicide. An entry in the notebook reads: 'The Hellenic character—a native joyousness, exultation in life, prominent therein, suicide not common—Ethics of Suicide—17.6.76.'[15] Hardy's last novel conjures up a frightening vision of the replacement of culture by consciousness, of a communal (*Gemeinschaft*) society by an associative (*Gesellschaft*) corporation, but it also tries to exorcise that vision by an instinctive reliance upon the mores and assumptions of the bygone traditional order. In his dramatic and moral perspective on the world without tradition, Hardy comes very close to the position enunciated by Allen Tate:

> It means that in ages which suffer the decay of manners, religion, morals, codes, our indestructible vitality demands expression in violence and chaos; it means that the men who have lost both the higher myth of religion and the lower myth of historical dramatization have lost the forms of human action; it means that they are no longer capable of defining a human objective, of forming a dramatic conception of human nature; it means that they capitulate from their human role to a series of pragmatic conquests which, taken alone, are true only in some other world than that inhabited by men.[16]

Many readings of *Jude the Obscure*, because they have a positivistic bias, fail to come to terms with the cultural consciousness in the novel. They have missed out on the novel's inverted celebration of the Wessex ethic in the face of every disruption and counter-movement. The fact that the misguided careers of Jude and Sue and their overdependence on self-generated intellectual ideals are the negatives of the novel has been lost sight of in the critical enthusiasm about modernist stances. What the novel presents as an antithesis has been mistaken for the thesis. Even the 'contemporary' readings of *Jude*, Hardy regretted, were preoccupied with 'the antitheses in Jude's life'. (1912 Preface) The point has been made, then, that the ultimate conclusions about self and society in *Jude the Obscure* are the same as in the other Wessex novels.

If *Jude* is a novel concerned in many of its key situations with cultural change and uprooting, it is also undeniably a metaphysical statement about the inevitability of frustration and pain in human life. Jude begins with a precocious sense of the fortuitous absurdity of life 'feeling...his existence to be an undemanded one'. (p. 37) He feels insupportably alone and menaced on the desolate landscape of his rook-scaring childhood: 'All around you there seemed to be something glaring, garish, rattling, and the noises and glares hit upon the little cell called your life, and shook it, and warped it. If he could only prevent himself growing up! He did not want to be a man.' (p. 38) His subsequent experiences would seem a systematic rationalisation of his tragic prescience were it not for the irrefutable circumstantial plausibility of everything that happens. However, Jude's life does become 'a tale told by an idiot', one long process of subjection to all those 'glaring, garish, rattling' forces of denial and doom. Hardy brings out the fundamental idiocy of life in a number of telling ways. So consistently is Jude defrauded of his noblest intentions, so pathetically put down at every step he takes towards happiness by an intractable conspiracy, that all the incongruous details of his story—the pig's pizzle, the nauseating effervescence of blood and beer, the closed gates of Biblioll, the involuntary inconsistencies of the woman he loves, leading up to the scenes of his unlamented death in a lonely tenement with Job's curse on his lips—seem figures in an integrated allegory of the tragic human condition. The predatory pervasiveness of mental and physical violence in the novel gives a central significance to Phillotson's statement that 'Nature's law be mutual butchery' (p. 327) or to Sue's awareness that 'the First Cause worked automatically like a somnambulist, and not reflectively like a sage'. (p. 362) But in all this *Jude* still remains a typical Hardy novel. The two most predominant strands in Hardy's fictional personality have always been a belief in the rural matrix as an ideal of sanity, and a powerful philosophical vision of cosmic absurdity. It is true that *Jude* explores the tragic nature of human life with an unsurpassed thoroughness, but it is also at the same time demonstrably concerned with the deficiencies that follow upon the erosion of the communal ethic and forms of life.

Notes

1. Edmund Gosse, 'Mr Hardy's New Novel'.
2. See Florence Emily Hardy, *The Life of Thomas Hardy, 1840–1928*, pp. 271–2.
3. See Irving Howe, *Thomas Hardy*, p. 138.
4. See John Holloway, *The Charted Mirror* (New York: Horizon Press, 1962), p. 107.

5. Ian Gregor, 'Hardy's World'.
6. Frederick P. W. McDowell, 'Hardy's "Seemings or Personal Impressions": The Symbolical Use of Image and Contrast in *Jude the Obscure*'.
7. Jean R. Brooks, *Thomas Hardy: The Poetic Structure*, p. 254.
8. Arnold Kettle, *Hardy the Novelist: A Reconsideration*, p. 12.
9. D. H. Lawrence, 'Study of Thomas Hardy' in *Phoenix*, p. 489.
10. See McDowell, 'In Defence of Arabella: A Note on *Jude the Obscure*'.
11. A. Alvarez, 'Jude the Obscure' in *Hardy: A Collection of Critical Essays*, p. 116.
12. Robert B. Heilman, 'Hardy's Sue Bridehead'.
13. Thomas Hardy, *Commonplace Book*, I, p. 191.
14. Durkheim's researches led him to conclude that there was a vital, though not logical, connection between what he called ' the march of civilization' and 'the rising tide of suicide'. See *Suicide: A Study in Sociology* (London: Routledge & Kegan Paul, 1966), p. 368. Writing in the same year that *Jude* appeared Durkheim viewed the new urban civilisation then spreading rapidly across Europe with profound dismay. He observed: 'We must not be dazzled by the brilliant development of sciences, the arts and industry of which we are the witnesses; this development is altogether certainly taking place in the midst of a morbid effervescence, the grievous repercussions of which each one of us feels.' Ibid., p. 368.
15. Hardy, *Commonplace Book*, I, p. 50.
16. Allen Tate, 'What is a Traditional Society?', *Collected Essays* (Denver: Alan Swallow, 1959), p. 301.

Conclusion

Each one of the major novels of Thomas Hardy, as we have seen, embodies and enacts the age-old forms of rural culture. Each is a novel return to the rural community in its more characteristic and recessive aspects. In content as well as form Hardy's fiction proclaims a rural sensibility. One of Hardy's major achievements as a novelist is his refusal to accept the antinomy between reality and dream which accounts for the exclusion, in rationalist theories of history and culture, of the metaphors through which we make sense of life. His novels bring the real and the imaginal into an effective relationship claiming them both as indistinguishable aspects of one whole of experience. In folklore and myths and legends, which are the lungs of rural culture, Hardy found a ready sanction for his 'partly real, partly dream' fictions of reality. Hardy is not a historian of the local and the ephemeral, but an explorer of the governing metaphors of rural life. He called himself 'a parish historian', but his parish was a paradigm of community before he had done with it even though it was a place on the map of England to begin with. He dearly loved his native Dorset and went to great lengths to incorporate some features of its life accurately in his novels, but he ultimately refused to be confined by historical or geographical boundaries. His interest in Dorset became fictionally productive only when Dorset became Wessex and, freed from the frigidities of annalistic history, the novelist's imagination began to play upon universally valid structures of community. His annoyance at the idea of treating Wessex as 'a utilitarian region which people can go to, take a house in, and write to the papers from' is well known.[1] Crude historical realism was, in Hardy's view, the bane of the novel and he fought a successful battle against the iron grid of Victorian realism by choosing to probe in his novels an order of life which carried an implicit sanction for the role of imagination in life and history. In doing so he revolutionised the meaning of realism in fiction as well as offered fresh insights into the felt history of the rural peoples.

Hardy the novelist and Hardy the rural historian thus stood creatively united. No wonder his style, with all its surprises of tone and idiom, seldom deviates from its one profound source; never ceases, in its dramatic functions, to be inventively mimetic of the voice of the culture of which he is the supreme historian. That explains the overwhelming integrity of Hardy's novels. They are not only novels *about* the rural way of life but are permeated with its mystique of experience and its immemorial habits of imagination. The rural tradition in the Wessex novels is not the product of a neopastoral literary stance, but part of the wider sociological context of the nineteenth century. Although rural literature and society go back to the dawn of human civilisation, it is only in the nineteenth century that the rural form of life becomes a central image of experience in literature and society. The distinction between the rural and the urban societies and their contrasting impact on the quality of human experience is a central concern of nineteenth-century sociology. In the writings of Toennies, Weber, and Durkheim, as well as in the novels of Thomas Hardy, there is an underlying vision of an organic rural society being increasingly eroded by the economic and cultural pressures of the day. Toennies's *Gemeinschaft-Gesellschaft* paradigm epitomises the working of the nineteenth-century rural imagination. The form of Toennies's perception of rural society is similar to that of Hardy's. They both have a distrust of descriptive history and see reality through images rather than facts. This is not to say that they posit an extra-historical dimension of reality or try to probe the historical condition through private myths. They only look at history from a point of view. Events become meaningful through a conception of events. History is defined by the experience of history.

In their evocation of the rural community there is a good deal of nostalgia as well in the sociologist as in the creative writer: 'A degree of nostalgia is built into the very structure of nineteenth-century sociology.'[2] In Hardy nostalgia is a major source of discovery and creation. The Wessex novels owe some of their most haunting moments to the action of memory. It is an answer to the inexorable mutability of life of which Hardy is all too aware. In a world where nothing abides, memory is the only instrument of integrity and continuity.

The idea seems to have received particular emphasis in Hardy's thinking as this entry in his journal indicates: 'memory is continuous. Though individuals die their offspring carry on the memory of all the impressions their ancestors acquired or received.'³ Hardy's nostalgia is a genuine and healthy nostalgia, not a self-defeating sentimental yearning. It is an 'involuntary memory' which can call up significant images, not romantic memorialising which issues in dead pictures. As such it is a corrective to purely rational perceptions. Hardy's nostalgia for a familiar rhythm of life is artistically necessary in the structure of feeling he dramatises. It is the kind of nostalgia which enabled the great sociologists of the century to use the rural matrix as a simulacrum of necessary social and moral attitudes and as an alternative to the chaos of rationalist and progressive assumptions. There is a fundamental unity between Hardy's emotive treatment of the rural community and its symbolic suggestiveness in the sociological landscapes of Toennies or Weber. Hardy's Wessex is a fictional construct like the sociologist's *Gemeinschaft*. It celebrates a standard of communal life and shows how a certain sort of society produces a certain sort of character. Wessex is more than a decimated district of south-west England. It is a moral touchstone, a country of the mind. Seen in the context of nineteenth-century sociology it acquires a psychic universality and cannot be indulged or dismissed as a pastoral make-belief. The Wessex novels are an artistic acknowledgement of the principles which gave to the nineteenth-century sociologist his whole mental and epistemological apparatus.

For a closing view of Hardy's sociological imagination we may look at 'The Dorsetshire Labourer', a sociological essay he wrote for the *Longman's Magazine* in 1883. The thirty-one page manuscript of the essay, kept in the Dorset County Museum, is heavily revised. Although described by Hardy as 'a merely descriptive article'⁴ it is not an excursion into journalism but betrays his novelistic preoccupation with non-quantitative forms of culture. The essay has an unmistakably impressionistic, polemical thrust. It is the work of an imaginative sociologist, not that of the local historian. It opens with a trenchant attack on rural stereotypes. The myth that Hodge is a 'degraded being of uncouth manner and aspect, stolid understanding, and snail-like movement'[5] is vigorously refuted. Hardy then takes the reader on a guided tour of the inside of a typical cottage demonstrating the quality of life in the cottage which is too often wrongly equated with its obvious material condition. Intimate experience of cottage life reveals that 'the characters, capacities, and interests'[6] of the cottagers cannot be rightly divined from the condition in which they exist. Their real history, their real character is 'impenetrable'[7] unless one acquires an innerness with them. They are often misrepresented or misjudged because there is a communication gap between them and their historians from 'the contrasting world of London'.[8] They appear unintelligent, uncouth, slovenly or wicked because of an 'inability' in those who write their history 'to see below the surface of things'.[9]

Characteristically, one of the central points of the essay has to do with such an impalpable, qualitative aspect of the labourer's life as the question of his happiness. In Hardy's view his happiness is incomprehensible to the outsider who concludes from his material condition that he needs must be unhappy:

> The happiness of a class can rarely be estimated aright by philosophers who look down upon that class from the Olympian heights of society. Nothing, for instance, is more common than for some philanthropic lady to burst in upon a family, be struck by the apparent squalor of the scene, and to straightway mark down that household in her note-book as a frightful example of the misery of the labouring classes.[10]

Their alleged misery is very often the invention of upper-class philanthropy or of those who do not share the native culture and can never, therefore, understand the true meaning of things for the cottager. It is this kind of correction of versions of history and common belief which makes Hardy more than a chronicler of facts; it makes him their interpreter. Another important point about rural society that emerges in the essay is that the basic structure of feeling in this society is resistant to historical change. The feeling of happiness in the nineteenth-century Dorset labourer is structurally identical with that of Piers the

Ploughman. The feeling is peculiar to a community, not to a historical generation. In making that point Hardy also, significantly, contrasts the possibilities of happiness in the village with those in the city:

> The pleasures enjoyed by the Dorset labourer may be far from pleasures of the highest kind desirable for him. They may be pleasures of the wrong shade. And the inevitable glooms of a straitened hard-working life occasionally enwarp him from such pleasures as he has; and in times of special storm and stress the 'complaint of Piers the Ploughman' is still echoed in his heart. But even Piers had his flights of merriment and humour, and ploughmen as a rule do not give sufficient thought to the morrow to be miserable when not in physical pain. Drudgery in the slums and alleys of a city, too long pursued, and accompanied as it too often is by indifferent health, may induce a mood of despondency which is well-nigh permanent; but the same degree of drudgery in the fields results at worst in a mood of painless passivity. A pure atmosphere and a pastoral environment are a very appreciable portion of the sustenance which tends to produce the sound mind and body, and thus much sustenance is, at least, the labourer's birthright.[11]

This is Hardy at his most representative. He is talking about the possibility of happiness in two contrasted sociological contexts—the field and the city—and he instinctively thinks in terms of metaphors—Piers the Ploughman—rather than in terms of a historical person. He is concerned with underlying structures, not circumstantial detail.

Hardy's portrait of the shepherd at a wet hiring fair is a highly evocative portrayal of a social phenomenon. He notices the changes which have come over the fair during the last few decades in such particulars as clothing and choice of colour. The Lady Day removals are described with the same vividness as in the novels—particularly *Tess*. As a result of the changes the village people are not as quaint and 'picturesque' as they had been at one time. But this is hardly a matter for regret: 'It is too much to expect them to remain stagnant and old-fashioned for the pleasure of romantic spectators.'[12] A more disturbing consequence of the change, however, is that the labourer's relation with the land he tills had become 'less intimate and kindly'.[13] In earlier years there has been a close community between labourer, farmer, and landlord. The labourer looked upon the landlord as a court of appeal in case of any grievance or difference of opinion with his employer. Now, the landlord is an unknown quantity. He is there one day and gone the next 'nobody thinks whence or where'.[14] Besides, he 'takes strictly commercial views of his man and cannot afford to waste a penny on sentimental considerations.'[15] This new type of landlord is not a development from within rural society, but 'a new comer'.[16]

Then follows a shrewd analysis of the pros and cons of the changes that have taken place. The economic benefits of the change are frankly acknowledged. The labourer earns more now and is more independent than in former times. The introduction of the threshing-machine has brought an increased demand for female labour. So, more and more women ought to take up the employment, but no:

> Quite the reverse do these lively women feel in the occupation which may be said to stand, emotionally, at the opposite pole to gathering in corn: that is, threshing it. Not a woman in the county but hates the threshing-machine. The dust, the din, the sustained exertion demanded to keep up with the steam tyrant are distasteful to all women but the coarsest.[17]

To prove the point, Hardy cites the strange case of the woman who was so dizzy after a day's work at the machine that she kept going round and round the field unable to find the exit. This emotional response to the threshing-machine is memorably rendered in *Tess*. It makes nonsense of Merryn Williams's claim that the threshing-machine in Hardy is not altogether evil, but even has potentiality for good.[18] The point is made that economic incentive in Hardy's world is not a man's or a woman's profoundest impetus. Apparent economic status is not a measure of well-being.

'The Dorsetshire Labourer' ends with a pregnant remark

on the implications of change in the village, which contains all Hardy's essential attitudes and perceptions:

> The changes which are so increasingly discernible in village life by no means originate with the agricultural unrest. A depopulation is going on which in some quarters is truly alarming. Villages used to contain, in addition to the agricultural inhabitants, an interesting and better-informed class, ranking distinctly above those—the blacksmith, the carpenter, the shoe-maker, the small higgler, the shopkeeper (whose stock-in-trade consisted of a couple of loaves, a pound of candles, a bottle of brandy-balls and lumps of delight, three or four scrubbing-brushes, and a frying-pan), together with nondescript-workers other than farm-labourers, who had remained in the houses where they were born for no especial reason beyond an instinct of association with the spot. Many of these families had been life-holders, who built at their own expense the cottages they occupied, and as the lives dropped, and the property fell in, they would have been glad to remain as weekly or monthly tenants of the owner. But the policy of all but some few philanthropic landowners is to disapprove of these petty tenants who are not in the estate's employ, and to pull down each cottage as it falls in, leaving standing a sufficient number for the use of the farmer's men and no more. The occupants who formed the backbone of the village life have to seek refuge in the boroughs. This process, which is designated by statisticians as 'the tendency of the rural population towards the large towns', is really the tendency of water to flow uphill when forced. The poignant regret of those who are thus obliged to forsake the old nest can only be realised by people who have witnessed it—concealed as it often is under a mask of indifference.[19]

This, then, is Hardy's response to rural history. First of all, he makes it quite clear that the disintegration and uprooting are the result of pressure from outside. This is an answer to those who insist unduly on internal pressures. Hardy joins issue with the statisticians on this point. His views are diametrically opposed to theirs. Should we, then, see and interpret the sociology of Hardy's novels in terms of contemporary registers of facts? The answer is, clearly, no. It is instructive, too, that Hardy moves from the consideration of the farm-labourer to the larger and, for him, much more significant problem of the destabilisation of a whole community of people—'the backbone of the village life'—who had lived in one spot generation after generation. It was in these middle-of-the-road people that Hardy found the central form of rural culture and it is their disappearance he regrets most for that reason. Hardy's view of defining social structures is quite explicit here. He conceived of these structures not in terms of stark economic polarities— haves and have-nots, landlords and labourers—but in terms of a community of people bound together by a shared instinct of association with a common environment. It was this sense of community which constituted a buffer between opposed econ- omic interests and made possible the psychological integra- tion of the rural peoples. The rapid disappearance of these classless members of the rural society meant the withering away of the rural forms of experience and of the cultural- moral centrality which made for an organic rural culture. All that was left for Hardy to do now was to make this socio- logical event the basis of his novels of the rural community, to find in the discontinued forms of experience a structure for his own deepest fictional urges. Because it is the most detailed expression of Hardy's view of rural society, 'The Dorsetshire Labourer' can be safely regarded as the mirror of the mind that created the Wessex novels.

This study, then, has substantiated the claim, with which it began, that Hardy's fiction is deeply engaged with forms of rural sociology in a way that calls for a fresh look at his novels. My reading of the major novels has, I hope, borne out my central argument that they are neither fictionalised history nor historical fiction but explorations of points of contact between history and fiction and assertions of the indispensable fictiveness of human histories. We must, on this view, abandon the notion of rural history as a reference to Hardy's fiction and see it as an essential tool of apprehension that at once makes Hardy a great novelist and a sociologist challenging comparison with some of the finest interpreters of nineteenth-century rural society. His novels are rooted in a homogeneous body of common experience that cuts across academic and political compartments of knowledge. He is a parish historian and a mythographer, a sociologist and a novelist. The seeming contradictions between reality and myth, history and fiction have been the stumbling blocks of Hardy criticism. To see the centrality of Hardy's sociological imagination in his novels is to see how they effect and celebrate a creative marriage between the native of Dorset and his novels of the archetypal rural community. The sociological imagination not only makes Hardy's novels plausible metaphorical accounts of a social process but unites them with a larger fiction called rural history to which they have been made out by Hardy's historical critics to be tangentially related. It has been my argument that the relationship between rural history and the Wessex novels is not thematic or referential, but genetic and organic. Hardy's novels are history *as* fiction, not history *and* fiction. If we would understand them we need humility and flexibility not only as critics but also as historians.

NOTES

1. See Preface to *Far from the Madding Crowd* (New Wessex edition, 1974).
2. Robert A. Nisbet, *The Sociological Tradition* (London: Heinemann, 1973), p. 74.
3. Thomas Hardy, *Commonplace Book*, I, p. 201.
   Cf. 'I am the family face; Flesh perishes, I live on . . .', 'Heredity', *Moments of Vision*.
4. Thomas Hardy, 'The Dorsetshire Labourer', p. 269.
5. Ibid., p. 252.
6. Ibid., p. 254.
7. Ibid., p. 253.
8. Ibid.
9. Ibid., p. 256.
10. Ibid., p. 255.
11. Ibid., pp. 254–5.
12. Ibid., pp. 262–3.
13. Ibid., p. 263.
14. Ibid.
15. Ibid.
16. Ibid.
17. Ibid., p. 267.
18. Merryn Williams, *Thomas Hardy and Rural England*, p. 177.
19. Hardy, 'The Dorsetshire Labourer', pp. 268–9.

Select Bibliography

Works of Hardy

PUBLISHED WORKS

Desperate Remedies (1871)
Under the Greenwood Tree (1872)
A Pair of Blue Eyes (1873)
Far from the Madding Crowd (1874)
The Hand of Ethelberta (1876)
The Return of the Native (1878)
The Trumpet-Major (1880)
A Laodicean (1881)
Two on a Tower (1882)
'The Dorsetshire Labourer', *Longman's Magazine* (July 1883), pp. 252–69
The Mayor of Casterbridge (1886)
The Woodlanders (1887)
Wessex Tales (1888)
Tess of the d'Urbervilles (1891)
A Group of Noble Dames (1891)
Life's Little Ironies (1894)
Jude the Obscure (1895)
The Well-Beloved (1897)
A Changed Man and Other Tales (1913)
Our Exploits at West Poley (1952)
An Indiscretion in the Life of an Heiress (1976)
Personal Writings, ed., Harold Orel. London: Macmillan, 1967
One Rare Fair Woman: Thomas Hardy's Letters to Florence Henniker, 1893–1922, eds.,
    Evelyn Hardy and F. B. Pinion. London: Macmillan, 1972
The Literary Notes of Thomas Hardy, ed., Lennart A. Bjork. Goteburg, Universitas,
    1974
The Complete Poems, ed., James Gibson. London: Macmillan, 1976
Collected Letters, Volume I (1840–1892), eds., Richard Little Purdy and Michael
    Millgate. Oxford: Clarendon Press, 1978

MANUSCRIPT MATERIAL

Commonplace Book, I, Dorset County Museum
Facts Notebook, II, III, IV, Dorset County Museum
Cache of Letters, Dorset County Museum
'The Ancient Cottages of England', Dorset County Museum, 2 pp.
'The Dorsetshire Labourer', 31 pp., 6 3/8″ × 7 7/8″, Dorset County Museum;
    sheets numbered by Hardy and signed at the end

Far from the Madding Crowd, 7 leaves, 6 1/8″ × 8 1/8″, numbered 2–18 and 2–24, Dorset County Museum; omitted from MS when revised

Biography (Notes and directions to F. H. for his biography), Dorset County Museum

Works on Hardy

BOOKS ON HARDY

Abercrombie, Lascelles, *Thomas Hardy: A Critical Study*. London: Secker, 1912.

Bayley, John, *An Essay on Hardy*. Cambridge: University Press, 1978.

Beach, Joseph Warren, *The Technique of Thomas Hardy*. Chicago: University Press, 1922. Rpt., New York: Russell & Russell, 1962.

Blunden, Edmund, *Thomas Hardy*. London: Macmillan, 1942. Rpt. 1951, 1967.

Brooks, Jean R., *Thomas Hardy: The Poetic Structure*. London: Elek Books, 1971.

Brown, Douglas, *Thomas Hardy*. London: Longman, 1954. Rev. ed. 1961; latest rpt. 1968.

———, *Hardy:* The Mayor of Casterbridge. Studies in English Literature 7. London: Edward Arnold, 1962. Latest rpt. 1973.

Butler, Lance St. John, ed., *Thomas Hardy After Fifty Years*. London: Macmillan, 1977.

———, *Thomas Hardy*. Cambridge: University Press, 1978.

Carpenter, Richard C., *Thomas Hardy*. Twayne's English Author Series 13. New York: Twayne Publishers, 1964. Rpt., London: Macmillan, 1976.

Collins, Vere H., *Talks with Thomas Hardy at Max Gate: 1920–1922*. London: Duckworth, 1928.

Cox, R. G., ed., *Thomas Hardy: The Critical Heritage*. London: Routledge & Kegan Paul, 1970.

Deacon, Lois, and Terry Coleman, *Providence and Mr Hardy*. London: Hutchinson, 1966.

Drabble, Margaret, ed., *The Genius of Thomas Hardy*. London: Weidenfeld & Nicolson, 1976.

Draper, R. P., ed., *Hardy: The Tragic Novels*. Casebook Series. London: Macmillan, 1975.

Frior, Ruth A., *Folkways in Thomas Hardy*. Philadelphia: University of Pennsylvania Press, 1931.

Gittings, Robert, *Young Thomas Hardy*. London: Heinemann, 1975.

———, *The Older Hardy*. London: Heinemann, 1978.

Gregor, Ian, *The Great Web: The Form of Hardy's Major Fiction*. London: Faber & Faber, 1974.

Grimsditch, H. B., *Character and Environment in the Novels of Thomas Hardy*. London: H. F. & G. Witherby, 1925. New York: Russell & Russell, 1962.

Guerard, Albert J., *Thomas Hardy: The Novels and Stories*, London: Oxford University Press, 1949. New York: New Directions, 1964.

———, ed., *Hardy: A Collection of Critical Essays*. Englewood Cliffs, New Jersey: Prentice-Hall, 1963.

Halliday, F. E., *Thomas Hardy: His Life and Work*. London: Adams & Dart, 1972.

Hardy, Emma, *Some Recollections*. London University Press, 1961.

Hardy, Florence Emily, *The Life of Thomas Hardy, 1840–1928*. London: Macmillan, 1962.

Hornback, Bert G., *The Metaphor of Chance: Vision and Technique in the Works of Thomas Hardy*. Athens, Ohio: Ohio University Press, 1971.

Howe, Irving, *Thomas Hardy*. London: Weidenfeld & Nicolson, 1968.

Hyman, Virginia R., *Ethical Perspective in the Novels of Thomas Hardy*. London: Kennikat Press, 1975.

Johnson, Lionel, *The Art of Thomas Hardy*. London: Matthews & Lane, 1894. Rev. ed., New York: Dodd, Mead, 1923; rpt., New York: Haskell House, 1973.

Kramer, Dale, *Thomas Hardy: The Forms of Tragedy*. London: Macmillan, 1975.

Kettle, Arnold, *Hardy the Novelist: A Reconsideration*. The W. D. Thomas Memorial Lecture. Swansea: University College, 1966.

Laird, J. T., *The Shaping of* Tess of the d'Urbervilles. Oxford: The Clarendon Press, 1975.

Lerner, Laurence, and John Holmstorm, eds., *Thomas Hardy and His Readers: A Selection of Contemporary Reviews*. London: The Bodley Head; New York: Barnes & Noble, 1968.

Lerner, Laurence, *Thomas Hardy's* The Mayor of Casterbridge: *Tragedy or Social History?* London: Sussex University Press, 1975.

Levi, Peter, *John Clare and Thomas Hardy*. The John Coffin Memorial Lecture, 1975. University of London: The Athlone Press, 1975.

McDowall, Arthur, *Thomas Hardy: A Critical Study*. London: Faber & Faber, 1931.

Meisel, Perry, *Thomas Hardy: The Return of the Repressed*. New Haven: Yale University Press, 1972.

Miller, J. Hillis, *Thomas Hardy: Distance and Desire*. Cambridge, Massachusetts: Belknap Press, 1970.

Millgate, Michael, *Thomas Hardy: His Career as a Novelist*. London: The Bodley Head, 1971.

Morrell, Roy, *Thomas Hardy: The Will and the Way*. Kuala Lumpur: University of Malaya Press, 1965.

Nevinson, Henry W., *Thomas Hardy*. London: George Allen & Unwin, 1941.

Orel, Harold, *The Final Years of Thomas Hardy, 1912–1928*. London: Macmillan, 1976.

Page, Norman, *Thomas Hardy*. London: Routledge & Kegan Paul, 1977.

Paterson, John, *The Making of* The Return of the Native. Berkeley and Los Angeles: University of California Press, 1963.

Pinion, F. B., *Hardy:* The Mayor of Casterbridge. Macmillan Critical Commentaries. London: Macmillan, 1966.

———, *A Hardy Companion: A Guide to the Works of Thomas Hardy and Their Background*. London: Macmillan, 1968. Rev. ed. 1976.

———, ed., *Thomas Hardy and the Modern World: A Symposium*. Dorchester: The Thomas Hardy Society, 1974.

———, *Thomas Hardy: Art and Thought*. London: Macmillan, 1977.

Purdy, Richard Little, *Thomas Hardy: A Bibliographical Study*. London: Oxford University Press, 1964.

Rutland, William R., *Thomas Hardy: A Study of His Writings and Their Background*. Oxford: Basil Blackwell, 1938.

Sankey, Benjamin, *The Major Novels of Thomas Hardy*. Denver: Alan Swallow, 1965.

Southerington, F. R., *Hardy's Vision of Man*. London: Chatto & Windus, 1971.

Stewart, J. I. M., *Thomas Hardy: A Critical Biography*. London: Longman, 1971. Second impression 1972.

Thurley, Geoffrey, *The Psychology of Hardy's Novels: The Nervous and the Statuesque*. St. Lucia, Queensland: University of Queensland Press, 1975.

Vigar, Penelope, *The Novels of Thomas Hardy: Illusion and Reality*. London: The Athlone Press, 1974.

Weber, Carl, J., *Hardy of Wessex: His Life and Literary Career*. New York: Columbia University Press, 1940. Second rev. ed., London: Routledge & Kegan Paul; New York: Columbia University Press, 1965.

———, *Hardy in America*. Waterville, Maine: Colby College Press, 1946.

———, ed., *The Letters of Thomas Hardy*. Waterville, Maine: Colby College Press, 1954.

White, R. J., *Thomas Hardy and History*. London: Macmillan, 1974.

Williams, Merryn, *Thomas Hardy and Rural England*. London: Macmillan, 1972, Rpt. 1974.

———, *A Preface to Hardy*. London and New York: Longman, 1976.

Wing, George, *Hardy*. London: Oliver & Boyd, 1963.

SHORTER STUDIES—ARTICLES, CHAPTERS IN BOOKS, OBITER DICTA

Anon., 'Adventures of a Novel: *Tess* after Fifty Years: Thomas Hardy and the Public Outcry'. *Times Literary Supplement*, 5 July 1941, pp. 322, 325.

Anon., 'Morals and Masterpieces'. *Times Literary Supplement*, 4 December 1943.

Agenda (Thomas Hardy Special Issue), Vol. 10, Nos. 2–3, Spring-Summer 1972.

Alcorn, John, 'Hardy: A Better World', *The Nature Novel from Hardy to Lawrence*. London: Macmillan, 1977, pp. 1–24.

Allen, Walter, *The English Novel*. London: Phoenix House, 1954, pp. 232–46.

Anderson, Carol Reed, 'Time, Space, and Perspective in Thomas Hardy'. *Nineteenth-Century Fiction*, Vol. 9, No. 3, December 1954, pp. 192–208.

Atkinson, F. G., 'Temperament as Motive in *The Return of the Native*'. *English Fiction in Transition*, Vol. 5, No. 2, 1962, pp. 21–9.

———, '"The Inevitable Movement Onward"—Some Aspects of *The Return of the Native*'. *The Thomas Hardy Year Book*, 1972–73, pp. 10–17.

Babb, Howard, 'Setting and Theme in *Far from the Madding Crowd*'. *Journal of English Literary History*, Vol. 30, No. 1, March 1963, pp. 147–61.

Bailey, J. O., 'Hardy's Mephistophelian Visitants'. *PMLA*, LXI, December 1946, pp. 1146–84.

———, 'Heredity as Villain in the Poetry and Fiction of Thomas Hardy'. *The Thomas Hardy Year Book*, I, 1970, pp. 9–18.

Baker, James, R., 'Thematic Ambiguity in *The Mayor of Casterbridge*'. *Twentieth Century Literature*, Vol. 1, No. 1, April 1955, pp. 13–16.

Bayley, John, 'Introduction' to *Far from the Madding Crowd*. New Wessex edition. London: Macmillan, 1974.

190 *Bibliography*

Beckman, Richard, 'Character Typology for Hardy's Novels'. *Journal of English Literary History*, Vol. 30, No. 2, June 1963, pp. 70–87.
Benvenuto, Richard, '*The Return of the Native* as a Tragedy in Six Books'. *Nineteenth Century Fiction*, Vol. 26, No. 1, June 1971, pp. 83–93.
Boll, T. E. M., 'Tess as an Animal in Nature'. *English Literature in Transition*, Vol. 9, No. 4, 1966, pp. 210–11.
Brick, Allan, 'Paradise and Consciousness in Hardy's *Tess*'. *Nineteenth-Century Fiction*, Vol. 17, No. 2, September 1962, pp. 115–34.
Bull, Philip, 'Thomas Hardy and Social Change'. *Southern Review* (Adelaide), 3, 1969, pp. 199–213.
Carpenter, Richard C., 'Hardy's "Gurgoyles"'. *Modern Fiction Studies*, Vol. VI, No. 3, Autumn 1960, pp. 223–32.
———, 'The Mirror and the Sword: Imagery in *Far from the Madding Crowd*'. *Nineteenth-Century Fiction*, Vol. 18, No. 4, March 1964, pp. 331–45.
Cary, Joyce, *Art and Reality*. The Clark Lectures, 1956. Cambridge: University Press, 1958, pp. 168–72.
Cavaliero, Glen, *The Rural Tradition in the English Novel, 1900–1939*. London: Macmillan, 1977, pp. 1–2, 3, 4, 6, 8, 15, 23, 30, 45, 46, 47, 48, 54, 63, 71, 78, 137, 140, 142, 149, 162, 173, 178, 193, 195.
Chapman, Frank, 'Hardy the Novelist'. *Scrutiny*, Vol. 3, No. 1, June 1934, pp. 22–37.
Clifford, Emma, 'The Child: The Circus: And *Jude the Obscure*'. *Cambridge Journal*, Vol. VII, No. 9, June 1954, pp. 531–46.
———, 'Thomas Hardy and the Historians'. *Studies in Philosophy*, LVI, October 1959, pp. 654–68.
Cockshut, A. O. J., *The Unbelievers: English Agnostic Thought, 1840–1890*. London: Collins, 1964, pp. 61, 119, 162–7, 179, 183.
Collie, M. J., 'Social Security in Literary Criticism'. *Essays in Criticism*, Vol. IX, No. 2, January 1959, pp. 151–8.
Cunningham, Vivian, *Everywhere Spoken Against: Dissent in the Victorian Novel*. Oxford: Clarendon Press, 1975, pp. 13, 15, 18, 24, 34, 37, 39, 43, 47, 63, 69, 73, 74, 80, 86f., 101f., 107, 110ff., 111, 126, 200ff., 204, 210ff., 279ff., 281, 283, 285ff.
Daiches, David, *The Novel and the Modern World*. Chicago: University of Chicago Press, 1960, pp 12–13, 26, 138. Fourth impression 1965.
———, *Some Late Victorian Attitudes*. London: Andre Deutsch, 1969, pp. 12, 38, 66, 68–86, 117.
Davidson, Donald, 'Futurism and Archaism in Toynbee and Hardy', *Still Rebels, Still Yankees, and Other Essays*. Louisiana State University Press, 1957, pp. 62–83.
Davis, W. Eugene, '*Tess of the d'Urbervilles*: Some Ambiguities about a Pure Woman'. *Nineteenth-Century Fiction*, Vol. 22, No. 4, March 1968, pp. 397–401.
Deen, Leonard W., 'Heroism and Pathos in *The Return of the Native*'. *Nineteenth-Century Fiction*, Vol. 15, No. 3, December 1960, pp. 207–19.
DeLaura, David J., ' "The Ache of Modernism" in Hardy's Later Novels'. *Journal of English Literary History*, Vol. 34, No. 3, September 1967, pp. 380–99.
Dike, D. A., 'A Modern Oedipus: *The Mayor of Casterbridge*'. *Essays in Criticism*, Vol. 2, No. 2, April 1952, pp. 169–79.

Dobrée, Bonamy, 'Thomas Hardy', *The Lamp and the Lute: Studies in Seven Authors*. First published, 1929; second edition, London: Frank Cass, 1964, pp. 18–37.

Drake, Robert Y. Jr., '*The Woodlanders* as Traditional Pastoral'. *Modern Fiction Studies*, Vol. VI, No. 3, Autumn 1960, pp. 251–7.

Eagleton, Terry, 'Thomas Hardy: Nature as Language'. *Critical Quarterly*, Vol. 13, No. 2, Summer 1971, pp. 155–62.

———, 'Introduction' to *Jude the Obscure*. New Wessex edition, 1974.

Eggenschwiler, David, 'Eustacia Vye, Queen of Night and Courtly Pretender'. *Nineteenth-Century Fiction*, Vol. 25, No. 4, March 1971, pp. 444–54.

Eliot, T. S., *After Strange Gods: A Primer of Modern Heresy*. London: Faber & Faber, 1934, pp. 54–8.

Evans, Robert, 'The Other Eustacia'. *Novel*, I, 1967–68, pp. 251–9.

Fayen, George S. Jr., 'Hardy's *The Woodlanders*: Inwardness and Memory'. *Studies in English Literature*, Vol. 1, No. 4, Autumn 1961, pp. 81–100.

Fernando, Lloyd, 'Thomas Hardy's Rhetoric of Painting'. *A Review of English Literature*, Vol. VI, No. 4, October 1965, pp. 62–73.

Fischler, Alexander, 'Theatrical Techniques in Thomas Hardy's Short Stories'. *Studies in Short Fiction*, Vol. III, No. 4, Summer 1966, pp. 435–45.

Fleishman, Avrom, 'Hardy: The Avoidance of Historical Fiction', *The English Historical Novel: Walter Scott to Virginia Woolf*. London: Johns Hopkins, 1971, pp. xvii, 28, 179–207, 208, 218.

Forster, E. M., *Aspects of the Novel*. London: Edward Arnold, 1927; rpt. 1963, pp. 89–90, 126.

———, 'Woodlanders on Devi'. *New Statesman and Nation*, 6 May 1938, pp. 679–80.

Friedman, Alan, 'Thomas Hardy: "Weddings Be Funerals" ', *The Turn of the Novel*. New York: Oxford University Press, 1966, pp. 8, 27–8, 38–74, 110, 170, 171.

Friedman, Norman, 'Criticism and the Novel—Hardy, Hemingway, Crane, Woolf, Conrad'. *Antioch Review*, Vol. XVIII, No. 3, Fall 1958, pp. 343–70.

Furbank, P. N., 'Introduction' to *Tess of the d'Urbervilles*. New Wessex edition, 1974.

Gibson, Wilfrid, 'Hardy's Short Stories'. *The Bookman*, LXXIV, June 1928, pp. 148–9.

Gindin, James, 'Hardy', *Harvest of a Quiet Eye: The Novel of Compassion*. London: Indiana University Press, 1971, pp. 2, 5, 10–11, 17, 19, 21–2, 65, 66, 78–101, 112, 113, 127, 163, 164, 179, 274, 303, 351, 358.

———, 'Tying the Work with the Man'. *Virginia Quarterly Review*, Vol. 48, No. 1, Winter 1972, pp. 153–7.

———, 'Towards Literary Biography'. *Modern Language Quarterly*, Vol. 37, No. 1, March 1976, pp. 82–92.

Goldberg, M. A., 'Hardy's Double-Visioned Universe'. *Essays in Criticism*, Vol. VII, No. 4, October 1957, pp. 374–82.

Gose, Elliott, B. Jr., 'Psychic Evolution: Darwinism and Initiation in *Tess of the d'Urbervilles*'. *Nineteenth-Century Fiction*, Vol. 18, No. 3, December 1963, pp. 261–72.

Gosse, Edmund, 'Mr. Hardy's New Novel'. *Cosmopolis*, Vol. 1, No. 1, January 1896, pp. 60–9.

Graves, Robert, *Goodbye to All That*. London: Jonathan Cape, 1929. Rev. ed., London: Cassell, 1957; rpt., Harmondsworth: Penguin Books, 1960, pp. 248–51.

———, Gregor, Ian, 'What Kind of Fiction Did Hardy Write?' *Essays in Criticism*, Vol. XVI, No. 3, July 1966, pp. 290–308.

———, 'Jude the Obscure', *Imagined Worlds: Essays on Some English Novels and Novelists in Honour of John Butt*, eds., Maynard Mack and Ian Gregor. London: Methuen, 1968, pp. 237–56.

———, 'Hardy's World'. *Journal of English Literary History*, Vol. 38, No. 2, June 1972, pp. 274–93.

Gregor, Ian and Brian Nicholas, 'The Novel as Moral Protest: *Tess of the d'Urbervilles*', *The Moral and the Story*. London: Faber & Faber, 1962, pp. 123–50.

Griffith, Philip Mahone, 'The Image of the Trapped Animal in Hardy's *Tess of the d'Urbervilles*'. *Tulane Studies in English*, XIII, 1963, pp. 85–94.

Gwynn, Frederick L., 'Hamlet and Hardy'. *Shakespeare Quarterly*, Vol. IV, No. 2, April 1953, p. 207.

Hagan, John, 'A Note on the Significance of Diggory Venn'. *Nineteenth-Century Fiction*, Vol. 16, No. 2, September 1961, pp. 147–55.

Hardy, Barbara, *The Appropriate Form*. London: The Athlone Press, 1964, pp. 6–9, 24, 36, 47–8, 51, 53, 70–5, 81–2, 109, 132, 135, 181.

———, 'Thomas Hardy', *Tellers and Listeners: The Narrative of Imagination*. London: The Athlone Press, 1975, pp. 175–205.

Hassett, Michael E., 'Compromised Romanticism in *Jude the Obscure*'. *Nineteenth-Century Fiction*, Vol. 25, No. 4, March 1971, pp. 432–43.

Hawkins, Desmond, 'Hardy as a Countryman'. *Country Life*, 6 January 1977, p. 28.

Heilman, Robert B., 'Hardy's *Mayor*: Notes on Style'. *Nineteenth-Century Fiction*, Vol. 18, No. 4, March 1964, pp. 307–29.

———, 'Hardy's Sue Bridehead'. *Nineteenth-Century Fiction*, Vol. 20, No. 4, March 1966, pp. 307–23.

———, '*Gulliver* and Hardy's *Tess*: Houyhnhnms, Yahoos, and Ambiguities'· *Southern Review*, Vol. 6, No. 2, 1970, pp. 277–301.

Herbert, Lucille, 'Hardy's Views in *Tess of the d'Urbervilles*'. *Journal of English Literary History*, Vol. 37, No. 1, March 1970, pp. 77–94.

Holloway, John, 'Hardy', *The Victorian Sage: Studies in Argument*. London: Macmillan, 1953, pp. 244–89.

———, 'Hardy's Major Fiction' and '*Tess of the d'Urbervilles* and *The Awkward Age*', *The Charted Mirror*. London: Routledge & Kegan Paul, 1960. New York: Horizon Press, 1962, pp. 94–107, 108–17.

Holmes, Theodore, 'Thomas Hardy's City of the Mind'. *Sewanee Review*, Vol. LXXV, No. 2, April-June 1967, pp. 285–300.

Hough, Graham, 'The Novel as Exploration'. *The Listener*, 53, 20 January 1955, pp. 111, 114–15.

Howe, Irving, 'A Note on Hardy's Stories'. *The Hudson Review*, Vol. XIX, No. 2, Summer 1966, pp. 259–66.

Howells, W. D., 'Pleasure from Tragedy', *Criticism and Fiction and Other Essays*, eds., Clara Marburg Kirk and Rudolf Kirk. New York: University Press, 1959, pp. 150–3.

Hyde, William J., 'Hardy's View of Realism: A Key to the Rustic Characters'. *Victorian Studies*, Vol. II, No. 1, September 1958, pp. 45–59.

———, 'Theoretic and Practical Unconventionality in *Jude the Obscure*'. *Nineteenth-Century Fiction*, Vol. 20, No. 2, September 1965, pp. 155–64.

Hynes, Samuel, 'Hardy and Barnes: Notes on Literary Influence'. *The South Atlantic Quarterly*, Vol. LVIII, No. 1, Winter 1959, pp. 44–54.

———, 'Hardy in His Times and Places'. *Modern Language Quarterly*, Vol. 34, 1973, pp. 325–30.

Ingham, Patricia, 'The Evolution of *Jude the Obscure*' (Part I). *The Review of English Studies*, Vol. XXVII, No. 105, February 1976, pp. 27–37.

———, 'The Evolution of *Jude the Obscure*' (Part II). *The Review of English Studies*, Vol. XXVII, No. 106, May 1976, pp. 157–69.

Jacobus, Mary, 'Tess's Purity'. *Essays in Criticism*, Vol. XXVI, No. 4, October 1976, pp. 318–36.

James, Henry, 'Hardy's *Far from the Madding Crowd*'. *The Nation*, 24 December 1074. Reprinted in *Literary Reviews and Essays on American, English and French Literature*, ed., Albert Mordell. New York: Twayne Publishers, 1957, pp. 291–7.

Karl, Frederick R., '*The Mayor of Casterbridge*: A New Fiction Defined'. *Modern Fiction Studies*, Vol. 6, No. 3, Autumn 1960, pp. 195–213.

Keith, W. J., 'Thomas Hardy and the Name "Wessex" '. *English Language Notes*, Vol. VI, No. 1, September 1968, pp. 42–4.

Kettle, Arnold, 'Thomas Hardy: *Tess of the d'Urbervilles*', *An Introduction to the English Novel*, 2 Vols. London: Hutchinson, 1953. Second ed., 1967, II, pp. 45–56.

Kiely, Robert, 'Vision and Viewpoint in *The Mayor of Casterbridge*'. *Nineteenth-Century Fiction*, Vol. 23, No. 2, September 1968, pp. 189–200.

Klingopulos, G. D., 'Hardy's Tales Ancient and Modern', *From Dickens to Hardy*, Vol. 6 of the *Pelican Guide to English Literature*, ed., Boris Ford. Harmondsworth: Penguin Books, 1958, pp. 407–20.

Knoepflmacher, U. C., 'The End of Compromise: *Jude the Obscure* and *The Way of All Flesh*', *Laughter and Despair: Readings in Ten Novels of the Victorian Era*. Berkeley, Los Angeles: University of California Press, 1971, pp. 202–30, 231 *passim*, 232 *passim*, 237, 239, 240.

Kramer, Dale, 'Unity of Time in *The Return of the Native*'. *Notes and Queries*, New Series, Vol. XII, No. 8, August 1965, p. 305.

Long, Andrew, 'Literary Chronicle'. *Cosmopolis*, Vol. I, No. 1, January 1896, p. 84.

Larkin, Philip, 'Wanted: Good Hardy Critic'. *Critical Quarterly*, Vol. 8, No. 2, Summer 1966, pp. 174–9.

Lawrence, D. H., 'Study of Thomas Hardy', *Phoenix: The Posthumous Papers of D. H. Lawrence*, ed., Edward D. McDonald. London: Heinemann, 1936. Latest rpt. 1970, pp. 398–516.

Leavis, Q. D., 'Hardy and Criticism'. *Scrutiny*, Vol. XI, No. 3, Spring 1943, pp. 230–7.

Lerner, Laurence, '*Tess of the d'Urbervilles*: A Behaviourist Complaint', *The Truth-Tellers*. London: Chatto & Windus, 1967, pp. 113–21.

The Letters of T. E. Lawrence, ed., David Garnett. London: Cape, 1938, pp. 408,

424, 427, 429, 430, 441, 442, 460, 471, 473, 475, 482, 498, 503, 564–7, 578, 582, 592, 593, 667, 668, 869.

Lodge, David, 'Tess, Nature, and the Voices of Hardy', *Language of Fiction: Essays in Criticism and Verbal Analysis of the English Novel.* London: Routledge & Kegan Paul; New York: Columbia University Press, 1966, pp. 164–88.

———, 'Introduction' to *The Woodlanders.* New Wessex edition, 1974.

Lowe, Robert Liddell, 'Three New Hardy Letters'. *Modern Language Review*, Vol. LIV, No. 3, July 1959, pp. 396–7.

Lynd, Robert, 'A Hardy Heroine' (1928), *Books and Writers.* London: J. M. Dent & Sons, 1952, pp. 178–82.

Marrot, H. V., ed., *The Life and Letters of John Galsworthy.* London: Heinemann, 1935, pp. 217, 264, 416, 418, 438, 458, 459, 462, 463, 469, 480, 481, 494, 507, 510, 549, 550, 568, 578, 622, 699, 749, 751, 753.

Marshall, George O. Jr., 'Hardy's *Tess* and Ellen Glasgow's *Barren Ground*'. *Texas Studies in Literature and Language*, I, 1959–60, pp. 517–21.

Marshall, William H., 'The End of the Quest', *The World of the Victorian Novel.* New York: A. S. Barnes, 1967, pp. 34, 93, 99, 127–8, 404–24, 456, 466, 480–1.

Martin, E. W., 'Thomas Hardy and the Rural Tradition'. *Blackfriars*, XXX, June 1949, pp. 252–6.

Matchett, William H., '*The Woodlanders* or Realism in Sheep's Clothing'. *Nineteenth-Century Fiction*, Vol. 9, No. 4, March 1955, pp. 241–61.

Maxwell, J. C., 'The "Sociological" Approach to *The Mayor of Casterbridge*', *Imagined Worlds*, ed., Maynard Mack and Ian Gregor. London: Methuen, 1968, pp. 225–36.

May, Charles, E., '*Far from the Madding Crowd* and *The Woodlanders*: Hardy's Grotesque Pastorals'. *English Literature in Transition*, Vol. 17, No. 3, 1974, pp. 147–58.

May, Derwent, 'Introduction' to *The Return of the Native.* New Wessex edition, 1974.

McCullen, J. T. Jr., 'Henchard's Sale of Susan in *The Mayor of Casterbridge*'. *English Language Notes*, Vol. II, No. 3, March 1965, pp. 217–18.

McDowell, Frederick P. W., 'Hardy's "Seemings or Personal Impressions": The Symbolic Use of Image and Contrast in *Jude the Obscure*'. *Modern Fiction Studies*, Vol. 6, No. 3, Autumn 1960, pp. 233–50.

———, 'In Defence of Arabella: A Note on *Jude the Obscure*'. *English Language Notes*, Vol. 1, No. 4, June 1964, pp. 274–80.

Meibergen, C. R., '*The Woodlanders* by Thomas Hardy'. *Englische Studien*, LI, October 1917, pp. 226–47.

Meynell, Viola, ed., *Friends of a Lifetime: Letters to Sydney Carlyle Cockerell.* London: Jonathan Cape, 1940, pp. 274–315.

———, *The Best of Friends: Further Letters to Sydney Carlyle Cockerell.* London: Rupert Hart-Davis, 1956, pp. v, 24–5, 29, 31–2, 34, 39, 45, 54n, 61, 63, 78, 81, 118, 167, 199–200, 224.

Miller, J. Hillis, *The Form of Victorian Fiction.* Notre Dame: University of Notre Dame Press, 1968. Second rpt., 1970, pp. xi, xii, 1, 4, 7–16 *passim*, 19, 24, 25, 26n, 49n, 53, 60ff., 60, 74f., 88, 96, 100, 114, 115, 117, 133, 138.

Millgate, Michael, 'Hardy's Fiction: Some Comments on the Present State of Criticism'. *English Literature in Transition*, Vol. 14, No. 4, 1971, pp. 230–8.

Mizener, Arthur, '*Jude the Obscure* as a Tragedy'. *Southern Review*, VI, Summer 1940, pp. 193–213.

——, 'The Novel of Doctrine in the Nineteenth Century: Hardy's *Jude the Obscure*', *The Sense of Life in the Modern Novel*. London: Heinemann, 1965, pp. 55–77.

Moore, John Robert, 'Two Notes on Thomas Hardy'. *Nineteenth-Century Fiction*, Vol. 5, No. 2, September 1950, pp. 159–63.

Morrell, Roy, 'Thomas Hardy and Probability', *On the Novel*, ed., B. S. Benedikz. London: Dent, 1971, pp. 75–92.

Moynahan, Julian, '*The Mayor of Casterbridge* and the Old Testament's First Book of Samuel: A Study of Some Literary Relationships'. *PMLA*, Vol. LXXI, No. 1, March 1956, pp. 118–30.

——, '*Pastoralism as Culture and Counter-Culture in English Fiction, 1800–1928: From a View to a Death*'. *Novel*, Vol. 6, No. 1, Fall 1972, pp. 20–35, esp. pp. 31–3.

Murphree, A. A., and C. F. Strauch, 'The Chronology of *The Return of the Native*'. *Modern Language Notes*, Vol. LIV, No. 7, November 1939, pp. 491–7.

O'Connor, Frank, 'Thomas Hardy', *The Mirror in the Roadway: A Study of the Modern Novel*. London: Hamish Hamilton, 1957, pp. 14, 61, 166-7, 237–50, 273.

——, *The Lonely Voice: A Study of the Short Story*. London: Macmillan, 1965. First published 1962, p. 216 *passim*.

O'Grady, Walter, 'On Plot in Modern Fiction: Hardy, James, and Conrad'. *Modern Fiction Studies*, Vol. XI, No. 2, Summer 1965, pp. 107–15.

Osgerby, J. R., 'Thomas Hardy's *Tess of the d'Urbervilles*'. *The Use of English*, Vol. XIV, No. 2, Winter 1962, pp. 109–15.

Page, Norman, 'Hardy's Short Stories: A Reconsideration'. *Studies in Short Fiction*, Vol. XI, No. 1, Winter 1974, pp. 75–84.

Paris, Bernard, J., ' "A Confusion of Many Standards": Conflicting Value Systems in *Tess of the d'Urbervilles*'. *Nineteenth-Century Fiction*, Vol. 24, No. 1, June 1969, pp. 67–79.

Paterson, John, '*The Return of the Native* as Antichristian Document'. *Nineteenth-Century Fiction*, Vol. 14, No. 2, September 1959, pp. 111–27.

——, '*The Mayor of Casterbridge* as Tragedy'. *Victorian Studies*, Vol. III, No. 2, December 1959, pp. 151–72.

——, 'The Genesis of *Jude the Obscure*'. *Studies in Philology*, Vol. LVII, No. 2, January 1960, pp. 87–98.

——, 'The "Poetics" of *The Return of the Native*'. *Modern Fiction Studies*, Vol. VI, No. 3, Autumn 1960, pp. 214–22.

Pinck, Joan B., 'The Reception of Thomas Hardy's *The Return of the Native*'. *Harvard Library Bulletin*, XVII, 1969, pp. 291–308.

Pinion, F. B., 'The Composition of *The Return of the Native*'. *Times Literary Supplement*, 21 July 1970, p. 931.

Porter, Katherine Anne, 'Notes on a Criticism of Thomas Hardy'. *Southern Review*, 6, Summer 1940, pp. 150–61.

Pritchett, V. S., 'The Anti-Soporofic Art'. *New Statesman*, LXXVI, 6 December 1968, pp. 793–4.

Purdy, R. L., 'MS Adventures of Tess'. *Times Literary Supplement*, 6 March 1943, p. 120; 26 June 1943, p. 307.

———, 'A Source for Hardy's "A Committee-Man of The Terror" ', *Modern Language Notes*, Vol. 58, November 1943, pp. 554–5.

Reed, Henry, 'For Younger Readers'. *The Listener*, 48, 9 October 1952, pp. 599–600.

Roberts, James L., 'Legend and Symbol in Hardy's 'The "Three Strangers" '. *Nineteenth-Century Fiction*, Vol. 17, No. 2, September 1962, pp. 191–4.

Sankey, Benjamin, 'Henchard and Faust'. *English Language Notes*, Vol. III, No. 2, December 1965, pp. 123–5.

Schwarz, Daniel R., 'The Narrator as Character in Hardy's Major Fiction'. *Modern Fiction Studies*, Vol. 18, No. 2, Summer 1972, pp. 155–72.

Schweik, Robert C., 'Theme, Character, and Perspective in Hardy's *The Return of the Native*'. *Philological Quarterly*, XLI, 1962, pp. 757–67.

———, 'Character and Fate in Hardy's *The Mayor of Casterbridge*'. *Nineteenth-Century Fiction*, Vol. 21, No. 3, December 1966.

———, 'Form and Matter in Hardy's Fiction: Some Current Theories and Methods of Analysis'. *English Literature in Transition*, Vol. 19, No. 2, 1976, pp. 133–8.

———, 'Fictions in the Criticism of Hardy's Fiction'. *English Literature in Transition*, Vol. 20, No. 4, 1977, pp. 204–9.

Scott, James F., 'Thomas Hardy's Use of the Gothic: An Examination of Five Representative Works'. *Nineteenth-Century Fiction*, Vol. 17, No. 4, March 1963, pp. 363–80.

Sherman, George Witter, 'The Wheel and the Beast: The Influence of London on Thomas Hardy'. *Nineteenth-Century Fiction*, Vol. 4, No. 3, December 1949, pp. 209–19.

Smart, Alastair, 'Pictorial Imagery in the Novels of Thomas Hardy'. *The Review of English Studies*, New Series, Vol. XII, 1961, pp. 262–80.

Southern Review (Thomas Hardy Centennial Issue), VI, Summer 1940.

Squires, Michael, '*Far from the Madding Crowd* as Modified Pastoral'. *Nineteenth-Century Fiction*, Vol. 25, No. 3, December 1970, pp. 299–326.

Stallman, Robert Wooster, 'Hardy's Hour-Glass Novel'. *Sewanee Review*, 55, April–June 1947, pp. 283–96.

Starzyk, Lawrence J., 'The Coming Universal Wish Not to Live in Hardy's "Modern" Novels'. *Nineteenth-Century Fiction*, Vol. 26, No. 4, March 1972, pp. 419–35.

Stevenson, Lionel, 'Hardy in Two Centuries'. *Yale Review*, Vol. 60, Autumn 1970, pp. 126–30.

Stewart, J. I. M., 'The Integrity of Hardy'. *English Studies*, n.s.l., 1948, pp. 1–27.

Stone, Donald David, *Novelists in a Changing World*. Cambridge, Massachusetts: Harvard University Press, 1972, pp. 50, 70, 72, 73, 74, 75, 76, 77, 78, 94, 105, 176, 252, 302, 303, 357.

Strong, L. A. G., 'Dorset Hardy'. *Essays in Criticism*, Vol. 1, No. 1, January 1951, pp. 42–50.

Swigg, Richard, 'Thomas Hardy and the Problem of the "Middle Distance" ', *Lawrence, Hardy, and American Literature*. London: Oxford University Press, 1972, pp. 3–31, 58–80.

Tanner, Tony, 'Colour and Movement in Hardy's *Tess of the d'Urbervilles*'. *Critical Quarterly*, Vol. 10, No. 3, Autumn 1968, pp. 219–39.

Taube, Myron, ' "The Atmosphere...from Cyprus": Hardy's Development of Theme in *Jude the Obscure'. Victorian Newsletter*, No. 32, Fall 1967, pp. 16–18.

Toliver, Harold E., 'The Dance Under the Greenwood Tree: Hardy's Bucolics'. *Nineteenth-Century Fiction*, Vol. 17, No. 1, June 1962, pp. 57–68.

Tomlinson, May, '*Jude the Obscure'. The South Atlantic Quarterly*, Vol. XXIII, No. 4, October 1924, pp. 335–45.

Tomlinson, T. B., 'Hardy's Universe: *Tess of the d'Urbervilles', The English Middle-Class Novel*. London: Macmillan, 1976, pp 131–47.

Trent, W. P., 'The Novels of Thomas Hardy'. *Sewanee Review*, Vol. 1, No. 1, November 1892, pp. 1–25.

Van Dyke, Henry, '*Tess of the d'Urbervilles', The Man Behind the Book: Essays in Understanding*. New York: Charles Scribner's Sons, 1929, pp. 283–305.

Van Ghent, Dorothy, 'On *Tess of the d'Urbervilles', The English Novel: Form and Function*. New York: Rinehart, 1953. Rpt., New York: Harper & Row, 1961, pp. 195–209.

Wain, John, ed., 'Introduction' to *Thomas Hardy: Selected Stories*. London: Macmillan, 1966.

Weatherby, H. L., 'Old-Fashioned Gods: Eliot on Lawrence and Hardy'. *Sewanee Review*, LXXV, April–June 1967, pp. 300–16.

Weber, Carl J., 'Hardy and *The Woodlanders'. Review of English Studies*, Vol. XV, No. 59, July 1939, pp. 330–3.

———, 'Ainsworth and Thomas Hardy'. *The Review of English Studies*, Vol. XVII, No. 66, April 1941, pp. 193–200.

———, 'A Masquerade of Noble Dames'. *PMLA*, Vol. LVIII, No. 2, June 1943, pp. 558–63.

———, 'Care and Carelessness in Hardy'. *Modern Language Notes*, Vol. 4, No. 1, January 1953, pp. 41–3.

———, 'Our Exploits at West Poley'. *Nineteenth-Century Fiction*, Vol. 7, No. 4, March 1953, pp. 307–8.

Webster, Harvey Curtis, 'Borrowings in *Tess of the d'Urbervilles'. Modern Language Notes*, Vol. XLVIII, No. 7, November 1933, pp. 459–62.

Welsh, John R., 'Egdon Heath Revisited: Ellen Glasgow's *Barren Ground', Reality and Myth*, eds., William E. Walker, and Robert L. Walker. Nashville: Vanderbilt University Press, 1964, pp. 71–9.

Wheeler, Otis B., 'Four Versions of *The Return of the Native'. Nineteenth-Century Fiction*, Vol. 14, No. 1, June 1959, pp. 27–44.

White, William, 'Dreiser on Hardy, Henley, and Whitman: An Unpublished Letter'. *English Language Notes*, Vol. VI, No. 2, December 1968, pp. 122–4.

Williams, Raymond, 'Thomas Hardy'. *Critical Quarterly*, Vol. VI, No. 4, Winter 1964, pp. 341–51.

Winfield, Christina, 'Factual Sources of Two Episodes in *The Mayor of Casterbridge'. Nineteenth-Century Fiction*, Vol. 25, No. 2, September 1970, pp. 224–31.

Winters, Yvor, 'Robert Bridges and Elizabeth Daryush'. *The American Review*, Vol. VIII, No. 3, January 1937, pp. 353–67.

Woolf, Virginia, 'The Novels of Thomas Hardy', *The Common Reader*, Second Series. London: The Hogarth Press, 1932. Rpt. 1948, pp. 245–57.

———, 'Pages from a Diary'. *Encounter*, Vol. 1, No. 1, October 1953, pp. 5–11.

Yevish, Irving A., 'The Attack on *Jude the Obscure:* A Reappraisal Some Seventy Years After'. *Journal of General Education*, 18, January 1967, pp. 239–48.

Zabel, Morton Dauwen, 'Hardy in Defense of his Art: The Aesthetic of Incongruity'. *Southern Review*, 6, Summer 1940, pp. 125–49.

Index